Praise for *ELEVATE*

"Insightful, practical, and full of wisdom . . . *Elevate* is for those who know they have so much more potential but struggle with things holding them back. Deitch transforms decades of experience and thought into a clear path to better awareness about the obstacles and practical action."

**—Shawn Achor, *New York Times*
best-selling author of *The Happiness Advantage***

"As I approach my 80th year, I firmly believe that if you stop learning, you should lie down and let them throw dirt on you, because you are already dead. Read *Elevate*, and you'll learn some new ways of not only thinking about life but, more important, doing life."

**—Ken Blanchard, coauthor of *The New One Minute Manager*®
and coeditor of *Servant Leadership in Action***

"*Elevate* offers the clues to do just what the title suggests. If you want strategies for keeping your life on a continuous upward path, this book is for you. Success in life is multi-dimensional, and Joe Deitch touches on all dimensions. This book is a great read for everyone at any point in life."

—Luke Campbell, Olympic gold medalist and professional boxer

"*Elevate* is a treasure trove of Joe's discoveries as to why and how we make the choices in life that have led us to where we are today . . . *Elevate* is his gift to the world and his quest to share his 'journey of increased awareness and enhanced performance.'"

**—Leanda Cave, world triathlon champion and first woman in history to win
both the Ironman Triathlon and Half Ironman in the same year (2012)**

"I told Joe Deitch months ago after I read the draft of *Elevate* that I could not wait for it to be published. Read it, study it, think about it, and implement it. Real happiness and success is not about what you know, what you do, or how much money you make. It is about who you are."

**—Lee Cockerell, former executive vice president,
Walt Disney World Resort and best-selling author of *Creating Magic***

"*Elevate* draws upon science, literature, religion, and our bodies to create a rational blueprint for self-discovery and improvement. It describes ways to change our lives today that help us rise to our potential. Don't just read it—use it!"

—David Dodson, Professor, Stanford Graduate School of Business specializing in entrepreneurship, and philanthropist

"With *Elevate*, Joe Deitch has achieved something remarkable: adding something distinctive and valuable to an oversaturated self-help market. By integrating Awareness and Action, the book links inner and outer, East and West, ancient and modern, spiritual and scientific into one eminently practical volume that will elevate every life to higher achievement and fulfillment."

—Philip Goldberg, author of *American Veda*

"From a pioneer in the financial planning industry, I expect practical advice. From a Tony Award-winning Broadway producer, I expect entertainment. Joe Deitch is both of those people, and this book delivers on both of those expectations."

—Adam Grant, *New York Times* best-selling author of *Give and Take*, *Originals*, and *Option B* with Sheryl Sandberg

"I've known Joe as a successful entrepreneur, a solid and trusted leader, an innovator, a friend, and now as an author. Joe's humility has enabled him to listen to everyone, to question everything, and to then reflect and derive wisdom from his life's experiences. *Elevate* will help us all improve the quality of our lives."

—Steven E. Karol, former YPO International President

"Joe has written an inspiring primer filled with wisdom. He is a master of brief, bite size, streetwise nuggets and takes you on an easy ride to success in business and in life."

—Stephen P. Kaufman, Professor, Harvard Business School and retired chairman and CEO of Arrow Electronics, Inc.

"Joe Deitch lives and breathes continuous self-challenge, and through that, self-improvement. In *Elevate*, he delivers what most great teachers do: He makes you believe you are capable of more than you realize—and pushes you to grow. This book can help you enter a new phase of your life with more insights leading to more fulfillment and more happiness."

—Dr. Ed Mascioli, MD, physician, venture capitalist, biotech CEO

"Joe is one of those rare people who has achieved much success in many different businesses. But what I also admire in him is his ability to truly savor his life and relationships. In *Elevate*, he distills the principles and practices that have worked for him and so many others. It is an insightful and eminently actionable book. I only wish I had read it many years ago, and I will send copies to my daughters."

—Sanjiv Mirchandani, President, Fidelity Clearing and Custody Solutions

"Reading this book is like accepting an invitation to an inspiring, enlightening conversation with a good friend. Joe's reflective questioning woven throughout nudges us toward greater understanding of ourselves and how to reach our potential in any field or endeavor. The insights are timeless and will provide guidance throughout life's stages. This book is perfect for a recent graduate or anyone navigating a life transition."

—Lynne Mooney Teta, Headmaster Emerita, Boston Latin School

"This wonderful book is full of life-changing wisdom from a man who has lived its insights. Joe Deitch digs deep and shares what we all need to know for greater adventures in life and work. I will enthusiastically recommend this illuminating treatise from the heart and mind to everyone I know."

—Tom Morris, former professor of philosophy at the University of Notre Dame and author of *If Aristotle Ran General Motors*, *True Success*, and *The Oasis Within*

"I've known Joe Deitch, professionally and personally, for many years. Evident in every conversation we have had is that Joe is a thoughtful, fascinating man, with great insights on life and business."

—Jack Nicklaus, *Sports Illustrated*'s Individual Male Athlete of the 20th Century and winner of a record eighteen major professional golf championship titles

"Destined to be a modern classic, *Elevate* tackles perceptions about life and common sense, gives them bones, and shares actionable direction. It left me knowing more about what makes me tick and gave me the tools to make impactful and lasting changes to my life."

—Les Otten, *Inc.* magazine Turnaround Entrepreneur of the Year and former vice chairman of the Boston Red Sox

"This is a large-hearted and graciously written handbook for existing. No crystals, nothing 'funny,' just a followable, easy-to-digest guide up the mountain of life, where Deitch proffers up a better view and clearer air. There's a treasure house of consciousness-expanding stories, quotes, and insights threaded together with practical how-to approaches to the business of work, health, and love. Deitch doesn't preach or promise so much as share his own life's aha moments with a self-deprecating wink, as if you were sharing a profound laugh with a new pal over a nice fireside beer. In short: reading this book will make you a better person."

—Amanda Palmer, rock star, crowdfunding pioneer, TED speaker, and author of *The Art of Asking*

"Joe Deitch has accomplished a miracle—a self-help book that really helps. Do yourself an enormous favor: If you buy only one self-help book, make it this one."

—Martin Sandler, award-winning author of more than seventy books, two-time Pulitzer Prize nominee, and five-time Emmy Award winner

ELEVATE

AN ESSENTIAL

GUIDE TO LIFE

—

JOSEPH DEITCH

GREENLEAF
BOOK GROUP PRESS

This book is intended as a reference volume only. It is sold with the understanding that the publisher and author are not engaged in rendering any professional services. The information given here is designed to help you make informed decisions. If you suspect that you have a problem that might require professional treatment or advice, you should seek competent help.

Published by Greenleaf Book Group Press
Austin, Texas
www.gbgpress.com

Distributed by Greenleaf Book Group

For ordering information or special discounts for bulk purchases, please contact Greenleaf Book Group at PO Box 91869, Austin, TX 78709, 512.891.6100.

Design and composition by Greenleaf Book Group
Cover design by Greenleaf Book Group

Cover image ©ostill. Used under license from Shutterstock.com

Publisher's Cataloging-in-Publication data is available.

Trade Paperback ISBN: 978-1-62634-469-3
Hardcover ISBN: 978-1-62634-522-5
eBook ISBN: 978-1-62634-470-9

Part of the Tree Neutral® program, which offsets the number of trees consumed in the production and printing of this book by taking proactive steps, such as planting trees in direct proportion to the number of trees used: www.treeneutral.com

TreeNeutral

Printed in the United States of America on acid-free paper

18 19 20 21 22 23 24   10 9 8 7 6 5 4 3 2 1

First Edition

To my mother and father,

who gave me the gift of life.

"Yesterday I was clever, so I wanted to change the world.
Today I am wise, so I am changing myself."

—Rumi

"If you are not willing to learn, no one can help you.
If you are determined to learn, no one can stop you."

—Anonymous

CONTENTS

Part Two: Action

Foreword

As a writer, I am regularly asked, "So, what do you read?" My vague answer is a little of everything. If pressed to be more specific, I say that I read contemporary fiction to keep refining my craft and because I love a great story. I read nonfiction texts on neuroscience, psychology, and medicine to keep learning and because these subjects will forever fascinate me. And my favorite genre is self-help. I love reading these books because I'm committed to continually growing, and the tools, frameworks, and reminders offered in these books teach me to live and love bigger.

I met Joe Deitch on Cape Cod in the summer of 2015. Soon after, he mentioned that he was writing a book. I braced myself. Everyone and their uncle's neighbor's daughter's dance teacher are writing books. Very few people are writing great books.

He said his book was about the wisdom he had discovered in his quest to understand how to live the best life possible. Self-help—my favorite! I was intrigued but still skeptical. And although I wanted to read it, I hesitated. Joe and I had just started dating. What if his book was terrible? I'd probably have to break up with him.

I already knew Joe to be a brilliant businessman; highly educated; intellectually curious about everything from physics to fashion; adored by friends, colleagues, and family; and living a life that appeared remarkably balanced in mind, body, and spirit. But he was tackling such a BIG subject. I've read books with a similar objective by Deepak Chopra and Eckhart Tolle, Jen Sincero and Gabrielle Bernstein, titles that illuminate how to live mindful, fearless, loving, badass lives; books that have transformed the way I live. The standard here was formidable.

Pushing past my reservations, I asked if I could read it. From the first page, I was captivated, fascinated, and impressed. And best of all, I was thrilled—we could continue dating.

Elevate explores the questions that seem to baffle us all. How do we overcome fear and ingrained habits to live more fully and authentically? How do we live and love without limitations? How do we become more consciously aware of ourselves, of what we say and do and how we react, of the ongoing chatter in our heads, of the world around us? How can we live the biggest, most successful, happiest life possible?

The answers to these questions in *Elevate* are enlightening, powerful, simple to absorb, and transformational. They are a set of elegant tools that I now carry with me. I use them every day and with ease. They are lessons I share with family and friends. They've given me a lens to recognize habits, beliefs, and ways of being that don't work, and so I can let these go. Obstacles are now possibilities. Frustration can be turned into fascination. Insights and skills for realizing the fullest potential in every relationship and endeavor are clear and inviting.

I am forever changed by the words on these pages.

You will be, too.

—Lisa Genova
New York Times best-selling author of *Still Alice*

Suggestions for How to Use this Book

"I went to a bookstore and asked the saleswoman, 'Where's the self-help section?' She said if she told me, it would defeat the purpose."

—George Carlin

The information in this book is drawn from a multitude of sources and was organized according to the perceptions and priorities of its author. But we are all different people, in singular situations. Therefore, I encourage you to approach the book in whatever manner benefits you the most. Toward that end, here are a few comments and suggestions that have proven helpful for others:

Take your time, and go at your own pace. While generations' worth of insights and understanding can be summarized in one volume, it's not realistic to assume that one can digest it all in a few days, or even a few weeks. It took decades to integrate and organize, and I'm still learning more every day.

Pushing our boundaries can be exhausting. When we grow and evolve, we become different people at every stage. This can be challenging, since growth means seeing and appreciating things that have eluded us in the past, or that we have historically avoided. But since you've picked up this book, you're probably ready to confront some barriers, look under rocks, open doors, and venture forward. Even so, be prepared for a few internal hurdles and surprising roadblocks. Just take them in stride. Safety and comfort can be the enemy of learning and growth. Discomfort is a doorway; don't run from it. When in doubt, adopt an attitude of curiosity.

Appreciate the interplay between awareness and action. One of the primary reasons *Elevate* is different from other guides to an optimal life is that it connects both our internal and external journeys; it integrates our improvement in fundamental skills with a greater awareness of ourselves and others. Once you embrace this connection, life will never be the same.

Read the material in the order presented . . . or not. While this book is organized with a particular flow in mind, if you're drawn to a specific topic, by all means go there. But if you do skip ahead, please keep in mind that some of the underlying concepts may have been explained earlier. This is especially true of the chapter on Awareness and of Insight 1, which are central to much of the book. You may choose to read the book in order from the beginning, but also jump around periodically as your needs and moods dictate. Whatever works best for you.

Create a Stairway of Success. In terms of implementing the advice in *Elevate*, start with the low-hanging fruit. If you're looking to change and improve, make it easier by focusing on the simple stuff first. One of the benefits of this approach is that your self-image and confidence will grow with each new accomplishment. And so will your energy.

Use Elevate *as a reference manual.* This isn't intended to be a read-it-and-move-on kind of book. Consider it a resource. Keep it handy.

Take the best and disregard the rest. There's a wealth of powerful information and insights to benefit from here, but if you doubt or disagree with a particular idea, feel free to set it aside for the moment. One reader may be greatly helped by certain sections and less so by others, while another person will have the exact opposite reaction. It all depends on where you are in life, what you need now, and what you're open to at the moment. Focus on what works best for you rather than getting bogged down with what might not feel right yet.

Find out for yourself. Play with the concepts. Don't take my word for everything. Consult with others. Do some research on the Web. Experiment. Give it a try, and see what happens.

Learn more about how you're wired and what's really important. While every journey should serve its primary objective, most people have multiple objectives. To further complicate matters, our goals are not always consistent, complementary, or even conscious. Take note of how things affect you. Every interaction provides insights into your psyche and your past conditioning. Everything is a learning opportunity. How we react to stimuli and what we choose to move toward and away from provide valuable clues about what we really care about, what makes us tick, and why.

Learn from what he and she said. In addition to organized information and personal examples, this book also contains many quotes from others that cut through the clutter and convey ideas and perspectives in a helpful way. Some quotes brilliantly condense a concept. Some are entertaining or memorable. And often the person quoted possesses substantial credibility and represents an important part of our shared heritage.

Be prepared for fundamental changes. As we change, so does our world. The more we learn and grow, the more our world improves. And as we grasp the insights and adopt the universal skills in *Elevate,* something miraculous happens: We transition away from dividing activities and opportunities into what we have and have not learned (*I can do this, but I can't do that;* or, *I am this, but I'm not that*). Little by little, we realize that we have the tools to do virtually *anything*—and that changes *everything.*

So what are you waiting for? Turn the page!

I Was Half Right

As a boy, I often thought the world was crazy. I constantly saw grownups doing dumb and self-defeating things—like smoking cigarettes, eating horribly unhealthy food, and drinking alcohol to excess. None of the consequences (whether heartburn, hangovers, heart disease, or cancer) seemed to provide sufficient motivation for them to change. I also watched them endure dead-end jobs and miserable relationships. Why couldn't they see how restrictive and destructive their habits and choices were? And, if they could see, why did they persist? They were clearly unhappy and unhealthy, so why didn't they choose the seemingly obvious, more intelligent alternatives? Why didn't they practice what they preached?

I saw adults cling stubbornly to their beliefs and argue passionately for the superiority of their politics, religions, sports teams, and everything else they identified with. They didn't seem to realize that their worldviews were primarily inherited and heavily influenced by other people and outside circumstances.

Later in life, as I grew into an adult and became more experienced and self-reflective, I gradually understood that I had been right. More accurately, I'd been half right: People *are* easily influenced, short-sighted, self-destructive, and frequently wrong. But I also discovered something much more important and powerful: I was essentially just as blind and biased as everyone else! *How could that be?*

This revelation, as fascinating as it was humbling, led to profound personal transformations as my mind continued to open. My late wife, Robbie, a gifted psychologist, often said, "People change when they're ready." Evidently, I was ready. My interest in psychology, growth, success, and happiness kicked into high gear. I started exploring voraciously, learning everything I could from anyone who might have something to teach me. I turned to both Eastern and Western philosophies, as well as to modern science. I essentially became my own lab rat, learning from my successes, and even more from my failures.

But oh, what I would have given for a great road map! Time and time again, I found myself yearning for answers. How could I speed up my learning curve? *What was I missing . . . and why?* And it wasn't just about me: How could I help the other people in my life, those I lived and worked with and cared so much about? How could we avoid the myriad unnecessary mistakes and missed opportunities that cause us so much pain and frustration? Surely there must be a better way.

My experience is hardly unique. That's why most of us share the same fantasy: *I wish I could go back in time knowing what I know now.* Such a delicious idea! The heartbreak and humiliation we could have avoided. The fighting and frustration we could have side stepped. The now-obvious solutions we could have implemented.

As parents, we try to spare our children the struggles we suffered. My wife and I sure tried our best to pass along what we believed to be valuable lessons to our son at every opportunity. And yet, he often had to find his own truths, just as we had to when we were young. While we could take some credit for making his journey easier, I constantly wondered how we could have done better. There was a wealth of wisdom available to us—filling up massive libraries and a vast Internet—*but how did it all fit together?* Where was that practical and reliable road map I yearned for?

$$\infty$$

In many respects, my desire for such knowledge has become my life's work. However, while it has always been satisfying to help and entertain others with an insight here and a nugget of information there, the decision to craft a book and to combine what I had learned into a cohesive whole forced me to search for a deeper understanding of what works and why; to discern the underlying truths of the insights and practices I acquired and to figure out how they all fit together.

It has been an exhilarating process. Every step of the way has been a learning experience, and this journey of increased awareness and enhanced performance has been rewarding at every turn.

In addition to my basic concerns about happiness and success and how to achieve them, I was especially fascinated by why we often avoid sensible solutions and proven pathways. Also, why do we thrive and excel in some aspects of our lives and totally miss the mark in others? How can we be so clear here and so clueless there? What's going on—or *not* going on, as the case may be? Fortunately, as we probe deeper and open up further, we understand more and more. Sincere curiosity—an open heart and an open mind—is the path to enduring growth.

This manual you are about to read provides the kind of integrated system of powerful insights and practical answers I had always searched for—an approach to life that explores what really works, and why . . . and what we can do about it. By using this framework, we can better understand, implement, reference, and continuously refine the best of the best practices in every area of our lives.

Elevate contains what I consider to be the most profound insights and transformative practices I have discovered on my ongoing quest to elevate my awareness as well as my success and happiness. Over time, these discoveries radically transformed my life, both professionally and personally, and I have verified their efficacy while training, coaching, and teaching thousands of people in my businesses and personal encounters.

This book is divided into two parts: "Awareness" and "Action." Like the ancient symbol for yin and yang, these two halves of our lives (our internal and external journeys) are perfectly complementary, and the essence of each resides in the heart of the other. Together they form a dynamic and continuous spiral of growth that reinforces itself—creating, in the process, a veritable Stairway of Success.

I realize this book can never be complete since the universe is infinite and our knowledge is limited. And yet we must try. Consider it an attempt to organize much of the wisdom that has been handed down to us by those who have already traveled this path, as well as a platform to build upon. This wisdom is not mine. It is ours. May it serve us well.

—**Joseph Deitch**

PART ONE

—

Awareness

Awareness: The Portal to Knowledge and Growth

"When you really pay attention, everything is your teacher."

—Ezra Bayda

I have a pair of beige, stonewashed jeans that I love. A friend of mine once made the mistake of calling them gray, so I corrected her. A spirited disagreement ensued, and I enlisted the help of various passersby to prove my point. Bizarrely, they all agreed that the jeans were gray, not beige. How could this be? Clearly, I'll have to ask more people until I get the answer I want . . .

—

Awareness is the ability to perceive what is going on—or *not* going on—in the world around us and within us. Awareness is about paying attention, and it pertains to both the conscious and subconscious realms.

Paying attention is proactive. *It is a conscious act that expands our consciousness.* Attention fosters awareness, and expanded awareness is our springboard to elevated understanding and growth. True attention entails looking, listening, and learning without prejudice. Conversely, restricted awareness translates to limited information and diminished understanding, which leads to unnecessary mistakes, stagnation, or worse.

Increased awareness is a journey of self-discovery. It is not just an intellectual exercise. Our essence resides in our body and in our soul, not just in our mind. Therefore, we must go and listen and feel wherever and however we can. We must sense and confront our blockages and biases if we are to be open and grow. And if we allow ourselves to be fascinated, learning comes more easily.

The appreciation of awareness and the enormous role it plays in our lives could certainly qualify it as being a major insight in its own right. However, I present it here as the primary theme of part one. It also permeates all of the ten skills in part two. Awareness influences and enables all that we are and all that we strive for.

But growth and fulfillment don't just depend on increasing how much information we take in. We also have to consider the validity and reliability of that information. And we need to understand how and why everything fits together.

Paradoxically, too much information can contribute to our becoming less aware, especially if that information is narrow and biased. This is problematic in today's world, as our options for data, news, and commentary expand exponentially, while our viewpoints become increasingly segmented and subjective. As a result, people tend to seek out and value perspectives that are consistent with their own self-interest, self-image, and worldview. Without open-minded discourse and discovery, this self-selection adds to the long list of cultural and political issues that divide us. We take sides, and those sides become more and more polarized and politicized. This is the antithesis of elevated awareness, understanding, and growth.

The Potential and the Path

"When the student is ready, the teacher will appear."
—Attributed to various sources

The magnitude of our potential becomes apparent if you consider the huge leaps forward humanity has made each time we expanded and enhanced our awareness. Think about eyeglasses, the microscope, the telescope, the photograph, hearing aids, radio and television, recording devices, and the Internet. The truly big personal breakthroughs are like acquiring a new sense. When someone who is born deaf can suddenly hear, or a blind person is miraculously gifted with sight, it's *Aha! Eureka!* Nothing will ever be the same.

Most of us have experienced such transformations. Falling in love is celebrated in song and story because it utterly changes our world. Likewise, going through puberty is akin to being reborn, as we become profoundly different, and, as a result, so does the world we inhabit. Then of course, there's the combination of love and rebirth we experience when we have our first child. All of a sudden, we understand and appreciate things we never did before. We *know* that which had previously been hidden from us.

The list goes on, but the point is the same: *We understand more, because we become more.* Conversely, we become more by understanding more. There is so much more to life than we can possibly comprehend and experience; and when our awareness expands, so does our world . . . and it becomes increasingly wondrous.

The big question is *How do we expand our awareness?* How can we elevate awareness, and thereby grow in wisdom, love, and fulfillment? There is no correct box to check, no simple one-size-fits-all answer. Awareness is not a school quiz that can be passed by reading and memorizing some facts. It's a journey that is fueled by our intent to be open, honest, and free. It begins when we realize that our comprehension is in fact limited, it continues when we follow that realization with a desire to break free of artificial constraints, and it unfolds when we move forward toward knowing our vast potential. From those precious moments on, a new course can be charted as we discover worlds that had been previously hidden or obscured.

Looking back at my younger self, I can now appreciate how shortsighted I often was, not to mention stubborn and argumentative, as I strove to show people why *they* were wrong. My ego, my emotions, and my inexperience regularly caused me to defend my beliefs and actions instead of opening up and listening to others— and to my inner self, my intuition. Sound familiar?

One of the points that all wise men and women agree on is this: *If we want our world to improve, we should work on ourselves first.* That's where the significant gains are to be found. Focusing on the inadequacies of others, or the unfairness in the world, is often just a trap of our own making as we resist looking in the mirror.

There is certainly no shortage of techniques available to increase awareness and gain clarity—from yoga, meditation, and breathing exercises to psychotherapy and cognitive skills, changing habits, and more. While this book identifies a number of such methods throughout, part one focuses on five transformational insights with enormous implications for our daily life.

In many respects, these insights are disruptive—even revolutionary—in that they can radically change the way we see the world and ourselves. This can be challenging in the best sense of the word. Like most healthy challenges, the insights stretch us and enlarge our capacities. Above all, they are liberating. When properly understood and absorbed, they help free the mind from past conditioning and unveil a new realm of possibilities.

Many so-called problems only arise in the first place because we're stuck in our perception of the world, and that limited awareness defines our reality. We see it often with teenagers who may be filled with angst over some social concern like how they look or dress, or being out of sync with their peers, or feeling inadequate, or experiencing romantic confusion. Granted, these are common issues for adults as well, but the interesting thing about teenagers is that often nothing their parents or any other adult can say makes a difference. Then one day, the problem is somehow resolved and just goes away—not necessarily because a logical solution appeared, but because the teenager literally grew up a bit—both physically and psychologically. The prefrontal cortex continues to develop during the teenage years, and what was once a major concern in the teenager's life is now perceived from a higher vantage point.

Granted, adults can get stuck too. There are innumerable opportunities for frustration in life, but also for breakthroughs and consequent advancement to elevated perspectives. A common example is how we often repeat deep-rooted behavioral patterns without even realizing it. We think we're making a cogent decision about specific circumstances when we're really just having a pre-programmed reflexive response.

Another typical trap is being unrealistic and unreasonable. For example, people are forever seeking a fulfilling and "balanced" life. They want to be passionately engaged but not stressed. They want to please everyone and also gratify themselves. They want to be 100% into their careers, 100% into their families, and 100% supportive of their personal needs and desires, including the desire to serve others and improve the world. They want, they want, they want. But time and energy are real constraints. You simply can't fit a gallon of desires into a quart container. And yet we continually try to do just that. What we need is a different approach. A bigger bottle would also help. So how do we grow our capacity for awareness and nurture our ability to continually become more aware?

The "answer" doesn't come in a formula or a one-sentence

aphorism. Rather, the path to ongoing enlightenment begins by loosening our death grip on our opinions, beliefs, and ingrained behaviors. When we let go, we create space to let in new insights and observations. As we explore we expand, and we become more aware. Letting go and opening up allows us to confront repressed feelings and fears, and allows love and compassion to flourish. That's why one person's "answer" might offer little insight to someone else. If two blind men are traveling down a path and one of them suddenly gains sight, does his description of the view allow the other person to attain vision? The common reality for most people seems to be that awakening comes bit by bit with every elevation of attitude, awareness, and understanding.

Everything Provides Insights

While the road to greater awareness begins with the deceptively simple decision to be more open and openly curious, there is one particular practice that I highly recommend as you proceed with this book and go through your daily life. *Pay attention to how you react to the various stimuli you encounter.*

Every idea, every person, and every interaction provides an opportunity to observe how we react to life in its infinite expressions. When we pay close attention, we may notice that our reactions are expressions of our fears, desires, and predispositions. Like a Geiger counter or a divining rod, our reactions provide critical clues at every step. If certain concepts, beliefs, situations, or people rub us the wrong way—more than might reasonably be expected, or more than they affect others—we should see it as an opportunity to wonder why. What's going on in our subconscious that we're not fully aware of? What in our background might explain such a reaction?

While it's hard to see what we can't see, we can be sensitive to the responses and associations those ideas and experiences trigger.

We can also ask our friends and family what they think about how we interact with the world, since they observe us from unique vantage points.

Don't limit this practice to adverse reactions. It also pays to ask why we're extremely fond of someone or why we crave something. And if the reaction, whether good or bad, pleasant or unpleasant, is especially strong, there is probably even more gold to be discovered on that trail.

As you embark on this journey of discovery, feel free to experiment. Consider trying things you might not normally do, and watch how you respond. For example, give up TV or other electronic obsessions for a week; take different routes to work; try out various exercise routines; compliment people more often; tell the important people in your life how much they mean to you; learn to speak a new language; take up a musical instrument; travel to exotic places. And exotic places need not be far away; you can start by spending time with people who are nearby but seem to be very different from you. Visit diverse restaurants, churches, and neighborhoods. The list is endless, and so are the lessons you stand to learn.

Play detective. You may notice that the very contemplation of change initiates a reaction, and not necessarily a comfortable one. What does that mean? What are you afraid of? What does it feel like? What does it remind you of? Where did it come from?

If you approach each of the insights, implications, and applications that follow with curiosity, you'll observe that there are many veils to part and doors to open. And still more behind those. If you're ready to let the light in, there's no adventure more exciting . . . or rewarding.

1

Our Perspective Is De Facto Limited and Distorted

"A great many people think they are thinking
when they are merely rearranging their prejudices."

—William James

*I grew up in Boston, in a poor, working-class neighborhood. On one side of
my street were triple-deckers (multifamily apartment buildings), and on the
other side was the public housing we called "the projects." I lived in one of
the triple-deckers, but most of the kids were in the projects, so that's where
we played. It was a melting pot of white and black, mostly Christian, plus a
few Jews like me. But that's not how I categorized the other kids. I divided
everyone up based on whether or not they were fun and friendly.*

*When I was twelve, we moved to another blue-collar neighborhood.
This one was all white, and I was the only Jewish kid. For the first time in*

my life, I experienced anti-Semitism. I no longer felt welcome. It was weird and uncomfortable, and I looked for friends elsewhere. Prejudice was a new experience for me, and it didn't make any sense. It certainly didn't seem fair.

Years later I realized that anti-Semitism is just one example of people being fearful of others whom they perceive to be different, whether because of religion, nationality, age, education, political preferences, or other factors. The irony is that Jews have a word for "the others." It's goyim. I had always heard that word, but it wasn't until I was on the receiving end of prejudice that I saw it for what it really was.

—

We are all somewhat blocked, biased, and blind. For starters, we are residents of a single point in time and space, able to sense only what is available at that location, that time, and that vantage point. We can't see what's happening across town or even behind our backs—let alone everywhere else in the vast expanse of existence. Plus, we see only a limited portion of the electromagnetic spectrum (only about 0.0035% is visible to the human eye) and hear only a limited range of sound waves. There are entire realms of reality we don't even know we're missing.

Listen to astrophysicists talk about the universe, and you will be awestruck by how much we know about the cosmos. Likewise, listen to neuroscientists talk about the brain, and you will be amazed by how much we've learned about our gray matter. On the other hand, you will also be humbled when you contemplate how much we still *don't* understand about our external and internal universes.

To complicate this further, we tend to generalize about what little we do know. As we grow up, we encounter limits to how many facts we can memorize and how many individual skills we can acquire. We begin to utilize guidelines, rules of thumb, and conceptual frameworks to understand the world; and we group our myriad choices into right and wrong, practical and impractical, desirable and problematic, friend and foe, pleasurable and painful, and many other categories.

Unfortunately, our tendency to oversimplify and generalize in order to navigate the complexities of life also distorts our perceptions. Together with our various prejudices and predispositions, this natural inclination can cause us to exclude uncomfortable or contradictory information, discount people who disagree with us, and even marginalize entire segments of the population. When we do this, we often end up ignoring relevant information, rejecting sound advice, and ultimately making poor choices.

A key to dramatic growth is to recognize an amazing paradox: By accepting and actually embracing our limitations, we allow ourselves to open up to the knowledge, experience, and insights of others.

We can best connect with those we come in contact with, as well as with the collective consciousness of all beings, only when we let down our defenses and adopt a more open attitude. As we become more open and accepting of others and appreciative of what they have to offer, they open up more to us in return. This approach not only improves our relationships with others, it also reveals more about everything else in our world.

Cognitive Science and Psychological Constraints

"Real knowledge is to know the extent of one's ignorance."
—Confucius

Not only are we limited by physics and biology, we are further influenced and constricted by psychological factors such as fears and desires; cultural factors like personal histories, religious traditions, and educational training; and by all the complexities of our diverse environments. We are intellectually, psychologically, and emotionally molded as soon as we emerge from the womb, if not earlier, and the conditioning continues with every interaction from then on. We are not just blocked and blind; we are also decidedly *biased*. We all like to think we're open-minded and objective when it comes to evaluating situations and people. But are we? A huge body of research in physics, biochemistry, and psychology says we're not.

Generally, people like people who are like themselves. We prefer to watch news reports and read opinion pieces that bolster our preconceived ideas rather than seek out alternative viewpoints. We also tend to remember information that conforms to our views and forget evidence that contradicts them. We even decide where to live, who to associate with, and who to vote for based primarily on the desire to foster a community of people like ourselves.

We are also very good at rationalizing. The phenomenon of *cognitive dissonance* describes the tension we feel when confronted with two conflicting thoughts or feelings, and our compulsion to resolve that tension. We modify our views of people and situations to support our self-image and life choices. Suppose you want to join a club (or team, company, or organization), and the club makes it really hard to get accepted. If you finally get in, you're likely to express a very high opinion of that group, even if you're somewhat disappointed in it, so you don't have to admit that it wasn't worth all the trouble. And if you're *denied* membership, you're likely to be very critical of the organization so you don't have to accept that you're "not good enough." Similarly, people who are spurned by someone they're attracted to might come to think that same person is less appealing after all, and they're really glad it didn't work out.

Another well-known phenomenon is the *false consensus* effect, whereby people tend to overestimate the extent to which their own opinions, beliefs, values, and preferences are normal and representative of how others supposedly think and act. This mind-set leads to conclusions that do not necessarily exist, i.e., a "false consensus." It also applies to groups where people assume that many or most others think as their faction does. And because these people and groups rarely interact or acknowledge those who disagree, their belief is bolstered. One of the important and unfortunate byproducts of this perspective is that we generally disrespect or devalue those who disagree, assuming that something is wrong with them.

A related cognitive bias is called *illusory superiority* (also "the above-average effect"). This occurs when people—usually 75% or more—overestimate their own qualities and abilities, and consider themselves to be better than their peer group on various measures such as intelligence, awareness, appearance, work ethic, and so on. While you too may consider yourself to be smarter, better looking, more charitable, and more conscientious than average, this is generally a statistical falsehood. Interestingly, while illusory superiority is common in the United States, some other cultures err significantly in the other direction in accordance with their social mores.

Don't assume that because you're worldly, well educated, and well intentioned you're free of bias. Research consistently reveals how much our unconscious preconceptions influence our judgments. For example, college students have been shown to rate an academic article higher if the author has a male name as opposed to a female name. In a 2012 study, Yale researchers asked 127 subjects to evaluate job applicants based on their resumes. The resumes were exactly the same, but half were assigned male names and half female names. You guessed it. The subjects gave the men higher ratings and said they were more likely to hire them based on their qualifications. It didn't matter whether the evaluators were male or female. And get this— the subjects were all scientists, who are trained to think objectively. Like all forms of prejudice, gender bias is more prevalent in some communities today than in others, but the larger point is that we're all subject to unconscious biases; these are merely some of them.

From Limited to Liberated

"He who knows nothing is closer to the truth than he whose mind is filled with falsehoods and errors."

—Thomas Jefferson

What we perceive and know is necessarily incomplete. But that is *not necessarily* bad news, because when we recognize and embrace our limitations, something magical begins to happen: We automatically position ourselves to rise above those very limitations. That is the paradox of the human condition. If we humbly accept that our experience of reality is constrained, we immediately loosen the chains that bind us, and we begin to expand.

Suppose you've spent your whole life inside the walls of a building. Maybe it's a perfectly comfortable building—a mansion, or a palace even—and it seems to have almost everything you need and want. Then you learn there's a great big world outside those walls, and you've actually been restricted and constrained all along. You've essentially been living in a prison. What if you then discover a set of keys that unlocks the doors? Would your feeling of imprisonment turn to one of liberation?

Perhaps. Some people would still feel more comfortable staying in that building, because venturing out can be scary, or at least uncomfortable. As Abraham Maslow, one of the first psychologists to study happiness, said, "In any given moment we have two options: to step forward into growth or to step back into safety." When it comes to the limitations of consciousness and perception, we have access to myriad windows, doors, and keys. And *that* is liberating—or at least it can be.

The more I understood and embraced this notion, the more I was able to value the experience and viewpoints of others. Like most people, I used to have a knee-jerk reaction when people disagreed with me, especially when I was heavily invested in an idea—whether psychologically, operationally, or financially. I wanted them to be wrong, because then I wouldn't have to change anything or lose any momentum. But I learned that my life improved dramatically when I *truly* wanted to listen to people, to learn what they knew, and what they thought, and how they experienced life from their vantage points. I found that this attitude gave new meaning to the old saying "When the student is ready, the teacher will appear."

Acknowledging my own limitations pried me loose from many of the delusions, fears, misconceptions, and conditioned responses that were standing in my way. It was the starting point of an ongoing process of small and large advances, punctuated by new information, sudden insights, and the occasional big *Aha!* moment. That process will assuredly continue as long as I remain attentive and open to learning, and the same is true of everyone.

Deluged by myriad bits and bytes of data, we make choices at every moment of our lives. If our perceptions are clouded or constrained, then our decisions will be suboptimal. They may not even be conscious; instead, our decisions may amount to nothing more than automatic responses to stimuli based on our current desires and past conditioning. But when we begin to remove these obstacles, we find we have heightened sensitivity, greater cognitive clarity, and more astute discernment—all of which lead to more creative analyses, wiser choices, and far more satisfying outcomes. It all begins with awareness—and a decision to open those doors and windows.

An enormous sense of calm and well-being can result from letting go and opening up. If you are really motivated to grow and lead a more fulfilling life, you will turn the realization of your own limitations into your greatest asset. You can expand your capacity for perceiving, learning, and knowing, and start to take greater advantage of the incredible resources we all have access to.

We're Blind Men Bluffing

> "It's easier to fool people than to convince them
> that they have been fooled."
>
> **—Mark Twain**

Did you ever play the poker game Blind Man's Bluff? I remember sitting with my friends in a circle as the dealer passed one card to each of us, face down. Simultaneously, we would pick up our card without looking at it and hold it face out on our forehead, so we could see everyone else's card, but not our own. Then the betting and bluffing began. As with any poker game, the winner was the person with the highest score (best card) who stayed in the game by matching or exceeding all the bets. If you've never played, the actual experience is fun and illuminating.

What a perfect metaphor for how we see the world. And how we don't. Just as we can see aspects of other people's realities that they can't seem to see themselves, our own perceptions are likewise limited. We have to bet, bluff, and blunder our way through much of life, because we're not fully aware of all the cards we're holding or showing to others.

Imagine how different Blind Man's Bluff would be if you knew what card you were holding! That's how different life can be when you make a genuine effort to become more self-aware. Knowledge is power. And what knowledge could be more powerful than self-knowledge?

Unfortunately, most people find it just as difficult to change how they perceive themselves as they do the world around them. This is totally understandable. Why should we doubt what we can see (or think we see)? On the other hand, if everything is clear and obvious, why do so many people disagree about so many things? What's *really* going on?

In addition to having limited perspectives and psychological biases, we block certain things from our conscious minds for functional reasons—and the power of self-preservation can be remarkably strong. Starting as children, we use defense mechanisms to build walls in our psyches that keep troublesome or overwhelming thoughts and feelings at bay. As we grow, many of those childhood defenses stay with us, even though we no longer need their protection. By the time we're adults, they're deeply rooted and unrecognizable. Unrecognizable to *us* that is. Our friends can often see our "issues"—the playing cards on our foreheads—just as we can see many of theirs. The trick is to better see, and understand, our own machinations. Therein lies the advantage—there is no true bliss in ignorance.

Making the choice to begin seeing ourselves accurately, warts and all, is a powerful step in our growth. Only when we recognize our shortcomings can we begin to remedy them. Only when we perceive our true strengths can we leverage their power. And only when we seek what we don't know can we really start to learn.

Consider the following:

- Do you think you delude yourself in any way? If so, why?

- Are you prepared to see it all—the good, the bad, the beautiful, and the feared? If not, why not?

- Are you willing to ask your friends what cards you're holding and to truly listen to what they have to say?

Know Thyself

"Knowledge of the self is the mother of all knowledge."
—Khalil Gibran

Legend has it that the wisest men in ancient Greece traveled to Delphi and inscribed the words *gnōthi sauton* ("know thyself") at the entrance to the famous oracle for every truth-seeking pilgrim to see. Fortunately, since ancient times, we have had teachers, coaches, and counselors to help guide us to better understand ourselves. In my own experience, the talent of the teacher can be much more important than the particular discipline they practice.

When you marry a shrink, as I did, it's understood that therapy is going to be in your future, and that it can be a valuable process of discovery and healing. One day, after a few contentious discussions, Robbie "suggested" that I meet with a particular psychiatrist, whom she described as both talented and well suited to men like me. Apparently, I was a bit headstrong and wedded to my own ways and my particular views of the world.

Therapy was fascinating. It was also fun at the beginning, because I got to talk about myself all the time—my favorite subject back then. At one point though, my therapist mentioned that I seemed to have issues around intimacy, and they were exerting a big influence in my psyche. He said I would do well to take a serious look at what he was noticing. That's when we had our first argument.

After thanking the dear doctor for his observation and recommendation, I explained that the particular fear he said was in my head simply wasn't there. He listened, then once again suggested that the issue seemed to be quite prominent and was negatively affecting my relationships. I calmly and firmly let him know that I was inside my head all day, every day, and had been so for my entire life. Furthermore, I took pride in being both intellectually curious and honest. *He* on the other hand was *outside* my head and had been there for only a few hours altogether. Therefore, in any discussion of what was actually in my head, I was the only true authority. I was right and he was wrong. But he didn't back down, and I became increasingly annoyed. He simply ended the discussion by saying, "I guess we'll find out."

Two weeks later, I saw it! The therapist was right. It was as if he had told me there was an elephant in the room; but since I couldn't see it, I fervently believed it wasn't there. Then I saw the elephant! How could this be? How could something so big, so important, so obvious to someone (and possibly many others) on the outside be hidden from me, the guy on the inside? Apparently, I had never looked closely with eyes wide open before. Maybe I could finally see it because the doctor provided helpful clues and I respected his expertise. Then again, maybe I was simply ready. After all, I hadn't been forced to go into therapy; I chose to go on that inward odyssey.

When my next session rolled around, I ran into my therapist's office and excitedly told him he was right. But this was just the beginning, because I realized something vital: If there was one thing in my head I couldn't see, it stood to reason there were others as well.

I had always considered myself intelligent, perceptive, and honest. Now an important door had been opened, and I found myself thinking, *What else is hiding within? What other issues and obstacles am I missing? There have to be a lot of them. And I can't wait to find out what they are!*

Because we're human, there will probably always be corners of our psyches that we're unable or unwilling to peer into because of deep-seated fears, conflicting emotions, and other limitations. But recognizing those restrictions and working to overcome them is a big part of self-knowledge and personal growth. It's part of the ongoing process of opening doors and parting veils—an incredible journey of continuous discovery and delight. It can also translate to increased energy and ability, as we no longer deploy resources to maintain unnecessary defense mechanisms and justify conflicting perceptions. It creates more space for learning and feeling, for expanding both the head and the heart.

As long as we think we have it all figured out, we shut the door on further growth. Acknowledging our limitations is often just what we need to shake us out of our mental stupor. And here's an added bonus: Other people really appreciate it when we openly and easily acknowledge our own limitations and therefore demonstrate that we value what they have to say. It has certainly made me a lot more enjoyable to work with than when I was a bit of a know-it-all.

There Is Always More to Learn

> "The whole of life, from the moment you are born to the
> moment you die, is a process of learning."
> **—Jiddu Krishnamurti**

You may be thinking, *What you've said may apply to most people but not to me. I know exactly who I am. I'm brutally honest with myself.* If so, I would urge you to think again. No one knows himself or herself as well as they think they do, or as well as they can.

Consider this experiment conducted by Dr. Gerald Bell, the founder of the Bell Leadership Institute and a professor at the University of North Carolina. Dr. Bell asked a large sampling of sixteen-year-olds this question: "On a scale of one to ten, how well do you think you know yourself?" Like most teenagers, the subjects thought they knew themselves quite well. Their answers clustered in the eight and nine range.

Next, Dr. Bell gathered a group of forty-year-olds. "Think back to when you were sixteen," he told them. "In retrospect, how well did you actually know yourself at that time, on a scale of one to ten?" The average answer was *four*! Looking back, those test subjects knew perfectly well that their self-awareness as teenagers had been severely limited. I'm sure you can relate. Personally, I might give my sixteen-year-old self an even lower grade.

But there's more. Dr. Bell went on to ask the same forty-year-olds, "How well do you think you know yourself now?" Like most people, they felt they had learned a lot over the years and had become much more introspective in midlife. Their scores were in the eight to nine range.

You can probably guess what happened next. Dr. Bell asked a group of seventy-year-olds to think back to when they were sixteen. "How well did you know yourself then?" he asked. Many of them gave their sixteen-year-old selves a score of one to two. Then he asked, "How well did you know yourself when you were forty?" The scores were in the four to five range. Apparently, they continued to learn a lot between forty and seventy! And so can we. In fact, as I approach seventy myself and look back on my forty-year-old self, the study mirrors my own experience.

This has served as a useful reminder to me: Don't get complacent. Don't fool yourself into believing you have no more blind spots or that your view of the world is uniquely accurate. Don't ever think there is nothing left to learn about yourself and the people around you. Nothing is more important than self-knowledge and self-awareness. And every event, every person, and every situation we encounter is a teacher.

Go Deeper

> "The learning and knowledge that we have, is, at the most,
> but little compared with that of which we are ignorant."
>
> **—Plato**

A major turning point in my professional life occurred when I enrolled in a program for business owners and company presidents at Harvard Business School. It was an extraordinary learning experience that helped me turn around my company and my life. One of the many compelling takeaways was an expression that our marketing professor frequently repeated: "Look at the fish."

The saying derived from a story about the legendary zoologist and natural history professor, Louis Agassiz. Dr. Agassiz would begin the education of his new students by having them look at a preserved fish specimen and describe what they saw. After that, Dr. Agassiz would ask them to take a pencil and draw a detailed picture of the fish. Drawing the fish forced the students to look closer.

Then he asked them to redraw the same specimen, this time in color. He asked his students to look at the fish more carefully, to see it from different angles, and to consider basic questions, such as "How did the fish swim?" "How did it eat?" "How did it breathe?" and "How did it procreate?" Sure enough, the students saw something new each time, and their renderings reflected their new perspectives and deeper understanding.

"Look at the fish" became the battle cry and guiding light for all our courses in that Harvard program. Look deeper, see more, and understand more. It's been a personal mantra of mine ever since—a reminder that there is always something more to discover and something important to learn. We may be inherently blocked, biased, and blind, but we can be *less* blocked, *less* biased, and *less* blind. When we're willing to accept the challenge of opening the doors of perception wider and wider, we can take giant steps toward achieving everything we want in our personal and professional lives.

Curiosity Leads to Clarity

"I think, at a child's birth, if a mother could ask a fairy godmother to endow it with the most useful gift, that gift should be curiosity."
—Eleanor Roosevelt

It's not always obvious how much we should listen to our own inner voice as opposed to the voices of others, or how much weight we should assign to our own analysis versus the calculations of others when we're making decisions. Being obstinate about our convictions can lead to trouble. But so can giving in when we have a strong belief about something. Some of the greatest innovators in science, statecraft, industry, and religion persevered with single-minded devotion despite being told they were wrong, or even crazy. But those seemingly stubborn mavericks were also insatiably curious people, explorers who sought answers to burning questions and put their beliefs to the test: Buddha, Plato, Leonardo da Vinci, Isaac Newton, Thomas Edison, Madame Curie, Albert Einstein, Walt Disney, Steve Jobs, the Dalai Lama, Oprah Winfrey, J. K. Rowling, Angela Merkel—the list goes on and on.

Instinct and intellect are powerful resources and both need to be listened to and respected. They need to live and work together. We have to take our intuition seriously while we examine the evidence. We have to be as expansive and open-minded as possible without being gullible or indiscriminate. We have to have the courage of our convictions without becoming so inflexible or fanatical that we shut ourselves off from the truth and push others away. The truth tends to reveal itself little by little as we go deeper. We need as many vantage points as we can get until we have clarity.

I personally strive to be open-minded enough to sincerely listen equally to my own analysis and inner voice and to those of others. I do my best to carefully consider all ideas and advice until the right path becomes clear. But when is that? When is the searching over?

In discussing this specific question with a diverse group of intelligent, experienced, and introspective people, the most common answer is: "When you know." While that may sound a bit nebulous, most people will agree that the sense of knowing that occurs when a person has reached that point is actually quite distinct. And when I'm still not sure which way to go, I do know this: I need to keep looking further and deeper until I *do* know. This doesn't necessarily mean that I stand still until I'm 100% certain, but rather that at some point, the scales tip, and it feels right to go one way or another. Only then, when reason and intuition align, do I take action with clarity, comfort, and conviction.

Turn Frustration into Fascination

"You don't drown by falling in the water; you drown by staying there."
—Edwin Louis Cole

Expanding our awareness is serious business, but it can also be a lot of fun. That's why Zen masters are often depicted as both stern and jolly. They appreciate this key paradox: While mindfulness (the state of being conscious and aware of what arises in the moment) requires our full attention, we also have to let go to let in. And while finding the truth may require rigor and discipline, the path to greater awareness and openness is often to lighten up and enjoy the journey.

Rather than torture ourselves and others about our shortcomings, we can approach life with an attitude of curious delight. And the delight part is just as important as the curious. Both work to open and elevate. One of my favorite pieces of advice to myself and to others is "Turn frustration into fascination!"

People always ask me for an example of this concept in real life. The list is theoretically endless, because throughout each day we all experience people and situations that bother us. It could be the frustration of being late because a cab driver went the wrong way, the disappointment of someone letting us down, a meal being overcooked in a restaurant, or people not listening to our advice or ignoring our requests. Like I said, it's theoretically a long list.

But in all of these examples, who is suffering? *Me.* And what am I learning? *Nothing*—other than perhaps not to depend on others. But that attitude leads to isolation and extra work as I end up micromanaging people or doing everything myself. Plus, I too make plenty of mistakes, and I still end up with that frustration. So where's the growth in this approach? Where's the joy in life if we're constantly getting upset?

Fascination is much more enjoyable than frustration, and it's far more productive. By attempting to sincerely understand something, we become open and curious, which is a great starting point for learning and growth. And asking questions is a wonderful point of entry to a state of fascination. For example, these are some of the questions I ask myself when I get unsettled:

- Why would someone do this, or act this way?
- Would I ever do this? Why?
- Why does this bother me so much?
- What does this type of situation relate to or remind me of?
- What's the real reason I (or they) haven't changed?
- What could I do differently next time?

- How can I make this journey of discovery into an enjoyable game?

- Who can I ask to join me in this exploration?

- How will other people respond if I treat them with love and appreciation instead of anger and contempt? Why don't I do that?

- And ultimately: *If this situation helps me learn something valuable about myself and others, is it a problem or a gift?*

This orientation toward fascination, and the questions we can ask to explore it, can be incredibly powerful and productive. And usually, the more upset and frustrated we are, the more we have to learn and gain. Give it a try and decide for yourself.

2

Our World Is a Mirror of Our Mind

"We don't see things as they are, we see them as we are."

—Anaïs Nin

When I was fifteen or sixteen, I kept a diary for a while. Then I put it away somewhere and forgot about it. At some point during my moves to college, to the Virgin Islands after graduation, and then back to Boston, the diary disappeared. Its loss wasn't really an issue since I never even thought to look at it, and I certainly remembered everything about those formative years— high school, after-school jobs, clubs, friends, parties, girls, sports, getting my driver's license, my family . . .

Years later, I was going through some boxes and chanced upon that old diary. Excitedly, I started reading all about those fabulous teenage times. Except, apparently, they weren't so fabulous. It appeared I wasn't always the happiest of kids. My father had been experiencing declining health and almost annual heart attacks for four years, and he died when I was seventeen. He had withered away right before my eyes, giving up his full-time employment and growing weaker and weaker. It affected the entire family. I had conveniently diminished the impact of other circumstances as well. The life I remembered overall was vastly different from what my diary revealed. Apparently, I had rewritten history in my head.

—

Fast forward to me at sixty years old, sitting with a small group and listening to Patrick Connor, an exceptional spiritual teacher, explain how our world (i.e., the reality that we perceive) is a reflection of what goes on inside our heads and hearts—in effect, a mirror of our thoughts and feelings. He built his argument with impeccable logic, and it all made perfect sense. Then he said something so startling that it sent my mind reeling. "It's never too late to have a happy childhood." *Huh?*

He explained that we're always "translating" events through our various filters; therefore, if our perception of reality is suspect, our memories are also questionable. Not only because we're blocked and biased to begin with, but also because our initial memories are a function of our mood at the time they are formed, the way we attach meaning to things, and numerous other factors. This is especially true of children, whose sense of reality is further impeded by limited knowledge, experience, and understanding and whose emotional states change with the wind.

Since our childhood perceptions were distorted to begin with, and we continued to modify them every time we reviewed our mental files to fit whatever story we were trying to tell at the time, how can we take our memories as gospel? Therefore, why not apply a much more pleasing and practical lens to them? Why not focus on the good rather than on some childhood hurt that we're hanging on to—especially since that remembered hurt probably didn't happen the way we think it did?

Is this really possible, I wondered? Is my teacher accurate? Is it "right" to do this? And if we do, what are the implications? No matter how I analyzed it, I kept coming back to this thought: *If we truly do rearrange reality all the time, why not make the process serve us better? Why not focus on the good and the useful?*

According to my diary, I had apparently done exactly that with my teenage years. But that was an unconscious act. Should I now act consciously to review my life? Should I modify my internal filters and interpretations to edit my autobiography as I previously perceived it? Could I?

To be sure, many of my origin "stories" centered around hurts and harms and shortcomings. Growing up poor wasn't always easy, and my parents certainly weren't perfect. Nor was I. All of a sudden, it became clear to me that the meanings I had attached to things were not only suspect, but often subversive. Many times, I portrayed myself as a victim to serve some long-forgotten argument, or some subconscious need. I realized there were many memories—from childhood and later—that accentuated the negative in ways that didn't serve me well, and those memories had become entrenched in my narrative over time. *Hmmm.* I needed to think about this.

Reading that diary was a turning point in my life. What I discovered underscored what Patrick had said: *The world we live in—the life we perceive—is a perfect reflection, a mirror image, of our internal reality.*

And because we move in concert with the stories we create for ourselves, life becomes a self-actualizing process, a self-fulfilling prophecy. But the even more profound realization was that we have the ability to modify and improve our reality, to decide what to focus on and how to frame things—to impact not just our present and our future, but also our past. For example, we can literally choose to be grateful, loving, and joyous all the time. Consider the consequences!

This was one of the most surprising and revolutionary insights of my life. And while the logic may make perfect sense, the underlying premise is not necessarily intuitive. We believe that the world out there is precisely as we see it . . . because that's how we see it. We're caught in a circular and self-reinforcing illusion. But if everyone perceives a different reality based on their unique physical and psychological attributes, their histories, needs, and desires, then whose reality is accurate? The point is, our so-called reality, the world we think we live in, is actually a contrivance. It's a projection of what we perceive, think, feel, and believe at any given moment. That may sound depressing, but it can be quite the opposite. It can be empowering. Why? Because, *if our reality is contrived, it can be adjusted . . . and elevated.*

Above and Beyond Rewrites

> "The real voyage of discovery consists not in seeking new landscapes, but in having new eyes."
>
> **—Marcel Proust**

We actually modify our reality every day. Every moment in fact. Every time we take in a new piece of information, our views, attitudes, and decisions adjust accordingly. Every time we add a desire, or provoke a fear, or introduce a new idea or emotion, our world changes. Our world feels vastly different when we win compared to when we lose . . . or when we think we lose. It feels different after a restful sleep compared to after an exhausting or discouraging experience. In fact, our world is always different than it was before, because we're always different, and so is our attitude.

While it makes perfect sense to adjust our lenses to focus on the good and the useful in our lives, there's a related process we can pursue to improve our existence: *The most fundamental and effective way to change our lives for the better—now and moving forward—is to focus on internal upgrades rather than chasing external reflections.* The time-honored path to enlightenment—or at least fulfillment—is to expand and elevate our awareness, and with it our understanding, ability, and appreciation. With a greater perspective, we better understand that "the Emperor has no clothes." We see the illusion for what it is, and we stop subjecting ourselves to destructive and unproductive interpretations of our world.

The recipe for a better life begins by looking within and upgrading our attitude and our perceived reality. Granted, we have to address external matters and make decisions about our obligations and opportunities, our environments, and our relationships, but that will only get us so far. Because "out there" is just a reflection of "in here." The real recipe for happiness, success, and well-being is to work first and foremost on what's inside of us. And yet, we tend to do the exact opposite. Most of us spend our lives trying to conquer and change our external world, never realizing that the world is just a reflection of our head and our heart.

Is this just too simple to be true? Is adjusting our outlook and expanding our consciousness really the basic formula for success and happiness? Yes, it is both that simple and that true. But it's also tricky since we can't see what we can't see, and we humans are famous for deluding ourselves. Awareness arrives incrementally as we gain elevation. It's challenging to fully understand this insight at first, and it's even harder to internalize and consistently act upon it. But once you start to travel along this path, you'll begin to see it expressed all around you. And the higher you go, the more you see.

Once I was introduced to this concept, I regularly saw it expressed in books; I began to hear it from yoga teachers, psychologists, and gurus; I saw it in philosophical quotes and scientific references. It was similar to what happens when you buy a new car and suddenly see the same model all over the highway.

Here are some illustrations that might shed more light on the premise and how it manifests, as well as the opportunities that arise when we better understand the cause-and-effect between our inner and outer words:

Physical filters. If you think a rose is red, then that's what it is. Unless of course, you're color blind, in which case what you see as red is a bit different from what others see. Or if you're totally blind, colors don't exist at all in your world. We could come up with similar examples for sounds, smells, and tastes, but the conclusion is always the same—our perception of what's out there is a function of our ability to sense, what we focus on, and the meaning we assign to it.

Emotional filters . . . and drivers. If we're happy, our world feels wonderful. If we're miserable, our reality reflects that instead. And if we're in love, life can be utterly amazing. Consider the example of two people who are similar in every way, but one receives horrible news while the other learns about something glorious. What happens to their consciousness? What would happen to yours? How would the two different messages affect your state of mind, your sense of being, the way you interact with others? Do we really want our happiness to always depend on which way the wind is blowing, and who's blowing it? Wouldn't it be wonderful if we could gain more control?

One way to assume more control is to hit the pause button periodically and give ourselves a little breathing room. In fact, taking a few deep breaths is often a perfect way to calm our body, create some space, and gain perspective. By being less reactive, we can better choose the meaning we attribute to things.

How we attach meaning. How we define and frame the world around us creates our so-called reality. The stories that we tell ourselves and others are arbitrary and subjective. This includes the way we characterize the people, places, and events that populate those stories. And it's all in flux based on the meaning we ascribe to things at every moment. Therefore, perhaps we should learn to assign meaning in more nourishing ways.

For example, when we can't get into a performance we want to see, a restaurant where we want to eat, or a class we want to take, we can get stuck in the associated disappointment, or we can get excited about other potential opportunities that have now become possible—nature tends to fill a vacuum, and when we're open to serendipity, we're better positioned to welcome it in. Both views are valid, but one makes our world a happier place. But let's say that we continue to feel upset. Another approach would be to think of this event as a Geiger counter that has pinpointed some deep-seated issue we have. Lucky us that it happened, because now we get a chance to see something about ourselves that is normally obscured.

A classic marketing axiom tells us that the identification of a problem presents an opportunity to find or create a solution . . . and then market that solution. Therefore, "problems" can be good, and big problems can be better because they allow us to reap even bigger benefits. It's all in how we look at things. Clearly, one way of looking at things creates a much cheerier and more promising world, and all we have to do to live in that cheerier world is change our internal orientation and interpretation.

Another example that has become a powerful tradition in both my company and my family is this: Whenever we receive bad service somewhere, we celebrate. We really do. That's because long ago we realized that one reason our business thrives is because so many others fail to deliver great, or even good, service. They make us look wonderful by comparison; we didn't even have to do anything. So every time we discover another example of bad service, we say a silent "Thank you!"

The common denominator in all these examples is the meaning we attach to things. And we can improve it if we choose to.

What came first, the finger or the button? We often observe that certain people annoy us. We say they "push our buttons." This can be especially true of family members since they know us intimately, and they seem to know exactly how to provoke us. We fervently believe that *they do it to us.* We wish they would stop, and we try to get them to change. But what if we have it backward? *What if we're putting our button onto their finger (or right nearby where they can more easily push it)?* What if we're initiating the dance and they're reacting to our lead?

Obviously, all relationships are dynamic and complicated, but one way of looking at such button-pushing places the responsibility for our situation and our mood on someone else, while the other places the onus—and the opportunity—on us. We can make a lot more progress if we take responsibility for our actions and focus on improving ourselves rather than blaming others. This creates an opportunity to elevate ourselves. And when we elevate ourselves, we immediately elevate every single thing and person we interact with. Our entire world rises as we do.

Note the mind/body/being connection. Our physiology changes as we slow down our breathing. As a result, our world generally becomes clearer and more comfortable. In a related vein, when we do some aerobic exercise, we boost our endorphins and our mood usually follows. Also note how the quality of our sleep affects us so profoundly. Likewise, we are affected in various ways by caffeine, alcohol, and sugar. We clearly have the ability to influence our moods and either diminish or elevate our energy levels. We can improve everything in our world by raising our awareness, our energy, our self-image, and our outlook.

Seek and ye shall find. Keep looking, and be prepared to be amazed. We can start on the path to improvement by better understanding how we function and why. What is our orientation? How did it come to be? How is it helping or hindering us? What meaning are we attaching to things—and why? By looking closely, and shining a light on our consciousness, we can become more conscious and less controlled by external circumstances. It's utterly fascinating.

∞

In the Zen Buddhist tradition, stories abound about masters who suddenly attain satori, or enlightenment. But enlightenment (deep and full development of awareness and knowing) normally arrives bit by incremental bit. Along the way, we have periodic *Aha!* moments, but they usually result from putting in a lot of effort. Similarly, in everyday problem-solving, when a key connective piece of the puzzle suddenly appears, it may feel like the solution came in an instant, but that instant was generally preceded by a lot of prep work. As you continue to read through this book and explore elsewhere, you'll come across insights and applications that can help you enormously with that prep work. You'll find abundant opportunities to work on yourself and change your world.

We Are Biological Supercomputers, Subject to Programming by Ourselves and Others

"The neurochemistry of the brain is
astonishingly busy, the circuitry of a machine
more wonderful than any devised by humans."

—Carl Sagan

After graduating from college, I spent an idyllic summer living and working along the seashore on Cape Cod, outside of Boston where I grew up. The experience was so wonderful that I didn't want it to end. The sun, the warmth, the water, and the happy summer attitude were intoxicating. But eventually autumn came, the weather cooled, and my friends departed to pursue their careers, so I decided to find my slice of heaven elsewhere. I consulted a travel agent, did some research, and concluded that a tropical island sounded perfect. I borrowed the cost of a one-way plane ticket from my sister and flew to St. Croix in the US Virgin Islands. The island's slogan was "American Paradise," and that it was.

My first job was running the water sports concession at a little beach resort. On Day One, I learned how to snorkel. On Day Two, I was teaching others to snorkel. On Day Three, I learned the rudiments of sailing, and on Day Four I was showing others how to sail their own little boats. I was having a grand time.

Then one day my life changed unexpectedly when I met two flight attendants who had just arrived at the resort. They had recently taken a course in something called "mind control," and they told me wild and wonderful stories about learning to read minds and perform incredible feats of memory and other mental gymnastics.

For example, they said they'd learned how to wake up in the middle of the night without an alarm clock, at precisely the time they chose to get up. They also said they'd learned to memorize dozens of items at a time and then reel off the list in whatever order they were asked to. I found that hard to believe . . . until they demonstrated it for me. Then I took them a lot more seriously. I wondered what else they could do. Could they really read minds? More importantly, could I learn to do what they were doing?

The women explained that in addition to learning specific techniques, a critical part of the process was understanding our self-image and belief system, which acts as a homing device. We essentially do what's necessary to be the type of person we believe ourselves to be. If we want to elevate our game, they said, we need to elevate our self-image—we need to prove to ourselves that we're better than we think we are. And to learn something new, we first need to be open-minded about the possibility.

I was hooked and couldn't wait to learn more.

—

My First Brush with Mind Control

"You will act like the sort of person you conceive yourself to be."
—Maxwell Maltz

I coordinated my next visit to Boston with the dates of the mind control course the flight attendants had told me about. The program was everything they said it was and more. I quickly and easily learned how to remember long lists of items, forward, backward, and every which way; and I was also able to wake up within a few minutes of any random time I chose—or that was chosen for me.

My initial hunch that it was all a trick was indeed correct. But the "trick" was learning how to program our brains and bodies, and that turned out to be far more powerful—and far more *logical*—than I'd imagined.

That inner alarm clock works because, with a little practice, we can just as easily estimate the passage of time while we're sleeping as we can when we're awake. In fact, most people already experience this when they somehow *know* that it's time to do something, or when they regularly wake up a minute or two before their alarm goes off. As for the memorization, I accomplished it through a combination of calming and focusing the mind (the first step in self-hypnosis), visualization techniques, and pre-established "memory hooks." Today, such skills are taught in seminars around the world and are readily available on the Internet. But for me, at age twenty-two, they were nothing short of revelations.

In the second weekend of the course, we moved on to more sophisticated skills. We essentially learned to read minds. There were no parlor games or gimmicks. It required simply being more aware than we usually are and listening more deeply and more attentively than we normally do. It meant feeling the energy of other people and fine-tuning our intuition. Just as we are quick to sense the mood and intentions of our family, friends, and coworkers, so too can we divine other people's feelings and thoughts. And, with practice, as with any other skill, we get better and better.

It is beyond the scope of this book to describe all the details of these specific techniques. Suffice it to say I came to appreciate that what we often dismiss as mere guesses are usually valuable perceptions formed by conscious and subconscious knowledge, mixed with subtle yet powerful sensory data, all processed through a tremendously sophisticated biological supercomputer made up of the totality of our brain and body.

The instructors explained that the skills we strive to improve in all endeavors benefit from self-belief. Conversely, they are sabotaged by self-doubt. The development of the particular skills at this course was accomplished the old-fashioned way: through practice and validation. With each new technique I acquired, not only did my repertoire and the muscles of my mind improve, but so did my belief in myself and my appreciation of my potential. The new information substantiated my new and improved self-image. The course designers started with the easy stuff, so that with each improvement we became more eager and open-minded as we realized we could do more. I came to call this evidence-based progressive elevation of ability and self-image "The Stairway of Success," which we will explore and reference throughout the book.

I came away from that course knowing three things beyond any shadow of a doubt:

- We have far greater capacity for perceiving, knowing, and accomplishing than we realize.

- We are essentially biological supercomputers. We are subject to programming—by ourselves and others—often in ways we're not aware of.

- We can take charge of that programming. There is so much we can do to benefit ourselves, our loved ones, our enterprises, and our society. *Whether we seize that opportunity or relinquish the reins to others is our choice to make.*

The Supercomputer Within

> "Sitting on your shoulders is the most complicated object in the known universe."
>
> **—Michio Kaku**

In 1960, Maxwell Maltz published his best-selling book, *Psycho-Cybernetics*. It was the first mainstream book to compare the human mind to a computer, which was a revolutionary concept at the time. Back then, no one compared human beings to computers because (a) we barely knew what a computer was, since they had only recently been invented, and (b) our brains could do so much more than those clunky early calculating machines, which took up entire rooms and had less computing capacity than today's smartphones. But Maltz was struck by the comparison, and he understood the immense power of programming for man and machine alike.

A lot has changed since then. Not only has the capacity of our digital devices expanded beyond what very few people conceived of even twenty years ago, much less when Maltz wrote his book, but we have also learned a tremendous amount about the brain, the mind, and human consciousness, thanks to the combination of scientific discoveries and unprecedented access to traditional Eastern wisdom.

Now the comparison seems more like common sense. Only today we would have to say that human beings are more like biological *super*computers. As mind-boggling as today's computers are, no existing machine can come close to experiencing, understanding, feeling, creating, and doing what humans can. As Michio

Kaku wrote in *The Future of the Mind* in 2014, "It is remarkable that a gigantic, city-size computer is required to simulate a piece of human tissue that weighs three pounds, fits inside your skull, raises your body temperature by only a few degrees, uses twenty watts of power, and needs only a few hamburgers to keep it going."

I hear you saying, "Wait a minute! How can you say our capacity is greater than a computer's when we can't even do basic things like multiply a couple of three-digit numbers? Heck, an ordinary calculator can perform that calculation in a fraction of a second!"

The answer is simple: We're designed differently. We may not be programmed for instantaneous mathematical calculations (although we could be if we needed to be), but we are designed to create machines that can do it for us. We're also programmed for far more significant functions—like asking great questions and finding ways to answer them, creating art, making babies, building civilizations, and experiencing love and joy and fulfillment, all the while orchestrating countless biological functions, each one enormously sophisticated in its own right.

But the important question isn't "What can we do that computers can't?" or "How much more powerful must computers be to duplicate human capacity?" The questions that truly matter are the ones that point us toward our full potential and a better life today:

* If we are supercomputers, what are the implications?

* What are we currently doing with our incredible capabilities?

* What more can we do?

* How can we be happier and generate more love in our life . . . and how can we do the same for others?

* How do we program ourselves?

* How can we avoid being programmed by others in ways that harm or limit us?

A major reason most people are not performing near capacity is that they simply don't think of growth and achievement in these terms. They don't know how to program themselves effectively because they don't look at life that way. One critical consequence is that we allow others to usurp our domain and compromise our best interests with their own self-serving directives—meaning that we are being programmed by forces outside ourselves; and in our ignorance and neglect, we tolerate that situation.

As Maxwell Maltz wrote in his groundbreaking book, "It is no exaggeration to say that every human being is hypnotized to some extent either by ideas he has uncritically accepted from others or ideas he has repeated to himself or convinced himself are true." *We don't put up with having our computers hacked by others, so why cede control of our minds and our very beings to anyone else?*

Unlike mechanical computers, we humans don't come with an operating manual. The first step is to appreciate that we are programmable and reprogrammable. We know this from direct experience, and brain researchers have made great strides in mapping the mechanisms involved.

Not only can we modify our software, we can also transform our hardware. One key discovery in neuroscience is that our neurons are not fixed and unchanging like the wires in a machine. Rather, the brain is constantly reconfiguring itself by forming new neural connections. This capacity, known as neuroplasticity, allows our neural networks to adjust to new information and changes in the environment. This is additional proof that we're not stuck with the hand we've been dealt. Knowing we can reprogram our brains and create new neural connections is enormously liberating and energizing.

Beyond the Brain

"I . . . am not contain'd between my hat and my boots."
—Walt Whitman

The brain is as mind-boggling in its microscopic complexity as the Milky Way is in its astronomical complexity. According to researchers at Stanford University, the human brain contains about 200 billion neurons, and each one has about 10,000 neuronal connections called synapses. There are more than 125 trillion synapses in the cerebral cortex alone. And yet, when I say we are biological supercomputers, I'm not only talking about the brain. Scientists have discovered that we think, feel, and understand with our entire bodies, not just with the three-pound hunk of gray matter inside our skulls. In fact, every organ contributes to a cognitive and intuitive whole. The gut, for instance, contains so many neurons that some scientists call it the second brain, and its response time can be faster than that of the rational mind. Even the bottoms of the feet contribute to the whole: As doctors and massage therapists know, our soles have an extremely high concentration of nerve endings.

So why not take advantage of these discoveries to heighten our awareness, expand our knowledge, and get more attuned to formerly mysterious functions such as intuition and so-called extrasensory perception? The better we pay attention to our entire selves, the more we can learn, and the more we can grow.

My initial awakening to this second brain was in my early thirties. I had been working on a big investment offering that year and began to regularly suffer from severe stomach aches. I had long been affected by a so-called irritable stomach, so I responded by doing the "logical" thing: avoiding spicy and greasy food. But the stomach aches persisted. In the last six weeks of the year, I lost 20 pounds, dropping from 150 to 130 pounds, which did not look healthy on my 5′ 11″ frame. But it wasn't the food that was bothering me; it was the stress. My body was trying to tell me that I was betting the farm on that one deal, and that was a bad idea. Unfortunately, I did not pay attention. Like the frog in the story who stays in the water as the temperature increases incrementally and ultimately boils to death, I didn't understand what was going on until it was too late; meanwhile I got in a deeper and deeper mess. My body was desperately telling me that something was wrong, and it shouted louder and louder until I became ill.

In the end, my investment deal was concluded successfully, but the toll on my body was significant. It was a few years before I fully recovered. Since that time, I've paid much more attention to the various parts of my body and what they're trying to communicate. As I learned to listen, I became able to discern more and more. For example, there is a certain type of intestinal distress I experience that has proven to be cognitively driven rather than food-related; interestingly, it often appears before my conscious brain realizes there's a problem in my life that requires attention.

Intelligent awareness doesn't stop at the confines of our skin. In fact, it doesn't stop at all. We are continually getting data from everywhere, both within and without. Obviously, we are biomechanical beings, with arms and legs and supporting infrastructure. We are also chemical beings whose every function involves a sequence of molecular interactions so sensitive and sophisticated that little prescription pills can have a huge impact on us, mentally, physically, and emotionally.

However, we are also energetic entities whose influence and interactions extend well beyond our physical bodies. We generate electromagnetic and other types of energy from every cell, and we receive energy at every moment. We interact on a molecular, atomic, and subatomic level with the world around us—not just those objects in our immediate vicinity, but conceivably all the energy-emitting entities in the universe. And, depending on the specific type of energy, this transmission can occur at the speed of light. Our sense of sight, sound, smell, touch, and taste only represent a fraction of the detectable energy that scientists are aware of. Suffice it to say that there's a lot more going on. And, like the ripples in a pond caused by tossing a stone, waves of energy can eventually impact the entire system.

What mystics, metaphysicians, and philosophers have always said turns out to be demonstrably true: We are affected by far more than the information we take in through our five senses, because we are intricately and irrevocably, part and parcel of something bigger than ourselves.

We are ultimately connected to all and everything. Some call this universal consciousness, or the collective unconscious, or the hive mind, or the void. Some use religious terms like God or Brahman, while others stick to scientific concepts and the language of quantum physics and energy to explain our interconnectedness. However we conceive of our deep oneness with the universe we share, it's clear that our ability to transmit and receive information (which is, after all, a form of energy) transcends space, and perhaps time as well. It is virtually boundless. So, whether we prefer the language of physics or metaphysics, spirituality or neuroscience, when we examine the facts it becomes crystal clear that we are embedded in a virtually limitless web of energy and potential.

The Implications Are Enormous

> "If we did all the things we are capable of doing, we would literally astound ourselves."
> —**Thomas A. Edison**

The enormous power of our minds and bodies, coupled with our energetic link to potentially all and everything, unveils immense possibilities. Once we recognize that something deeper than words or even feelings is transmitted among human beings, we can start to become more conscious and more powerful programmers instead of being subject to so much unconscious programming.

Think of a time when you entered a room and began to feel suspicious or fearful. What was happening? Quite possibly, you were picking up on electromagnetic waves emitted by the other people present, and then you connected the feelings that arose inside you with other data points in your memory to deduce certain conclusions. In its own complex way, your brain put two and two together. By contrast, think of a time when you felt peaceful and safe upon entering a room. You may have been experiencing a different set of energy patterns—ones that were harmonious with your own.

In other words, each of us is both a transmitter and a receiver of energy. Like tuning forks, we send and receive information to and from one another through energy resonance. In fact, that's exactly what our senses do: They take in and discern the specific signatures of sight, sound, smell, touch, and taste—and perhaps a great deal more.

This basic everyday phenomenon can be utilized consciously and purposefully. For one thing, we can cultivate the ability to discern different energies, just as we train muscles for specific uses. The more we become acclimated to an environment, familiar with a feeling, or attuned to another person, the better we recognize that particular energy stamp. For example, you probably know if a family member is happy, sad, or mad as soon as they enter a room. And you know it with even more certainty when you observe their body language and they utter a few words.

The practical implications of this energy and information transmission are greater than you might think. One is the benefit that comes from being around talented, successful people, even if you can't speak to them. Years ago, my Tai Chi teacher told me about a time when his meditation practice was stuck on a plateau, and he found a new teacher who helped him rise to the next level. I asked, "What did he teach you? What did he say?" He revealed that his teacher didn't *say* anything. Simply meditating at the teacher's feet was enough to have a huge impact in the form of an energy exchange that my instructor called "transmission of mind"—a phenomenon that has been practiced for thousands of years in Eastern cultures.

While I had never given it a specific name before hearing my teacher's term, I had always known I was being strongly affected by others. Not only can they touch me, move me, and even awaken me, but I can also sense, imitate, and replicate their energy to varying degrees—I can learn and grow from their vibrations. For that reason, I've taken every opportunity to interact with exceptionally gifted and talented people, even if I could do so only for a short time. I've briefly passed through the lives of powerful personalities ranging from presidents of countries, titans of industry, and celebrated teachers to con men, comediennes, singers, socialites, and even one saint. In each case, their energy imprint was so specific and so strong that I can still remember it and how it felt.

What is especially fascinating is that I don't remember much of what they said or what I read in any of their books, but I vividly remember the essence of their energies from those personal encounters. The lessons they shared with me were woven into their energy imprints. In this way, I continue to benefit from their being, however distant in space and time.

That might sound esoteric or New Age-y, but think of some of the influential people in your past—a parent, an uncle or aunt, a teacher, a mentor—and notice that what you remember is not just something they said or did, but also the *feel* of their personality and essence. Their energy. That imprint contains a subtle form of knowledge, and we resonate with other people's energy output like a tuning fork. That's why your parents told you to hang out with the right people. That advice still applies today. Try it, but do so consciously and pay attention. You'll be surprised how much you can learn through the transmission of energy.

And that's just the input side. There's also output to consider: We can learn to transmit specifically designed and targeted energy when we communicate. We can exude love, confidence, friendliness, and other moods and feelings as the situation warrants. In practical terms, this boils down to communicating more effectively and having greater influence.

The key to improving how we impact others is to heighten our sensitivity to the energy and information we transmit, and to that which we receive. Like learning to ride a bicycle, it begins with conscious intent and effort, and it evolves into an automatic process as each subset of skills is practiced, mastered, and integrated. The same is true, of course, for other skills, from playing tennis to driving on the expressway to winning friends and influencing people.

Beyond Positive Thinking

> "When you change the way you look at things,
> the things you look at change."
> **—Max Planck**

Does the expression "Whatever you can conceive and believe, you can achieve" sound familiar? It might, because it's widely used in motivational speeches, self-improvement seminars, self-help books, and even churches. The statement, which has been attributed to Napoleon Hill, Andrew Carnegie, Johann Wolfgang von Goethe, and others, might sound like garden variety motivational blather, but it captures something profoundly true about human design and potential, and we now have a good deal of evidence to support its basic premise. For one thing, high-achievers, from sales reps to star athletes, use visualization and guided imagery to prepare for action by picturing desired outcomes in their minds. Such practices work because they modify the programming of the supercomputers we call "I" and "me."

Research demonstrates that what we conceive—that is, what we construct in our minds—produces activity in the brain that is strikingly similar, if not identical, to what happens neurologically when we experience the actual thing. The success of visualization has led to the development of more refined programming techniques.

Once we know where we want to go and what we want to accomplish, and we *believe* it, we can much more easily achieve what we've conceived. In part two of the book, we'll look at practical methods for realizing that promise by taking conscious control of the system. After all, what good is having a supercomputer with enormous capability if we don't know how to program it? And what's the use of knowing how to program it, if we don't actually do it? Or, worse yet, if we allow *others* to program us for their own benefit?

Many claims that are commonly promoted in the self-improvement world fail to live up to expectations because they are more wish-based than evidence-based, and computers tend to be rational, realistic, and fact-oriented.

Take the common practice of replacing negative thoughts with positive ones. In theory, this makes perfect sense, since negative beliefs can indeed be crippling. The problem is, the brain consults its previously stored information, and if it observes that our personal histories and demonstrated capacities contradict what the affirmation says, it kicks out an error message like "That's rubbish!" or "That does not compute!" Say you start taking guitar lessons and you're really bad at it, but you tell your brain that you're going to win a Grammy Award in the coming year. Your brain immediately calculates that your assertion is ridiculous. As a result, you end up with an inner conflict that undermines your avowed objective.

Fortunately, there are ways to install positive programs that are acceptable to the brain because they're realistic, correspond to reason and evidence, and can be continuously validated through action. If you really want to be a good guitar player, for example, trying to convince your brain that you're destined for immediate Grammy greatness is not as effective as this program: "I'm going to practice so I can have fun and entertain people with a few songs." To that, the brain says, "Sounds good to me. I'm all for it."

As we gradually rewrite our subconscious programming, our self-image improves accordingly. This is critical, because as Maxwell Maltz put it, "Our self-image, strongly held, essentially determines what we become." Like a homing device, our self-image orients our lives and largely determines our goals, choices, and actions. Therefore, it is essential to shape and maintain a positive self-image, and we can do that with realistic programming that nourishes our potential instead of undermining it. Then, with each genuine improvement we make, we start to realize that we can use the same principles to get better at other things. And when that turns out to be true, the big revelation occurs: We realize that we can get better at *every* thing. Based on this evidence, a new, more positive self-image arises, and it gets progressively reconfigured and reinforced until it permeates all aspects of our lives.

From the Abstract to the Concrete

"The only source of knowledge is experience."

—Albert Einstein

As amazing as all this sounds, I know you won't be truly convinced until you experience tangible rewards yourself. That's what happened to me forty years ago. What those two flight attendants told me was intriguing, but I didn't really believe how powerful the programming methods were—or truly understand them—until I experienced the techniques firsthand. Once I gave them a try, it wasn't long before I realized the women were right: Programming ourselves for improved functioning is as straightforward and logical as it is powerful. So is the equally important process of *de-programming* what has already been installed (by ourselves and others) and is not serving us well.

I demonstrate that simple truth to the students in my classes (generally business conferences, home office training, and periodic guest lectures) with the following method: First, I prime the pump by asking, "Do you know anyone who's an insomniac?" Most of them say they do. I then ask, "What do insomniacs typically say?" The answer is "I can't sleep."

That is an example of self-programming, I explain. By telling themselves, over and over again, that they can't sleep, those people are reinforcing their identity as insomniacs and perpetuating the very problem they say they want to solve. The brain has a picture of how insomniacs behave, and it acts accordingly.

I then ask, "Do any of you have trouble remembering names?" Most of them raise their hands. "Who is *really* bad at it?" I ask. A few people raise their hands. I ask them to explain what they mean. Almost all their answers include the words "I can't." I point out that they're doing the same thing as the insomniacs. The point is always well taken.

I then propose a test: "I'll give you a list of ten items. I want you to remember all ten." I reel off the names of ten familiar objects. A few minutes later, I have them write down the ten items. Most people remember six or seven, and some get only four or five. A few in the room score a bit higher, but rarely does anyone remember nine or ten.

Then I take the challenge myself, only I ask them to give me *twenty* items. I sit still, close my eyes, relax into a self-hypnotic state, and have someone name each item, allowing a few seconds between each one. Another person stands behind me and writes the words on a flip chart. I then reel off all twenty. In order. The students are invariably impressed.

I then name the items in reverse order. Then I ask the group to shout out numbers from one to twenty. If someone calls out "Six!" I name the sixth item on the list. If someone yells "Eleven!" I state the eleventh word. And so on, for all twenty.

The point isn't to show off (although it definitely feels good). It's to demonstrate that these mental skills can be learned. In fact, I tell them, *anyone* can do such things. All they need is the right method.

I offer to teach them how to do it in twenty minutes. They accept the challenge with a mix of hope and skepticism. After explaining how autosuggestion (i.c., self-hypnosis) works and teaching them some simple techniques, which are covered later in this book, I give them another ten items to remember. This time, about 90% of them remember nine or ten. The rest are in the seven to eight range. And in many cases, someone who got a three or four the first time around, now scores a nine.

"I thought you had bad memories," I say. "Well, do you or don't you?"

Now they're not so sure. They realize they may have programmed themselves to believe something erroneous and limiting, and they just disproved it. They are now much more open to what I really want to teach them—that their abilities and potential are much greater than they suspected. Their excitement is tangible as they begin to grasp the ramifications and possibilities.

That's what happened to me many years ago when I took that mind control course. I too thought I had a lot of limitations, only to realize that the conviction was just a self-imposed image based on a lack of knowledge and experience. Once I had some practical techniques under my belt, my self-image changed dramatically. That was the "believe" part of "Whatever you can conceive and believe, you can achieve." Now I knew I could program my mind, not just for memory games but for virtually anything.

We Can Leverage the Multiplier Effect for Exponential Gains

"Opportunities multiply as they are seized."

—Sun Tzu

In the early days of building my financial services business, Commonwealth Financial Network, we observed enormous disparities between the revenues generated by our top financial advisors and those from our lower-end associates. But the gap was far greater than one might reasonably assume. Even after discounting the outliers at the extremes of the bell curve, the highest earners, as a group, grossed twenty times more than our less productive people!

I already knew there was a big discrepancy between the best and the rest, but twenty times? How could that be? Were they twenty times smarter? Did they put in twenty times as many hours? We were determined to solve this puzzle so we could learn how to help everyone become more productive, which, of course, would also boost the company's earnings.

First, we gathered data about the advisors' abilities and work ethics. We also considered their product knowledge, efficiency, and communication skills; the quality of their office staffs; their use of technology; and other factors. The numbers revealed some helpful information: Person A knew approximately twice as much as Person B, and Person A was also twice as efficient as Person B. But "twices" like these could not account for twenty times as much productivity. In fact, nothing could. The math just didn't seem to work.

—

Eventually, we realized that the math did work, and the implications were enormous. The problem was in the faulty logic we used when thinking about the issue. We had been *averaging* the relevant strengths and weaknesses of every individual before comparing them to one another. But in reality, a person's various talents augment and reinforce one another. That is, the individual strengths improve all the other strengths, and likewise, the weaknesses diminish everything they interact with.

For example, if someone gains technological proficiency, that expertise will generally improve every area of her work. It will make her research, marketing, and operations better because technology affects everything. On the other hand, if a manager is a weak communicator, his whole operation will suffer because communication is critical in getting everything and everybody to move in the right direction, to coordinate actions, and to energize the team.

This realization led to the solution to our mystery: Instead of averaging, or adding and subtracting attributes, the key to understanding why some people produced twenty times more than others was to *multiply*. We had missed it because it wasn't intuitive. The simple mathematical examples that follow demonstrate exactly how this works.

Profound Implications

"I have a great respect for incremental improvement . . . but I've always been attracted to the more revolutionary changes."

—Steve Jobs

We usually assume that adding one positive element to a person or an organization will improve the results proportionately. That may be true if there is only one factor to consider. However, when total performance is made up of multiple factors, sometimes a single improvement in one area can trigger a dramatic chain reaction and increase the cumulative benefits not just by 10%, 20%, or 30%, but maybe by a few hundred percent—or more.

Imagine two individuals or organizations that are both extremely knowledgeable and talented across five categories (e.g., product quality, customer service, marketing, sales, and technical support) with one exception. While one is 100% proficient in all five areas, the other is 100% in four and achieves only 50% of their potential in the weaker area. The math might look something like this:

100%—100%—100%—100%—100%

versus

100%—100%—100%—100%—50%

At first glance, it's easy to see that the top performer is better than the other one, but certainly not twice as good. After all, he or she may be twice as good in that last category (i.e., 100% vs. 50%), but both people are equally wonderful in all the other categories.

But what if that last category was a measurement of efficiency? Now we can understand how the top performer could be twice as productive overall: Being twice as efficient in general, he or she is likely to be twice as productive. Therefore, to get the correct answer, we need to *multiply* the proficiencies, as you can see here:

$$1 \times 1 \times 1 \times 1 \times 1 = \mathbf{1}$$

$$1 \times 1 \times 1 \times 1 \times \tfrac{1}{2} = \mathbf{\tfrac{1}{2}}$$

1 (or 100%) is twice as big (or productive in this story) as ½ (or 50%).

Now, suppose we compare two other people in the same categories, where one is 80% proficient in all five categories and the other is 40% proficient in each. On seeing those numbers, most of us would initially assume that the first person is twice as productive as the second one, since 80% is the double of 40%. However, if we multiply the proficiencies instead of averaging them, the math for the first person looks like this:

$$.80 \times .80 \times .80 \times .80 \times .80 = \mathbf{.32768.}$$

The second person's combined score, on the other hand, is:

$$.40 \times .40 \times .40 \times .40 \times .40 = \mathbf{.01024.}$$

Seen from this perspective, the first person isn't just twice as productive as the second. He is potentially thirty-two times (.32768 / .01024) as productive! That's what we were observing in our business.

That's the power of the Multiplier Effect!

All of a sudden, the huge disparity in our advisors' productivity made sense. This astounding *Aha!* led to profound changes in the way we do business. And it didn't stop there, because we soon discovered that the inherent logic of the Multiplier Effect can generate extraordinary improvements in every area of life. But first we needed to better understand the mechanics and how to apply them.

For example, while the math might prove the point in the hypothetical scenarios just described, neither people nor organizations can ever be reduced to only a few characteristics. Therefore, it's best to think of the Multiplier Effect as a conceptual framework as opposed to a rigid formula.

This is not a new concept. The Multiplier Effect is a well-established principle in economics, and its basic rationale is rooted in a common axiom of both the ancient East and the modern West: *Everything within a particular system interacts with everything else.* Whether you're looking to build a business, advance your career, or win friends and influence people, success in any realm is the result of adopting and improving the particular success factors for that objective. And an appreciation of how everything interacts can easily make the difference between success and failure.

This leads to another powerful and related insight: *If the Multiplier Effect can multiply strengths, it can also multiply weaknesses!* Since all of our actions and attributes impact one another, the same logic about multiplying positive characteristics holds true for multiplying weaknesses, mistakes, and oversights—only in the opposite direction.

As you'll soon see, when we grasp the implications of the Multiplier Effect, we can consciously put the principle to work for us to generate exponential improvements in everything from our personal lives to the most complex organizations. Likewise, we can minimize unnecessary and unintended decline and deterioration.

The Mystery: Why Excellence Is So Hard to Imitate

> "We are kept from our goal, not by obstacles, but by a clear path to a lesser goal."
> —**The Bhagavad Gita**

If you look at the top performers in any field—business executives, entrepreneurs, attorneys, teachers, artists, athletes, and those in other important roles, such as parents, spouses, lovers, and friends—you find people who may only be moderately better than their counterparts in most specific skills, but who nevertheless soar above the pack in overall performance and success. Some even reach superstar levels. Why?

Because their strengths augment and multiply one another. Taken one at a time, their talents and skills may not account for a vast difference in success. But in combination, they work like compound interest, producing exponential gains that improve outcomes by orders of magnitude. Furthermore, if these people have any additional special talents, those talents improve all the others, and the gap widens even more.

But success isn't just a function of math; math is merely how we understand the process and measure the results. Success is primarily an outcome of focus and energy—the skillful application of purpose, passion, and resources. We don't get to the top of the mountain unless the objective is crystal clear, resonates with what we hold dear, and is pursued intelligently and energetically. This isn't new or esoteric, so why doesn't everyone, or every serious enterprise, do just that?

Some years ago, in an article in *Harvard Business Review*, renowned Harvard professor Michael Porter showed how this dynamic of interrelated strengths and weaknesses (i.e., the Multiplier

Effect) played out in the airline industry. He posed a very interesting and important question: *Why don't less successful companies simply imitate their most successful counterparts? Why doesn't everyone just copy the champions and deliver similar great service and quality products?*

It seemed like a practical question, because imitating superior achievers, whether corporate or personal, would appear to be an obvious strategy. But it's not common practice. Why is this?

Porter found two reasons: (1) it's not always easy to achieve true excellence in a given area. It takes a solid commitment and a great deal of time, effort, and resources to raise key skill sets to superior levels. And (2) hugely successful companies have *many* areas of excellence. This is a critical notion, because it might be feasible to imitate one or two competencies, but duplicating all of them is extremely difficult. "It is harder for a rival to match an array of interlocked activities," Porter wrote, "than it is merely to imitate a particular sales-force approach, match a process technology, or replicate a set of product features."

He used the example of Southwest Airlines. One of the reasons for the company's initial success, Porter pointed out, is that it had an array of advantages: great routes, quality technology, low-hassle seating, a competent and engaging staff, and low prices. And these were not stand-alone skills. Each one enhanced all the others. As a result, the overall benefits multiplied.

Now let's get personal and consider our individual situations. This is where it gets much more interesting, because we decide where to focus our time and energy—and where not to. *As a result, we are both the problem and the solution.*

Doing What Doesn't Come Naturally

"Where you stumble, there lies your treasure."
—Joseph Campbell

The Multiplier Effect shows that we can get dramatically better outcomes by focusing on areas with the most room for growth. That generally means addressing our biggest weaknesses. A big improvement in one fundamental weakness can boost a business's productivity and profitability dramatically. Similarly, an improvement in a weak aspect of our personal life can enhance our well-being and fulfillment by several orders of magnitude. The same goes for intimate relationships, athletic achievement, and anything else we care about.

The problem is, we usually do the exact opposite. We choose to fine-tune our strengths rather than face our shortcomings and weaknesses. In fact, that's partly why they became strengths and weaknesses in the first place—we nourished one and neglected the other, most likely because we enjoyed one activity more than the other, and it probably came more easily to us. Let's face it, focusing on areas of strength gives us pleasure, while dealing with our weaker attributes is usually unpleasant, often frustrating, and sometimes agonizing. As a result, we generally don't want to confront those weaknesses. Plus, sometimes we believe that we don't have to look at them because we're sufficiently successful doing what we do well, and we rationalize that we can just keep doing things the way we always have.

However, this tendency eventually catches up with us, and when it does, it poses problems. You probably know established people and businesses that haven't embraced new technologies because, historically, they were able to get away with their traditional approaches and legacy systems. It's most likely only a matter of time before they get eclipsed by competitors who can do things better, faster, and cheaper. Or, think of a company that has enjoyed dominance in its sector, but whose customer service is so poor that people don't want to deal with them. What are their long-term prospects once the competition closes the product gap and also offers first-class service? Likewise, too many individuals rest on their laurels, whether physical, financial, or anything else, only to fall or fail when their primary advantage fades away.

The biggest improvements we make usually come from upgrading areas of weakness and developing important skills and offerings we currently lack. Ignoring those challenges constrains growth and fosters stagnation—or worse. It becomes a vicious cycle: We tend to get weaker and weaker in the areas we avoid; and the weaker those qualities get, the more unpleasant they become, and therefore the more we want to avoid them. Because we tend to move toward pleasure and away from pain, the cycle perpetuates itself. Therefore, it's critical to recognize what's going on, and to understand our part in it so we can take corrective action.

There is also an additional benefit in confronting our areas of weakness and discomfort. We are enormously resourceful beings, and by demonstrating that we can make a significant difference if only we try, we not only raise our skill set and improve the issue at hand, we also strengthen our self-image.

Diminishing Returns vs. Milestone Opportunities

"I fear not the man who has practiced 10,000 kicks once, but I fear the man who has practiced one kick 10,000 times."

—Bruce Lee

In most instances, allocating additional resources to an existing strength will only bring about modest results. For example, the benefits from improving proficiency in one area from 90% to 95%

are not nearly as dramatic as those that come from raising an area of weakness and vulnerability from 50% to 80%. However, there are times when upgrading an existing strength enables us to break through a barrier and achieve a significant milestone. And that milestone can indeed be transformative.

Sometimes improvements of that nature can be monumental, raising an existing strength to such a level that, in effect, a whole new category is created. I know many "highly sought-after experts" in various fields who have increased their knowledge by 10–20% beyond the majority of their peers, but that 10–20% places them at the very pinnacle of their professions. They know more, they understand more, they command more respect, and thereby, they attract more business. They are considered the thought leaders, the authorities, "the best."

At Commonwealth, for example, we had always taken pride in providing world-class customer service, but at one point we decided to take service to an entirely new level. We explored this vision in numerous meetings, thinking through what we really wanted, what it would look like, and what it would be called. Finally, we decided that we wanted our service to be literally *indispensable*. It would be so incredible that our clients would feel that they couldn't do without us and would never even think of leaving us. Armed with this compelling new vision, we set to work exploring, understanding, and brainstorming how to bring it to life as our enthusiasm and creativity took root. I'm happy to say we not only succeeded in improving our customer service from world-class to indispensable, but the experience infused everything we did with a clarity and energy that greatly exceeded previous levels.

There are many other examples of breakthrough improvements: Amazon's 1-Click ordering didn't just make buying online easier; by creating an entirely new experience for customers, it was essentially a revolutionary new strength. Netflix did the same when it shifted from only delivering DVDs by mail to also streaming movies online. And, of course, there's Apple's iPhone, which transformed the smartphone into the worldwide phenomenon that we all know. Sometimes a commercial brand sets out to not just be better, but to create a new category. Think Four Seasons hotels, Whole Foods markets, Sonos music systems, or Uber.

I'm sure you can think of many other examples. It doesn't have to be something that alters an industry or requires a great investment. I know many people who transformed their lives by becoming brilliant cooks or joke tellers, or they learned to play guitar or give great massages, all with spectacular results. Some of the most popular people I know are great listeners and caring friends. What they all have in common is that they elevated an existing skill to an exceptional level, and that improvement had a significant impact on others.

Creatures of Habit

> "The chains of habit are too weak to be felt
> until they are too strong to be broken."
> **—Samuel Johnson**

We focus on our strengths not only because it gives us more pleasure than dealing with our weaknesses, but also because we are creatures of habit. Once a routine has been set and our infrastructure is neatly in place, we usually keep things just the way they are as long as the results are reasonably good and no big problem poses a threat. We choose the comfort of the status quo over the risk and fear of change, even when change is exactly what we need.

There's a classic example right on your computer's keyboard. The arrangement of letters on that keyboard goes by the nickname QWERTY, for the six letters on the left side of the top row. The system was created in the early 1870s when the typewriter was invented.

In order to minimize the jamming of keys on the early machines, the letters were arranged to separate the ones we use most frequently, purposely slowing the maximum pace someone could type.

Today's typewriters (i.e., keyboards) don't have mechanical levers, so key jamming has long ceased to be an issue. Studies have shown that other arrangements of letters would actually be markedly more efficient and enable us to type much faster, but we generally *haven't* changed our keyboard configurations. Originally, typewriter manufacturers didn't want to risk selling a machine that typists or clerks were not acclimated to. And typists didn't want to risk learning a new technique they couldn't employ at work if the machine there had the traditional configuration. So no one did anything.

I'm sure you can find examples in your own workplace and in your personal life. Exploring why we don't do what we know we should do is a fascinating area of inquiry. And in light of the tremendous gains to be had by igniting the Multiplier Effect, it becomes a vital question.

∞

"If you don't have time to do it right, when will you have time to do it over?"
—John Wooden

The Multiplier Effect represents a golden gateway to progress, especially for those who are willing to take up the challenge of working on areas of weakness. Opportunities for improvement abound and surround us. We can always find ways to overcome drawbacks and shortcomings, and often those very problem areas can be turned into strengths. We can even make the process enjoyable, as you will learn later in the book.

The Multiplier Effect is usually strongest when a key skill that is currently missing gets added, or when a weakness is significantly improved. It is also safe to say that the more fundamental a skill is, the bigger and broader the impact of upgrading it will be. Improving our aptitude for chugging beer is probably of limited value, for example, while improving our ability to motivate others can reverberate exponentially throughout all our relationships and enterprises. Likewise, enhancing our capacity to love—both others and ourselves—will yield enormous riches.

This leads directly to the next primary insight: Some skills are so universal and so fundamental that their impact ripples through the entirety of our lives.

There Are Universal Principles and Fundamental Skills that Fuel All Learning and Growth

"Excellence is achieved by the mastery of the fundamentals."

—Vince Lombardi

I had recently turned forty and was increasingly interested in the pathways to success in all areas of life, both for myself and others. In a Tai Chi class one day, my teacher and I were playing with the incoming energy of an opponent—how to feel it, move with it, neutralize it, and, if necessary, absorb and then redirect it. Once practitioners learn this powerful skill, they can use it to seemingly dance with the energy of much bigger opponents, and even turn it against them. When performed by a master, this ability appears to be almost effortless, bordering on supernatural.

Then came an epiphany when I realized that these methods for managing energy also applied to windsurfing, another sport I enjoyed. Windsurfers learn to sense the wind in relation to the position of their board, their body, and their sail. They adjust everything accordingly in order to capture the wind in the sail rather than struggle against it. They then direct that wind energy through their bodies and out through their legs and feet into the board. Likewise, sailors adjust the direction of the boat and the trim of the sail to capture the power of the wind and then use that energy to propel the boat while they direct it with the rudder. The more efficient their techniques, the more wind they capture, the less they struggle, the more successful their voyage, and the more fun they have.

This appreciation of energy flow also applied to tennis. I began consciously sensing the various energies involved in that sport—my own position, my opponent's, the incoming ball, and the torque of my body. It's a short leap to apply the same fundamental principles to virtually any sport. While this was certainly not a new discovery in any of these individual sports, the awakening for me was the concept of employing the same general principles to different activities.

—

A physicist friend was amused by my "discovery." He said that the principles I described are easily explained by basic laws of physics. However, while it was exciting (for me at least) to realize that the same laws of nature can be applied to a broad range of physical activities, my mind exploded in wonderment with my next revelation.

All of a sudden it dawned on me that the benefits of discerning, amassing, and managing energy also applied to business. Energy and communication channels flow within every organization and entity. They manifest in the form of ambitions, desires, and virtually every other human emotion, and they are influenced by both internal and external forces.

As with physical sports, the challenges are to:

- Sense and understand the type of energy that is being expressed

- Recognize its source

- Neutralize, cancel, or augment it, depending on what is most efficient and expedient

- Gather and store it when warranted

- Deploy and direct it as necessary

The principles an athlete employs to propel a ball, and a martial artist uses to overcome an opponent, are, in a business context, the essence of basic communication, goodwill, political currency, carrot-and-stick incentives, and other managerial tools.

It also dawned on me that, for all the same reasons, I could use these skills at home with my wife and son to foster greater awareness, reduce stress, avoid unnecessary struggles, and ultimately direct our family energies toward positive shared objectives. All of a sudden, a lot of things made much more sense. Discerning and directing energy was a universal skill! I could apply it essentially anywhere. That series of epiphanies about universal skills was the original inspiration for this book.

Many of our existing skills and talents can be applied to other areas of life, immediately, and with dramatic benefits. A favorite example of many women I know is the high-powered businessman who excels at his profession but is almost clueless as a husband and father. What he doesn't understand is that most of the basic skills and strategies that drive his professional success—having a clear and compelling vision, listening to his target audience, being aware of trends, recognizing and satisfying needs, creating agreed-upon strategies and tactics, accessing outside expertise, and creating customized incentives—can also be used in his personal life. Granted, the language and specific applications are likely to be somewhat different from the business or athletic versions, but the underlying logic, physics, and protocols are essentially the same. Conversely, skills that we cultivate at home, such as love, empathy, and appreciation, can also be employed (no pun intended) at work and elsewhere. It's a virtuous cycle.

The bottom line is that anyone who masters the fundamental and universal skills of life can pretty much go anywhere, do anything, and essentially meet any business or personal challenge with confidence, efficiency, and delight. You become an explorer whose all-purpose abilities allow you to navigate much more safely and effectively through virtually any environment.

Task-Specific vs. Universal Skills

> "I was lucky enough when it came to sports and work ethic to be taught some basics that continue to be important."
>
> **—Joe Namath**

Most how-to books teach task-specific skills. They prescribe specific actions aimed at achieving specific results: how to start a business, play better golf, improve your marriage, and so forth. A central insight of *Elevate* is that certain skills are so basic, so fundamental, so universally applicable that they drive achievement in every conceivable endeavor.

Does that sound far-fetched? Not if you realize that we've all grown up learning universal competencies and have depended on them all our lives. Remember the "three Rs"—reading, writing, and 'rithmetic? There are very few areas of life where the ability to read and write, and to add, subtract, multiply, and divide, are not relevant. Communication skills are another example: Where would you be, at work, at home, or at play, without the ability to speak to and listen to other human beings?

The philosopher Aldous Huxley described a world based on such broad-spectrum skills in his novel *The Island*. He imagined a utopian society that starts with a clean slate and creates an educational system that incorporates principles and practices that are basic to both the ancient wisdom traditions and modern science, such as awareness, meditation, and visualization. The results he described were transformative. The inhabitants had greater clarity, more confidence, less stress, better health, and more love and satisfaction in their lives.

As our understanding of these fundamental principles and practices has blossomed, many of them are being applied in a variety of settings throughout our culture. Programs have even sprouted up in preschools and elementary schools with predictably powerful results. Young minds are especially open and are naturally attracted to such enjoyable fundamental practices. One such program is Calmer Choice, which is based on the mindful awareness techniques that Dr. Jon Kabat-Zinn developed from Eastern and Western insights. Calmer Choice teaches young people how to effectively and safely manage stress and resolve conflict so that they live happy, healthy, and successful lives. Their goal is to provide skills that will diminish the risk of violence, substance abuse, and other self-destructive behaviors. Mindfulness allows the students to pay attention, on purpose, to what is happening right now, both internally and externally, with kindness and curiosity toward themselves and others. This provides the ability to better regulate themselves. In this awareness they realize they have choices in how they respond to internal and external stimuli.

Like tree branches, the disparate activities we engage in have similar roots and structures, just as our most important endeavors share similar paths to success. In other words, we can accelerate growth, achievement, and improvement by understanding and applying the principles that form the foundation for all achievement.

Ex-athletes, for example, don't succeed in their post–retirement days only by cashing in on their fame and connections; those factors merely open doors. Retired athletes who continue to flourish draw upon the same skills that helped them excel on the field or the court. They simply transfer them to their next career, redirecting techniques such as knowing how to practice and improve, how to work with teammates, how to listen, how to persevere through setbacks, and how to lead. Likewise, they know the value of coaching, cross-training, competition, and nutrition—all things that will put them at their best on game day, even if the game is now being played in an office. Consider how celebrities like Arnold Schwarzenegger, Jack Nicklaus, Jessica Alba, Dwayne Johnson, Oprah Winfrey, and many others applied the disciplines that made them great in one arena to similar levels of success elsewhere.

Unfortunately, not all people understand this critical insight and therefore fail to enjoy either success or satisfaction after they move on from the profession in which they excelled. They think they were great at that one thing, never realizing how transferrable all the associated skills are.

TURNING PROBLEMS INTO PUZZLES

> "The most common way people give up their power
> is by thinking they don't have any."
> **—Alice Walker**

By applying universal skills to different areas of life, another powerful element kicks in: We realize that we're not nearly as limited as we thought we were. Even the most confident people can see themselves as more constrained than they actually are. When we understand that we already know how to achieve much more than we currently do, and that we already possess many of the required skills that a new endeavor supposedly requires, a whole new world of possibility and probability opens before us.

In a very real sense, we are primarily limited by our beliefs and self-image. But when each step of improvement brings proof of our skill, competence, and ability to accomplish our goals, we understand, on a very deep and powerful level, that we can do much more and do it more easily. As a consequence, our belief in ourselves increases, and we venture more confidently into new territory. Our capacities expand, which in turn elevates our self-esteem and self-confidence, as we strive for still higher levels. This further enhances our capacities. And on and on it goes in an ever-ascending spiral.

At a certain point, a powerful, new mindset gets established. Now, when we're faced with a new challenge, instead of responding with the self-limiting refrain of "I can't do that" or "But I haven't learned how to do that yet," we react with the enabling, energizing realization that "I have the basic skills to attempt and accomplish just about anything."

Steve Martin is a perfect example of this principle in action. In an article in the *Los Angeles Times*, he wrote, "My whole career has been, 'If I can do this, then I might be able to do that.' If I can write comedy, maybe I can do stand-up. If I can do stand-up, maybe I can act in a movie. If I can act in a movie, maybe I can write a screenplay. If I can write a screenplay, maybe I can write a play. If I wrote a play, and music, then maybe I could write a musical."

Once you ascend the Stairway of Success, you show up eagerly and confidently for every opportunity, no matter how new and different it appears to be. One of my favorite examples of the enormous difference this mental orientation can make is based on a story told by the philosopher George Gurdjieff. Growing up in Turkey, Gurdjieff benefited from an educational system organized around solving puzzles rather than memorizing facts. As a result, he came to see the challenges life presented as a series of puzzles to be solved. Instead of thinking, "I don't know what to do because I've never faced this before," or, "I can't do such and such because I haven't learned how to do it yet," he would think, "Oh, here's another puzzle. I'll figure it out." His life was filled with examples of solving puzzles and ingeniously overcoming obstacles as he traveled the globe, amassing experiences, successes, and followers.

Inspired by Gurdjieff's example, I learned to frame challenges as enjoyable puzzles to be solved rather than as intimidating predicaments. Like many of us, I had already done this intuitively, but Gurdjieff's description of his education deepened my awareness and reinforced my commitment to the practice. Ever since, I have found this approach to be incredibly beneficial and empowering. And it applies across the board, no matter which area of life I'm engaged in at the moment. Turning situations from problems into puzzles is a universal principle with enormous ramifications.

Some of the basic requirements of puzzle-solving and success are so simple that people often overlook them. For example, Benjamin Franklin's famous saying, "Nothing ventured, nothing gained," and Woody Allen's similar suggestion that "Eighty percent of success is just showing up," point to one of the most profound observations about achievement in any endeavor. As you'll see in the first skill in part two of this book, the mere act of "Asking" can unlock the answers to virtually any puzzle imaginable.

Successfully applying universal skills to a wide range of situations not only changes some of our default programming, it also changes our general outlook and self-image. Instead of feeling helpless in the face of unknown outside forces, we gain a healthy perspective, a firmer sense of control, and far greater strength.

IMPLICATIONS FOR EDUCATION

> "If you think education is expensive, try ignorance."
> —**Derek Bok**

This insight about universal skills has important ramifications beyond our individual lives and the success of our organizations. Properly understood and implemented, it can radically impact our overall systems of education and training. Some of the greatest gains we make as a society will come from upgrading how we prepare people for life.

Much of our current approach to education evolved from a historic need to fill specific jobs that fueled local and regional life. This trend accelerated after the Industrial Revolution, when businesses needed to fit cogs into society's ever-growing machines, and specialization increasingly became the norm.

But life has changed. Information is now available instantaneously, but wisdom is not, and education needs to adapt. If we move universal skills to the forefront, we can enhance the capacity of students at all levels to keep on growing, learning, and achieving throughout their lives. How odd is it that most high school students take an entire year of calculus, while we have no required public education courses on fostering interpersonal relationships, or little that applies puzzle-solving outside of math and science problems? This is not to suggest that calculus doesn't have value in some professions, but it is a skill that few people can even define, let alone remember and apply. If we are going to build better lives for one another, and a more successful society for future generations, we need to start by building a solid base of transferrable, applicable, universal powers.

From the practical, psychological, and educational standpoints, this is a game-changer. When the proverbial light bulb goes on in someone's head (or within a group) as they understand that their existing skills in one arena can be applied elsewhere, and perhaps everywhere, their world is transformed. Solutions immediately become more accessible, and big goals become more achievable. Opportunities multiply and beckon as self-images soar. I have seen this simple shift revolutionize individual lives, families, and organizations, and I see no reason it can't also generate a powerful transformation of society as a whole.

$$\infty$$

Now it's time to turn to part two of this book, where we focus on ten powerful action-oriented skills that you can employ everywhere and immediately. As you'll see, they're all enhanced by increased awareness and the five insights we just discussed. These ten universal skills are neither esoteric nor secret. Gaining competency in them will raise your level of accomplishment in any endeavor, from business to sports to interpersonal relations.

Bear in mind they do not constitute a complete list of universal competencies. They are merely a springboard to get you started. Once you understand and appreciate the concept of universality, you will begin to see examples of other such abilities all around you. Take advantage of them all and experience the greater power, joy, and freedom this knowledge brings.

PART TWO

—

Action

Action: Experiment, Experience, Adopt, and Refine

"You miss 100% of the shots you don't take."

—Wayne Gretzky

Adopting an attitude of experimentation is far more empowering and liberating than it might initially appear to be. I learned this firsthand some years ago when a psychologist questioned me about my tendency to be five or ten minutes late. Back then, I was punctual only when the consequences of being late were substantial. Otherwise, I was very cavalier about being on time. While it was not a dangerous or debilitating behavior, it annoyed others so much that I finally decided to change. And yet, I didn't.

The therapist and I discussed some of the reasons I couldn't fix this long-standing problem, but we didn't get very far. Then she asked this question: "What would it feel like if you experimented with being five minutes early for everything for just one week?"

Note that she didn't say I should change permanently or tell me what to do. If she had, I probably would have automatically resisted, and she no doubt knew that. She just asked a great question.

My instinctive answer was, "It would feel horrible." I had an irrational issue about always using every available second before moving on to my next activity. Like most people these days, my to-do list seemed inexhaustible. The thought of wasting time by getting someplace early was painful. That prompted her to ask, "Why would it feel so horrible?" and "What is the worst thing that could happen if you tried it for a few days?" She had me!

I looked at her, smiled, and said, "Oh, you're good!"

—

Obviously, nothing bad would happen if I arrived at appointments five minutes early. And by proposing an experiment that I controlled, my therapist circumvented my resistance. Plus, a temporary test was far more palatable and less threatening than committing to a permanent or indefinite change. I could see that it would not only be easy to try the experiment, it would also be a terrific learning experience.

Her two-step process of increasing my awareness and proposing an action/experiment that was easy and interesting turned what I would have seen as an imposition or an attack into a little adventure with no real downside. So, I tried it. I did the experiment. And, of course, it didn't hurt. I didn't suffer any pains or penalties. In fact, it actually felt a bit luxurious to be free of the anxiety I used to experience when I was running late. I confess that I still reverted to my old tardy behavior periodically because the underlying pull of old habits can be quite powerful. But I made a huge step forward that week, and I learned the value of *experimenting with change*. Equally important, the experience gave me a new understanding of what makes me tick and a great strategy for implementing future improvements.

Knowing that we can experiment with new behaviors and practices also gives us a powerful tool for interacting with others. When we suggest, rather than demand, a change in this manner, whether to a teenager, a teacher, a coworker, or a friend, we elicit a sense of curiosity and self-control—as opposed to them feeling pushed to do something they either fear or don't want to do.

Reading Is Not Enough

"To learn and not to do is really not to learn. To know and not to do is really not to know."
—Stephen R. Covey

If we are to truly evolve and grow, it's not enough to read about concepts. We must also incorporate them into our lives. Unless they are applied, and unless their worth is verified and validated through personal experience, their influence will be minimal. To really be effective, learning also has to be experiential. We must act upon ideas for them to be fully understood and eventually integrated. And then they need to be reinforced so that new habits and orientations can be cultivated.

There are things in life that we simply must experience in order to *know*. Someone can tell you what it feels like to experience or witness the birth of your first child, but the actual experience is in another realm altogether. The same is true of love. You can read sonnets, hear romantic songs, and understand the biochemistry, but until you experience love, it's all just a bunch of words.

You're about to explore ten universal skills that are indispensable tools for accomplishing virtually anything. In that respect, they're almost superpowers.

Each skill also reinforces and enhances the others, triggering the Multiplier Effect and more. Every incremental advance in each skill improves our overall ability and self-image, generating increasing gains in productivity, satisfaction, self-esteem, and enjoyment.

These ten skills are not just about changing your outer behavior; they're also about transforming your inner landscape. They're not just about *doing*; they're also about *being* and *becoming*. As you understand, adopt, and master each of these skills, you will be expanding your awareness and reprogramming yourself for the better. Expanded awareness and conscious actions reinforce, nurture, and elevate one another in a dynamic cycle of growth.

I urge you to approach the chapters to come with an open mind. You will no doubt find information that seems familiar to you. You might react at times with, "I already know that." And perhaps you do. Then again, maybe you only know some of it. Or you may be familiar with a proven technique, but you don't utilize it. If you find yourself resisting any of these powerful skills, ask yourself why, and don't stop asking until you get to the *real* answers. There is always something new to learn, and the journey of self-discovery is endlessly fascinating and rewarding.

Please note that the choice of these ten core competencies and the order in which they are presented is subjective. The skills in this book should not be considered definitive or complete. They have been distilled and organized to fit the structure of this book, and they overlap in many ways. However, their power is, nonetheless, enormous, and their applicability is wide-ranging. I encourage you to explore other universal and transformative skills as they call to you.

Be prepared for surprises. As you understand more, you will become more. As your senses and sensibilities grow, you will see everything differently. Situations that used to cause trouble may cease to be big issues, either because you have new tools to deal with them or because you simply don't see them as problems anymore. In the process, your view of yourself will also evolve, and that new self-image will reinforce your newly strengthened skills, which will further elevate your self-esteem, and so on. That's the Stairway of Success at work.

1

ASK and Receive

"Ask for what you want and be prepared to get it!"
—Maya Angelou

Imagine that your favorite uncle, an eccentric explorer, returns from a far-flung journey and brings you an incredible enchanted box. He says, "You can ask it any question whatsoever, and the box will provide the answers."

Now suppose you put the box to the test and find out your uncle is telling the truth. The box answers every question you come up with. Amazing, right? You would treasure and protect that box, wouldn't you? And you'd ask lots of great questions. You would learn to fashion questions to get the most out of its power. What a fun fantasy!

—

Well, you *do* have a magic box. We all do. It's called our brain—or, more accurately, the totality of mind, body, and spirit that I call the biological supercomputer that processes all the information we access as sensory, intellectual, and intuitive data. (Please note that references to "brain" in this book encompass the holistic and integrated brain, body, and spirit network of knowing, unless expressed otherwise.)

And that magic box *must* answer our questions. It can't *not* answer, because it's hard-wired for that purpose. Input a query and the brain cannot ignore it.

Don't believe me? Let's put it to the test: Ask yourself any question. For example, ask yourself if you're closer to five feet tall or ten feet tall.

What happened? Your brain answered immediately, didn't it? Of course it did. It *had* to!

Try asking it how old you are. See? Another quick answer.

Now, let's have some fun and ask a harder question: "How far does light travel in one second?"

I have asked this question to audiences for years, and the responses are fairly predictable. A small percentage answer with either the scientifically correct answer, 186,000 miles, or a very big number that's close to it. A larger group says something akin to "Very far" or something clever like "A light second." However, most people say, "I don't know." But notice this: Everyone answers the question. "I don't know" is, after all, an answer.

The brain is compelled to answer by its very nature—that's its job. It's a veritable answering machine. However, if your brain doesn't know the right answer, and you just stop there, nothing is gained. Instead, what happens if you ask yourself a follow-up question, such as, "Where can I find the answer to how far light travels in one second?" *Aha!* Your brain answers, doesn't it? That spectacular box operates automatically and magnificently, serving up answers without fail. The follow-up question is the key! Once we recognize the significance of the follow-up, a whole new world of understanding and opportunity opens to us.

The Best Answers Come from the Best Questions

"We keep moving forward, opening new doors, and doing new things, because we're curious, and curiosity keeps leading us down new paths."

—Walt Disney

The first step to achieving virtually anything we aspire to is *Ask*. Ask is the most deceptively simple—and one of the most powerful—of the ten core skills. In fact, it is *so* deceptively simple that most people don't appreciate its power. And because we have such easy access to so much information in today's wired world, there has never been a better time to be a competent asker.

When I give talks, whether to business audiences or lay people, I use the acronym MAP. It stands for Magic, Awareness, and Power. Asking creates Magic because it enables us to create something that didn't exist before. Asking raises Awareness because it opens pathways and possibilities that allow us to perceive more—of both the world outside of us and the world within. And asking bestows Power because when you ask the right questions, you can find out virtually anything, and nothing is more empowering than knowledge.

When Jeff Immelt, the former chairman and CEO of General Electric, was asked what it takes to be a modern business leader, he said, "I think it's humility, and the curiosity that comes with it." The big mistake people make, he added, is to stop asking questions. Which is precisely why, in Insight 1, we emphasized the incredible value of recognizing that our perspective is limited and distorted, that we are all blocked, biased, and blind to one degree or another. Acknowledging our limitations prompts us to start asking questions, and from that precious moment on we move from limited to liberated.

The problem is, most people don't know which questions to ask, how to ask them, or when to do the asking. Just as important, we're often *afraid* to ask questions, either because we don't want to admit we don't know something, or because we're wed to the status quo. Or, perhaps subconsciously, we're afraid to face the truth or some imagined terror. Sometimes, it's all of the above. While resistance to asking questions may be limiting and self-defeating, we can use it to our advantage by becoming aware of our resistance and asking ourselves some related questions, such as, "Why don't I want to improve my situation? What stands in my way? What am I afraid of?"

If you examine the road to any accomplishment, whether it's an earth-shattering new invention, a better golf stroke, healing an interpersonal conflict, increasing business, or reducing energy costs, it usually starts with asking a question. For example,

- "What do we have to do to make this happen?"
- "What is causing the problem?"
- "What does our target market *really* want?"
- "How can we fix this?"
- "How can I improve the situation?"
- "Who can help me?"
- "What needs to be done?"

And, often just as important,

- "Why haven't I been doing what needs to be done?"

Here's a story that many people in the northern climates will relate to: I used to hate the month of November. In Boston, with winter approaching, the leaves are usually either dull-brown or gone entirely by the beginning of that month, and the weather grows increasingly cold, raw, and dreary. Plus, once the clocks are turned back for Daylight Savings Time, the sun goes down in the late afternoon, and it's dark and bleak when we head home after work.

The only period in November that I looked forward to was Thanksgiving. It was always my favorite holiday—the food, the friends, the fun, and the gratitude all combined to make it a feast for all the senses. If only the rest of the month could be imbued with the same exhilaration and nourishment.

One day, I got fed up and decided to do exactly that. I would stop whining about November (much to everyone's relief!) and turn it into the best month of the year. I began with specific questions. I asked myself, *What would November look like if it were much more enjoyable? What can I do to make it better? What can I do to make it the* best *month?*

I quickly started coming up with great ideas to create a month-long celebration. In fact, the very process of planning and fantasizing was exciting. I greeted the next November with great anticipation and joy. I hosted parties, tried new things, planned a couple of small adventures, and gave treats to my friends, coworkers, and family members—and to myself. I took a trip. And I teamed up with others to create delightful and offbeat contests and anything else that seemed like a good idea. All this and more made that November glorious. I had succeeded in turning something I dreaded as bleak and dreary into a warm and wonderful good time. All because I had a clear purpose and asked targeted questions.

November in Boston stayed wonderful for several years. Then, as everyone in my life knows, I said, "Oh, screw it," and moved to Florida as soon as I could manage to. While I admit this somewhat tongue-in-cheek, the reality is that I had indeed transformed November. I just prefer to enjoy it in warmer weather now. Plus, that move was also a function of understanding that our options are virtually boundless, especially if we ask great questions. So now I spend each winter working in Florida, but I return to New England every year in late November to celebrate my favorite holiday with friends and family—and the cold days that come before and after Thanksgiving are all joyous.

Quit or Advance: The Art of the Follow-Up

"I was bold in the pursuit of knowledge, never fearing to follow truth and reason to whatever results they led, and bearding every authority which stood in their way."

—Thomas Jefferson

"The important thing is not to stop questioning."

—Albert Einstein

As mentioned earlier, we know that the brain *must* answer every question posed to it, and that one of those answers might be "I don't know." What happens then? If we respond by just giving up, nothing is gained. In fact, a lot is lost. In addition to missing out on opportunities, we also reinforce our self-perception of being limited and powerless. If, on the other hand, we simply ask ourselves some good follow-up questions, well . . . all shall be revealed!

One obvious follow-up question is "Where can I get the answer to that question?" These days, the most likely response will be "Look it up online." For questions of fact, that might indeed be the best solution. But simple searches are seldom enough when it comes to complex real-life questions. Instead, follow-up queries may lead you down a variety of Internet avenues, along with magazines, books, and videos—whether online or in traditional form. Chances are, they will also lead you to helpful human beings—like experts, coaches, people with relevant experience, and all the individuals in your life who know you, understand your specific situation, and can see you and your circumstances from perspectives you are not necessarily privy to.

In truth, *any* useful answer is a step in the right direction. The key is to keep asking, keep probing, keep drilling down. If you activate your natural curiosity, every answer you get may generate new questions, and then new answers, followed by more questions, and so on, in an ever-rising ladder of understanding.

In Japan, there's a formal follow-up process called "Why Why Analysis." It was first developed by Sakichi Toyoda and used extensively at Toyota Motors as part of their problem-solving training. (And in case you're wondering if the spelling of Toyoda and Toyota is accurate, it is. Thanks for "asking.") It consists of following up every answer with another "Why?" After five levels, the questioner feels clearer and clearer and usually arrives at the root cause. Personally, I think this technique was really invented by toddlers. Once they learn the power of asking "Why?" they wield it until they get a good answer or drive their parents nuts, whichever comes first. Perhaps it's time to bring back your inner toddler, but with a bit more diplomacy.

Recently, I struck up a conversation on a plane with the woman in the next seat. A trial attorney, she told me that she's very good at speaking in a courtroom, but often gets anxious in other situations, such as personal interactions. She said she's come to accept this as a fact of life, but it clearly bothered her. So I politely asked her some questions. While careful not to mimic a four-year-old, I probed deeper and deeper: "What don't you like about those situations?" "Has it always been that way?" "What are you afraid will happen?" "What would the consequences be if something were to go wrong?" "Did anyone in your family exhibit a similar trait?"

As she answered my questions, I could see a growing sense of discovery in her facial expressions. Then I asked, "Would you like to change this situation?" She said she would, so I followed up with "What would you have to do to improve it?" And so it went, with me asking a series of related questions.

I can't say for sure that our conversation changed her life, but I'm confident it had an impact. As we said goodbye, she thanked me and said something I've heard many times—"You should be a therapist."

Hearing that always makes me chuckle inside, because all I do is ask questions (hopefully in a kind and curious manner) and sometimes offer an example of similar challenges that I faced and the help I received from others. The fact that my late wife was a psychologist suggests that her approach rubbed off on me. Her insights and expertise certainly had an enormous impact on my life. In fact, many of the key moments in my own personal growth occurred when she or someone else with psychological insight asked me the right question at the right time—just like the therapist I mentioned earlier, who taught me to approach change as an experiment. That was just one example of how my wife used questions to explore issues such as what I wanted and why, and what I was afraid of and why. And that one question, "What's the worst thing that could happen if you try this?" has made a huge difference for me. Regardless of how big the perceived issue is, I quickly realize that a little experiment that I can control is much less intimidating. Whether we get stuck due to fear, bias, habit, or inertia, simply asking some questions allows us to see and understand so much more.

One of my favorite examples of the power of asking involves my son. When Matt was a toddler, I taught him an important skill. "Whenever someone says that you can't have something you want," I told him, "instead of complaining and crying and arguing, just ask them one simple question: 'What do I have to do to get it?'"

When Matt posed this question to people, they were obliged to answer. Plus, it was always fun to see the look on someone's face when this little boy asked such an adult question.

My suggestion to Matt initially got me into a bit of trouble with my wife. She was terrified that I might have created a little monster with a huge sense of entitlement. But it quickly became apparent to both of us that the approach worked wonders. Matt not only stopped whining as much when he heard "No," he also learned to be inquisitive and open-minded rather than emotional and closed-minded.

Naturally, increasing the likelihood of getting what he wanted made him happy. But the more important result was that the practice expanded the boundaries of his conceptual universe. He learned from experience that just about anything was possible if he approached it with an open, calm, and curious mind. He literally saw the world differently. As a result, he was spared some of the usual childhood disappointments, and the positive reinforcement instilled in him an appetite for ongoing experimentation and exploration. As a bonus, my wife and I were able to bypass some of the typical parenting struggles. We still had plenty of challenges, but we had created a new pathway to improvement. Matt is now a wonderful, well-adjusted business consultant who excels at asking great questions, brainstorming with others, and discovering wonderful solutions.

Enlist the Help of Others

"Knowledge is of two kinds. We know a subject ourselves, or we know where we can find information on it."
—Samuel Johnson

Our perception of reality is not only constrained by our physical limitations but also by our past experiences (or lack thereof), our conditioning, our fears, our desires, and so on. Basically, we're limited. That's just the way it is. Therefore, if we're looking for solutions, it makes a lot of sense to enlist the help of others to gain access to their experience, insights, and ideas.

To demonstrate this concept when I teach classes, I often start by finding someone in the room who plays tennis or some other sport at an intermediate level. I ask that person, "If you wanted to really improve your game, what could you do?" I usually get three to five answers, such as, "I should practice more," "I could join a tennis club," and "I could take some lessons." After that, the ideas dry up. Then I ask the rest of the group, "Is there anything else he can do?" Answers start flying: "Do strength training," "Sign up for tournaments," "Cross-training," "Eat better," "Get better equipment," "Work on flexibility," and so on. Within minutes, the group generates a far superior recipe for success than the individual alone could come up with.

Then we drill down further. I might zero in on coaching, for instance: "OK, what kind of coach should he get?" "Where can he find the best coach at the best price?" And so on. Once again, the plan quickly becomes better thanks to the input from others.

Continuing in this way, we consider other critical success factors, such as "How can he make the practice more enjoyable?" and "What else can he do to make sure he executes the plan?" "What carrots and sticks can we add to increase the probability of success?" and "Which of these activities should he prioritize to make it more fun, effective, efficient, and affordable?" After fifteen to twenty minutes, we have a thorough, practical, and results-oriented plan that's ready to implement. And all we did was ask questions and enlist others.

The Art of Asking

> "You create your opportunities by asking for them."
> —**Shakti Gawain**

Asking is a practical discipline as well as an enjoyable art form. It can be easily learned and practiced. Here are some tips that many have found helpful.

CLARIFY THE OBJECTIVE

The better the question, the better the answer. That's why it's crucial to get clear about what you're trying to achieve and why. What exactly is the problem that needs to be solved? Why do you think you haven't solved it yet? Where are you in conflict? What mystery needs to be unraveled?

If you are not clear about your needs and intentions, you might frame your questions in a way that takes you in a different direction and generates answers that don't get to the heart of the situation. But not to worry: If you stay open and curious, the clouds will clear, and little by little the truth will be revealed.

DIG DEEPER

Whether it's a personal matter, a business decision, or an existential dilemma, there is always a deeper level to penetrate; and persistently asking targeted follow-up questions of yourself and others will help get you there. Remember, however, that our brain has ingrained behaviors, and it's not always easy to change. Therefore, you may inwardly resist certain inquiries when the potential answers seem intimidating. We are masters of rationalizing to support the answer we want. But if finding the truth is important to you, the solution is to keep poking and prodding.

GET TO THE REAL ISSUE

In sales, there is a saying, "Don't just answer their questions; solve their problems." When a client or a prospect asks questions about your products or services, or demonstrates resistance of any kind, you need to first identify and understand their primary issues before you can offer a proper solution or an effective response. For example, if the person says, "I have to discuss it with my wife," or "I can't afford it," or any number of reasons to avoid saying "Yes," your task is to find the *real* objection. This is especially true when we realize that it's in everyone's best interest to have a satisfying long-term relationship rather than just make a quick sale. And it's just as relevant to friendships as it is in commerce.

Sometimes you can be straightforward and simply ask, "Why?" But the person sitting across from you may not even know why, or might not want to tell you why. In such instances, some hypothetical questions can shed light on the subject. For example, you could say, "If we can make this affordable, will you want to proceed?" If the person says "Yes," you can explore those solutions. If the person says "No," or "I'm not sure," price is obviously not the primary objection, so you probe further.

This is similar to the distinction psychotherapists make between "the presenting issue"—the troublesome matter that rose to the surface and prompted the visit—and the real underlying issues that are yet to be revealed and may not even be known to the client. A classic situation in family counseling occurs when parents drag their child to see a therapist because he's acting out and "has a problem." But, the chances are good that little Johnny's outbursts are a manifestation of the overall family dynamic rather than just his own issues. This is not the time for the therapist to jump to conclusions and blame it all on the parents. This is the time for targeted questions within a safe environment and room to explore. With proper inquiry, much is revealed and eventually understood by everyone involved.

People don't always respond to questions with complete candor at first, even to themselves. They prefer the convenient and comfortable way out instead. Nor do they always understand the situation fully. None of us does, especially when our own subconscious concerns play a role. Targeted questions, a compassionate enviroment, and time to reflect can help.

ENLIST THE HELP OF OTHERS . . . BUT MANAGE THE MANY

As the old saying goes, two heads are better than one. And three are better than two. And so on, but not indefinitely and not for every issue. Unless the process is properly managed, you can reach a point of diminishing returns because too many minds can cloud the conversation and undermine the outcome, just as too many cooks can spoil the proverbial broth.

In the right size group, with the right mix of personalities, talent, experience, and incentives, inquiring minds can perform miracles of mental mining. While some research suggests that five to seven people might commonly be the optimum number for a productive group, circumstances differ. Mix it up and make it safe. At work, we use all sorts of methods to tease out the best answers from everyone in the company: periodic surveys, weekly huddles, annual campaigns, contests, and team goals—all with imaginative rewards and incentives, and all to infuse the process with energy and make it fun.

The more diverse the minds are, the broader the range of viewpoints and the richer the results. Because we are all limited in one way or another, it makes sense to draw on the experiences and observations of people of different genders, ages, ethnicities, religions, professions, personalities, and socioeconomic backgrounds.

USE POSITIVE REINFORCEMENT

In the art of asking, carrots generally work better than sticks. Going outside the box, or even contemplating such a journey, can be daunting for many people. Therefore, we should use care and cultivate a positive environment during the asking process.

Whether in a group or with one person, make everyone feel heard and appreciated. When the atmosphere is positive, and it feels good to open up, people will not only share more readily, they will also be more open to hearing other points of view. For the most part, nothing shuts down creativity faster than criticizing someone or their ideas and beliefs, especially in front of others.

Admittedly, in certain high-stakes situations, pressure and the threat of negative consequences can be extremely effective, but not for all people and not all the time. The risk of alienating someone by applying negative energy is high, and over time it can lead to burnout and the burning of bridges.

Positive reinforcement can also be effectively employed in group situations when choosing the best solutions from all those put forth. In addition to accessing "the wisdom of the crowd," I use the following technique:

> After brainstorming a list of ideas, ask all the participants to identify their five favorites from all that were generated. (There's nothing special about five—pick the number you think best, based on the size of the group, the number of choices, or any other operational factors.) After tallying the results, it will quickly become apparent that the group, be it two or two hundred, has some consensus regarding the ideas that offer the greatest opportunity for success. Praise everyone for their participation and continue to explore how best to refine and execute.

This approach makes everyone feel that they are a valuable part of the process, and therefore they are more likely to support the eventual decisions as well as offer more suggestions and observations.

ASK OPEN-ENDED QUESTIONS

While asking specific questions to achieve targeted results is a fruitful strategy, sometimes open-ended questions lead to new discoveries—and it's a grand treasure hunt besides. Exploratory questions can help us find answers that we never considered or were dwelling in our subconscious. But no one is going to answer your exploratory questions unless they trust you and see you as an ally. They have to feel that you are on their side, or they shut down. There is a difference between asking helpful questions as opposed to conducting an interrogation. No one likes to be interrogated, especially in a group setting. But when people are asked thought-provoking, sincere questions by someone who is genuinely interested, they usually open up and offer meaningful answers.

I have a dear friend, Sanjiv Mirchandani, who I often call "the most interesting man in the world"—partly because he is intelligent, multifaceted, and well-traveled, but also because he is thoroughly intrigued by people and asks sincere, thought-provoking questions that spring from such fascination, compassion, and love of connecting, that people feel flattered when he inquires about their lives. I'm always amazed that they come away from encounters with Sanjiv saying how interesting he is, when in fact, *they* did most of the talking, and almost the entire conversation was about them. It works because Sanjiv sincerely cares and makes them feel comfortable and genuinely valued.

In gathering material for this book, many of my interviews started with three open-ended questions:

- What were the major revelations or *Aha!* moments in your life?

- What did they teach you in school that you didn't need, and what did you need in life that they didn't teach you in school?

- If you had only one opportunity to give advice to a child that would help him or her lead a successful and rewarding life, what would you say?

Besides the previous three questions, here are a few you might try when engaging with others (modify to best fit the people and the circumstances):

- What are your favorite activities, and what do you like most about them?
- If you had time, what new talents would you cultivate?
- Who are your heroes?
- What was the best vacation you ever had?

There's no end to the questions you can ask. The serendipitous responses that follow are likewise infinite, and the rewards often extend beyond the answers you get. Genuinely curious, open-ended questions put people into a positive state when those queries are directed toward positive feelings, such as memorable experiences, hobbies, aspirations, celebrations, children, and so on. These encourage more intimate and rewarding conversations. As a result, bonds are established and friendships are fostered.

SLEEP ON IT

Experiments show that taking breaks, temporarily suspending operations, and just plain getting away from it all can help generate insights and solve problems. It's called *incubation*, and it works because it lessens anxiety and frees the subconscious mind to put information together in ways that augment conscious analysis.

In fact, one of the most powerful ways to use the skill of asking is to pose clear questions to your own brain and put those questions to work while you're sleeping or otherwise relaxed. You may not realize it, but you're already doing this. That's why you sometimes wake up in the morning with the answer to a question you've been pondering; or why a solution to a vexing problem comes to you seemingly out of the blue when you're in the shower or driving or taking a walk. So, next time you hit a dead end in your quest to solve a puzzle or reach a conclusion, instead of grinding away, you might want to get away from it for a while and simply instruct your brain to play with it while you're relaxing.

The basic principle is simple: A quiet, relaxed mind is most receptive to exploration and most susceptible to suggestion or programming. That's why hypnotists start the process by calming the mind and putting their subjects into a state of deep relaxation. The same approach is used in self-hypnosis, also referred to as *autosuggestion*.

Try it. Before you drift off to sleep at night, direct your mind to focus on an issue that's baffling you. Your subconscious will do the processing while you're snoozing and often greet you in the morning with insights and answers.

INVITE THE UNIVERSE

We are connected to the energy of the universe, and we transmit and receive information beyond the confines of our physical bodies. This is a central teaching in the metaphysical traditions of both East and West. While some people dismiss this notion out of hand, it is actually supported by the known facts of physics and biology. Empirical evidence for the power of prayer, affirmations, and similar practices continues to grow.

Whether you see it as speculation or as a rational conclusion, the possibility that we have access to a free, unlimited cosmic data bank is intriguing. Don't get lost in the dogma. Try it out. Put the universe to work as a much bigger brain than your own, and see if it comes through. How can you do that? Pose your questions . . . and see what happens.

Experiment with Asking

"No one is dumb who is curious."
—Neil deGrasse Tyson

Asking, like any skill, has to be developed through understanding and practice, which ties back to that dynamic relationship between awareness and action. The payoff is tremendously empowering. You not only get answers to specific questions, you also expand the range of what you thought was possible. When you realize that you can get the answer to virtually anything, your imagination takes flight and your confidence soars. Confidence breeds optimism, and optimism breeds energy.

But don't take my word for it. Experiment with the power of asking in your own life. Start asking questions. Ask yourself and ask others. Ask experts and non-experts. Ask your coworkers, your family members, your friends. Ask old people and young people. Look things up. Probe deeper. And deeper still. Open the door behind the door. Then open the door behind *that* door. And keep opening doors as they present themselves. Along the way, you'll learn a lot! You'll also learn what kinds of questions yield the most insightful, revelatory answers.

I predict that if you get into the habit of asking, you will become far more productive—primarily because you'll be open to growth and change, and also because you'll be armed with highly usable information that orients your mind and turns your focus to the desired result. What's more, you'll come to see yourself and the world differently. When asking high-yield questions becomes a habit, and you're taking full advantage of every opportunity to learn, the world becomes utterly fascinating, and living in it becomes a more joyful and wondrous voyage.

Cost-Free and Available 24/7

"Our deepest fear is not that we are inadequate. Our deepest fear is that we are powerful beyond measure."

—Marianne Williamson

There is no limit to the number of great questions you can ask. There are no quotas and no restrictions other than those of your own making (e.g., you may be fearful of looking in areas of perceived vulnerability). In a related vein, when it comes to approaching others, you want to be careful and considerate, especially when asking personal questions. So be creative, be courageous, be kind—to yourself and others—and start asking.

If you find that you're reluctant to ask certain questions, turn the process inward and ask yourself why. Amanda Palmer, author of *The Art of Asking*, made this observation about the reticence to ask: "From what I've seen, it isn't so much the act of asking that paralyzes us—it's what lies beneath: the fear of being vulnerable, the fear of rejection, the fear of looking needy or weak. The fear of being seen as a burdensome member of the community instead of a productive one." If you're reluctant to ask, ask yourself if any of those issues are holding you back.

Some questions are so basic they can serve as touchstones for our lives—places we return to from time to time to get our bearings. Asking the following questions never fails to yield benefits. Feel free to come up with as many as you want. In fact, you can ask your intuition what questions might be most powerful and most productive. Start asking them of yourself, and when you want to know more, take the risk of asking others about yourself. They can see you in ways you cannot.

- What do I want?

- Why do I want it?

- What do I have to do to get it?

- Am I doing what needs to be done? If not, why not?

- Am I doing things that don't work and are even counterproductive? If so, why?

- What's influencing me that I don't fully understand?

- Do I have unproductive habits and thoughts that I picked up from my parents and others?

- What can I do to foster new, more productive habits?

- Do I have limiting beliefs that I wish to let go of?

- Which people give great advice?

- What questions could I ask them that might help me soar?

- What can I do to make today special?

- What can I do to make *every* day special?

- What new activity can I try that might add new dimensions to my life?

- What can I do to make my life more enjoyable?

- What can I do to make others happier?

- Why does making others happy make *me* happy?

Asking is the beginning of a process of learning and growth, and it can be incredibly powerful. But it's really only productive if you also implement the next skill—Listening.

LISTEN and Learn

"Courage is what it takes to stand up and speak; courage is also what it takes to sit down and listen."

—Winston Churchill

By 1985, I felt I had made it. The company I started in 1979, Commonwealth Financial Network, had just been acknowledged as one of the fastest-growing private businesses in the country. I was incredibly proud of that achievement. But rapid success created new challenges, and the flip side of my success was that I was in over my head and woefully unprepared for the innumerable operational issues that growth and changing times had presented. The good ship Commonwealth was faltering. In fact, while I didn't quite know it yet, we were headed for a shipwreck if we didn't correct our course quickly. Eventually, and luckily, I realized that the problem was not the boat but the captain. In order to fix the company, I would have to fix me.

In an uncharacteristic move for me at that time, I listened to the advice of others and agreed to seek help. I applied to Harvard Business School's Owner/President Management Program (OPM), a three-year executive program designed to help company presidents like me fill in the gaps in their education and experience. It had become painfully obvious that I had a lot of shortcomings. Like most of us, I had no idea how much I couldn't see and didn't know.

By the time I enrolled in the Harvard program in February 1987, things had gotten even worse. My leaky vessel was being battered by financial storms. The tax laws had recently changed significantly, dealing a devastating blow to much of the financial services industry. Then, eight months after the Harvard program began, the stock market crashed in October 1987. Financial companies were soon going out of business left and right—young firms and venerable institutions alike. I was now so desperate that I was finally ready to listen to anyone and everyone who might be able to help.

The Harvard program was a rescue ship, and it arrived just in the nick of time. Each year, I spent three weeks sequestered 24/7 at the "B School," along with 120 other company presidents from twenty countries. There was much to learn, and after each session, I tried to summarize my copious notes into a manageable list of insights and action items. Then I spent the rest of the year trying to implement what I had learned.

By the time I finished the program, I had condensed those lessons into a few hundred key points, taking up ten pages. But even that felt unwieldy. My goal was to have a pocket-size summary, a handy reference to help guide me throughout each day, especially at decisive moments. I sliced and diced some more, distilling relentlessly until everything was encapsulated on a single page with just thirty items to focus on.

Yet that, too, proved impractical. We humans have trouble focusing on more than a few concepts at a time. I thought and thought, and whittled away, probing for the essence of what I had learned and what I needed. Finally, I realized the most important lesson for me, the core takeaway from my three years spent with brilliant minds and experienced practitioners, came down to one powerful word: **Listen!**

—

I had thought I was a good listener, but I'd been deluding myself. I now realized that much of the time I had really just been waiting for other people to finish talking so I could politely explain why they were wrong. Up until then, I believed that much of my success in business had come from blazing my own trail, from *not* listening to those who disagreed with me, and from *not* listening to conventional wisdom. In reality, I *couldn't* listen. I was holding on to my existing beliefs and personal desires so tightly that little could get through to deter me from my ways. I had convinced myself that my previous successes had come as a result of my ability to see what others could not. I bought into that logic and acted accordingly.

In retrospect, a lot of my success had been the result of working harder than others, coupled with a talent for swaying people with my arguments and enthusiasm. Basically, I was a very good salesperson. So good, in fact, that I had even sold myself a bill of goods.

The Harvard program drove home something that now seems obvious: While I have a lot of valid observations and insights, so do other people. I'm often right, and so are other people, including many who see things differently from me.

"Listen" has been my North Star ever since. It is the essence of awareness and the indispensable complement of Skill 1—Ask. The basic message is this: Knowledge is power, so tune into more of it by learning to listen to both your inner and outer worlds. The alternative is to keep on banging your head against the limitations of your self-imposed prison and suffering the consequences.

The Art and Science of Listening

"We have two ears and one mouth so that we can listen twice as much as we speak."

—Epictetus

We learn a whole lot more when we listen than when we talk, whether in business meetings, family conversations, fact-finding missions, or casual chats. This may seem obvious, but acknowledging that truth and acting on it is not easy for many of us. It sure wasn't easy for me. I realized that my inability to listen was a function of being blocked, biased, and blind, and vice versa. To improve one, I had to improve the other: To listen well, I had to be less blocked, less biased, and less blind; and to be less blocked, biased, and blind, I had to learn how to listen better.

Once I realized that it was much more productive to assume that my own data and analysis were de facto limited or distorted, I came to love it when others disagreed with me, because the ensuing exploration was invariably rewarding. This has made me far more collaborative, not to mention more enjoyable, than I used to be. Now I learn so much more by listening. Not just because I'm paying more attention, but because other people are far more open and honest when they feel their comments are truly appreciated. When people know they're being heard, they feel validated, and the interaction is much more gratifying for everyone. As a result, my decisions, in both business and my personal life, are much better vetted and far more practical.

Who should we listen to? Anyone and everyone. Take it from Galileo, who said, "I have never met a man so ignorant that I couldn't learn something from him." The art of listening means treating what other people are saying with the utmost respect. In addition to this attitude of respect (which others can almost always feel), artful listening entails paying complete attention to the person speaking—their words, their intonation, their body language, and also what's *not* being said.

As ancient gurus and modern scholars have all pointed out, you cannot fully listen to someone and engage in another activity at the same time. This includes *thinking*. You cannot really listen while thinking about something else, or contemplating what you're going to say next. The other person deserves your full attention. Just as important, you deserve to have all the information you stand to glean if you give your full attention. When we truly listen, everything speaks to us—from the faint whispers within our own inner being to the abundant sources of information in our immediate environment, and all the way up to what has been called "Big Data" and beyond.

The Customer Is Always Right

> "You see, but you do not observe."
> **—Arthur Conan Doyle**

I had long dismissed the old saying, "The customer is always right," as a tired cliché. But at Harvard I learned that it actually points to something quite important. I came to understand that it doesn't mean the customer is necessarily ethically right, or correct about the facts, or accurate as to their conclusions. It's essentially a marketing axiom with both simple and sophisticated meaning. When customers say they want this or that, they're simply telling you what they believe will make them happy. In marketing terms, they're giving you the keys to the kingdom. So instead of telling someone what they *should* want or why they're wrong to want what they do, it may be much more productive to listen with respect and then respect their wishes.

But be aware there is often a difference between what people *say* they want and their actual underlying desires and objectives. As Henry Ford said about his groundbreaking automobile company, "If I had asked people what they wanted, they would have said faster horses." Thus, the better you are at listening to others, the more you can understand the breadth and depth and subtleties of what they're trying to tell you. If you begin with a genuine intent to fully hear the message, to truly understand what they want and why they want it, then it's much easier to satisfy them. The customer, or the marketplace as the case may be, is always telling us what it wants. When we understand and respect those messages, the struggle evaporates, and the profits soar. However, people don't always speak plainly or openly, and that's where the multileveled, multifaceted art of listening comes in.

And it's not just customers who are always telling us what they want; so are spouses, children, friends, and others. They too speak clearly at times and cryptically at others. I realized I had to listen to everyone in the same deep way and do so holistically—not just with my ears and intellect, but with all my senses, including my heart, my emotional intelligence, my intuition, and my subtle faculties that are always receiving information from the energy fields around us. It begins with a sincere intention to understand more. Then, with practice, we strengthen those muscles and create the conduits to increased awareness.

Everyone Is Somewhat Deaf About Themselves

"Put your ear down close to your soul and listen hard."
—Anne Sexton

The most important voice to listen to is the one inside our heads, because it filters, translates, and interprets everything else. The internal chatter we call "self-talk," for instance, speaks volumes. The problem is that it's often false. It speaks to us largely in the language of preconceived notions, old habits and attitudes, perceptions, beliefs, and internalized instructions that may have outlived their usefulness. It is influenced by our anxieties and desires, as well as our hard-wired instincts. It also speaks below our radar, in our subconscious. *So how do we distinguish between our intuition and inner truths versus our less trustworthy biases?*

Internal listening is a vital aspect of awareness and elevation; it involves being attuned to how we're feeling as well as to what our bodies are trying to tell us and what the voice of intuition is whispering. We can learn a great deal about ourselves as unique personalities if we direct our gaze inward and penetrate levels that are deeper than ordinary self-talk and self-analysis. This is one good reason to learn how to get centered and to quiet the usual mental chatter through mindfulness, meditation, and similar practices. The key word is *practice*. As with any other endeavor, the more we practice, the more attuned we become to subtleties and subtext, and the better we get. With practice and patience, we learn to differentiate between the associative and reactionary chatter vs. the deeper knowledge within.

There's much more to us than we realize, so when it comes to self-knowledge we have to take everything into account. Since we invariably have blind spots and biases about ourselves, we shouldn't limit our self-awareness to what we receive through our own internal listening devices. Our families, friends, coworkers, and even casual acquaintances possess insights, perceptions, and information we don't have. Finding out how they see us can be tremendously enlightening.

See Yourself from 360 Angles (but Be Prepared)

"I not only use all the brains that I have, but all that I can borrow."
—Woodrow Wilson

In terms of accessing the insights and ideas of others, a 360-degree analysis is a powerful tool frequently used in business and executive coaching. But it is also beneficial to anyone seeking overall improvement. It provides a comprehensive and confidential evaluation from individuals at all levels within your professional and personal universe: those you report up to, those who report to you, and those at the same level. In terms of validity, it's hard to beat.

But this recommendation comes with a caveat: Because of the confidential and comprehensive nature of the survey, the results are difficult to dismiss. You may find out that you're more respected and admired in some areas than you thought you were. But don't celebrate too quickly. You may also be in for a shock when your weaknesses are laid bare along with your strengths. And when you get consensus from all corners of your life about where you're falling short and need to improve, there's no place to hide.

I still remember the first time I came in contact with this expansive analysis. It was at a business seminar that was offered to members and their senior management teams of a professional organization I belong to. Two months before the scheduled presentation, confidential questionnaires were sent to the people above, below, and around us in our companies, as well as to individuals outside of work, whose names had been provided by each subject. When completed, the evaluations were mailed to an outside organization where the results were tallied prior to our meeting. I eagerly looked forward to getting my evaluation. After all, I wanted to grow, and therefore I wanted to listen—or so I told myself.

When the seminar leader prepped us for the survey results, there was a clear cautionary tone in his voice. He explained that the feedback we were about to receive had an exceptionally high level of validity because it did not come from one person but from *many* people with a variety of different relationships to us. There was, he said, a high probability that any themes that showed up consistently in the evaluations were accurate. He was warning us that we might get feedback we had not anticipated—and we might not like it. I could feel the mood in the room shift from celebratory to sober, and in some cases, tense.

The person sitting next to me was one of the key people at a company run by a friend of mine. He seemed to be an affable man, and his good humor didn't diminish a bit during these cautionary tales. But later, as we were reading over the results of our individual 360s, he did an abrupt 180. His face turned red, and he let loose a furious rant, cursing his coworkers and calling them idiots for their stupid evaluations. You might wonder what they had said about him, as did I. Well, he shared it with me as he belittled their observations. They said he was mercurial. They said he was overly emotional. They said he would sometimes have fits of inappropriate rage. I was incredulous. This guy was vehemently denouncing the evaluations while he displayed that exact same behavior before our very eyes. He simply could not hear the truth. I have no doubt he was an intelligent man. He was certainly somewhat successful. But when it came to self-awareness, he was not merely blocked but extremely well defended; and now he was decidedly on the offense, as well as offensive. I could only hope that he had the wisdom to read the report again and to fully consider what his colleagues were telling him. In other words, I hoped that he could listen.

In case you're wondering what I learned about myself that day, there weren't any scandalous revelations. However, there was one observation I found especially interesting and enormously helpful:

A number of people pointed out that while I was very patient and compassionate when working with our customers, I was decidedly less so with my staff and coworkers. How interesting! I clearly had the tools and the ability to foster relationships and promote progress, but I was only using them well in one arena. It reminded me of the story about the businessman who was brilliant in the office and a bust at home. The observations were especially ironic since I had been using that very example whenever I explained Universal Laws (Insight 5) to people while I was writing this book. Just another illustration that we all have a lot to learn.

Comprehensive analyses such as the 360 described here are invaluable tools for generating feedback that deserves to be listened to—but only if you're willing to be open and honest. If you're not, you'll get nothing out of it. In that sense, it's a metaphor for life in general.

If You Want to Get Better, Get Coached

"Everyone needs a coach. It doesn't matter whether you're a basketball player, a tennis player, a gymnast, or a bridge player."
—Bill Gates

Not long ago, during a course I was teaching to new employees, the topic of coaching came up. I knew that most people assumed that only the least proficient people needed to be coached, so I had to dispel that misconception right at the start. I turned to one of our staffers, who had been on the Canadian national ski team. Knowing full well what his answer might be, I said, "Fred, I'm sure that at your level you didn't need any coaches, right?"

"No, Joe," he said, "of course I needed coaches."

I asked how many coaches he had. I thought he'd say three or four and that information would surprise most people in the room, because they'd likely assume he had only one coach. But he said, "About ten." Ten! Even *my* mouth fell open at that point. Could it be that he was totally inept? Or, maybe the leadership thought he was so good that he was worth the investment?

Fred went on to explain that he and the other members of his team had coaches for strength and conditioning, nutrition, flexibility, psychology, equipment, and even a few specialized skiing coaches.

Nothing dispels the arrogance of "I don't need a coach" better than the reality check of world-class athletes. We think they're the last people on earth who need coaches, but in fact they have more coaches than anyone else, and they know exactly how to take full advantage of their expertise. I often make that point with business leaders who say that coaching is great for those below them, but that *they* don't need it. Elite athletes take their performance so seriously they seek out all the help they can get. Do you?

Even people who recognize the value of coaching in a specific domain—golf, for example—don't realize that talented coaches can help them in other areas of their lives too, whether in business, marriage, parenting, or personal development. Being able to work with an expert who understands you and your situation is invaluable. The right coach at the right time can help you improve virtually anything, sometimes by leaps and bounds, and save you enormous time and effort. But you have to be open to it. And if you're not, I guess that begs an interesting question, doesn't it? Listening is a critical skill at every point of our lives, and sometimes the voice of a good teacher is just what we need to hear. And we can be coached all the time if we simply ask others for their observations and suggestions. Friends, colleagues, and others who have gone down the path we're on can all be invaluable resources—if we ask, and if we listen.

If you want to get better, get coached. Most successful people I know have a "kitchen cabinet" of counselors—talented, trusted advisors they can turn to for specific kinds of recommendations, expert referrals, and candid opinions. And seeking assistance offers a fringe benefit: As Dale Carnegie said in his seminal book, *How to Win Friends and Influence People*, one of the best ways to make friends is to ask people for help.

Peeling Back the Onion

"Without self-knowledge . . . man cannot be free, he cannot govern himself, and he will always remain a slave."

—George Gurdjieff

Peeling back the proverbial layers of the onion to reveal and better understand what really makes us tick is one of the most productive journeys we can embark on. And it doesn't have to be painful or uncomfortable. Self-discovery can be an enjoyable adventure, a lifelong treasure hunt. As I taught my son when he was a child, it always pays to ask, "What's behind the door?" and "What's behind the door behind that door?" I also told him a big secret: There is always another door, each one more revealing than the previous. I advised him to be curious about each door and enjoy and appreciate every new opening.

However, as we've already seen, there is a limit to how much we can learn about ourselves by ourselves. That's where experienced therapists, counselors, and teachers come in. But most people don't want to expose themselves and their vulnerabilities, especially if they feel some measure of shame or guilt. Many erroneously feel that asking for help is a sign of weakness. And many of us have a knee-jerk reaction that says, "I don't need to see a shrink. I'm not crazy."

We take our cars to mechanics, we see doctors when we injure a body part, and we consult with lawyers, accountants, and other experts when appropriate; yet we generally resist turning to experts on sensitive psychological and emotional issues. But think about it: If you want to know more about yourself, who better to ask?

The same resistance to psychologists and therapy can apply to coaching, mentoring, 360-reviews, and other forms of professional assistance that might expose our weaknesses and vulnerabilities. We tend to guard our innermost feelings, wounds, conflicts, and dilemmas as if they were national security secrets, because we think that keeping them hidden protects our personal security. We may even keep them secret from ourselves. But knowing the truth about ourselves can be extremely liberating.

Getting the right help can facilitate the process of self-revelation. However, as in any profession, not all therapists, coaches, and counselors are created equal. Invest in the process—and yourself—by doing some research. Ask for referrals and meet with potential teachers before you sign on. Along the way, you will garner more information and get a feel for the proper "fit" with each one. Personal chemistry may vary, and trust can be as critical as talent, especially when dealing with sensitive issues.

Every Experience Is a Learning Opportunity

> "Learning is the beginning of wealth. Learning is the beginning of health. Learning is the beginning of spirituality. Searching and learning is where the miracle process all begins."
>
> **—Jim Rohn**

I struggled for nearly thirty years to grasp the meaning of something I once read by the spiritual philosopher Jiddu Krishnamurti. He said that *beautiful and ugly are essentially the same thing*. I sensed there was something profound in that enigmatic statement, but what was it? Many years later it came to me. We know that whether something is considered beautiful or ugly is in the eye of the beholder. What's more revealing is that the beholder's determination of what is beautiful and what is ugly is a valuable insight into the soul and psyche of that person. The beauty and the beast are mirrors. It's never actually about the object; it's really about us. Every person, situation, and idea is an interaction between the observer and the observed, and therefore, a potential source of knowledge. Every encounter is an opportunity to learn, not just about the object but about ourselves. Every encounter is therefore an opportunity to evolve. If we pay attention!

Some people seem to think that awareness is practiced only during meditation, but meditation is merely one form of practice. Anyone who wants to live a more fulfilled life can adopt an attitude in which life is an open classroom with boundless opportunities to listen and learn. The more we listen, the better we get. Increased awareness elevates us and expands our universe. And *every* experience and every interaction is an opportunity to exercise the muscles that take us there.

Pattern Recognition

> "your handwriting. the way you walk. which china pattern you choose. it's all giving you away. everything you do shows your hand. everything is a self portrait. everything is a diary."
>
> **—Chuck Palahniuk**

As we pay more attention to the world around and within us, we begin to notice things that may have escaped our detection previously. Eventually, we also start to see groups of things acting together in concert. We begin to notice patterns.

For example, while we may notice a particular response we have to something, we might assume that it was a conscious act based on specific facts and circumstances. However, with ongoing attention and curiosity, we may observe that we often behave that way in similar situations, and that the behavior is generally stronger (or weaker) than warranted. We may notice that our reaction is more an ingrained behavior pattern than an individual decision. In poker, a "tell" is a specific behavior that someone tends to exhibit in a given situation that communicates what they may be thinking or feeling. Or there are people like me who unconsciously revert to humor when they experience anxiety. Here's another example: When I first started psychotherapy years ago, I was late to the first session because of traffic. Then I was late to the second because I forgot something and had to go back to get it. The third time, it was because of an argument with my wife. By the sixth session, and a myriad of other excuses for being late, it became clear to even me that I was exhibiting a behavioral pattern. But once I saw it, I could listen and look deeper to identify the root cause.

Josh Waitzkin, the international chess master who was the subject of the book and subsequent movie *Searching for Bobby Fischer*, was a child prodigy. He explained in his book *The Art of Learning* that early on he began noticing certain configurations on the chessboard. He recognized common patterns, and then he recognized more complicated ones. As he got better at recognizing them, he could see them as they started to take form. He could then initiate countermoves before the opponent posed a more serious threat—he could get himself out of hot water before the water was barely warm.

The equally amazing part of Josh's story is that he then went on to study and compete in martial arts, soon becoming an international champion in that discipline as well. And while we may not immediately think of chess and martial arts as being similar, they are both strategic contests that require mastering the fundamentals and then building on them. They also require an inordinate level of attention and focus. Listening!

In *The Art of Learning*, Josh explains how both disciplines have patterns that can be exploited and defended against—if they are observed. His advice is to start with the simplest situations and evolve from there. While this may sound obvious, it's different from how most people learn chess. The game begins with all of the pieces on the board and an infinite number of variables. The same holds true of martial arts when two opponents square off against each other. And likewise, much of life can seem incredibly complicated. But if we begin by familiarizing ourselves with the simplest situations, we can better understand and build. In chess, that may mean just playing a game with two kings and one pawn (which is similar to what the end of a game may look like) and mastering that world. Then we can add more pieces and the attendant complications as we ultimately move backward toward the beginning of the game with all of the pieces on the board.

In martial arts, this could be as simple as playing "push hands" (an exercise where you try to push the other person off balance) but with only one hand, thereby making it simpler to sense your own energy and your opponent's. This makes it easier to notice how you react to certain stimuli, as well as understand what works, what doesn't, and why. In all areas of life, we can listen and learn more as we reduce the variables. Then, once we grasp simple patterns and how to work with them, we can build on a solid base.

All Data, Big and Small

"We are drowning in information but starved for knowledge."
—John Naisbitt

Back in the 1970s, John Naisbitt started tracking hundreds of magazines and newspapers. He and his staff literally counted the number of printed words and lines that were devoted to various themes. He was looking to identify topics and trends: What was the relative weight of newsworthy topics? Which trends were gathering force and which were slowing down, and at what pace? In 1982, he published a book whose title was a word he coined: *Megatrends*. It spent two years on *The New York Times* best-seller list, selling more than fourteen million copies. Now, four decades into the computer age, Naisbitt's method seems as quaint as an abacus or a quill pen. But the approach is still valid, and the need he tapped into is stronger than ever: Individuals and organizations must have easy access to data and trend analysis that they cannot gather on their own.

Listening goes well beyond what we can sense as individuals. It also includes being sensitive to the ever-expanding world around us. We all need information, and it needs to be reliable and accurate. To make decisions and take advantage of opportunities, as well as avoid unnecessary mistakes, we need systems to gather, sort, and process the wealth of information that's out there into a form we can use.

We live in an age where we can find out virtually anything with a speed and ease that would boggle the minds of the most knowledgeable people just fifteen or twenty years ago. Any business, enterprise, or entity that is not set up to take full advantage of the virtually unlimited information and analysis available is at a distinct disadvantage. That goes for both task-specific, granulated data and what has come to be called Big Data—collections of data so big and so complex they can't be processed by ordinary data-management tools.

We also need to fact-check. Not just our own observations and beliefs, but everyone else's—including what's written in this book. Not everything put forth on the Internet, TV, social media, or appearing in a well-known publication or written in a blog, is necessarily accurate or thorough. In the words made famous by George and Ira Gershwin in the hit musical *Porgy and Bess*, "It ain't necessarily so." Media is no longer controlled by a handful of responsible and respected stewards. Now everyone has a voice and the ability to deploy it; and the results are as varied as the perspectives and personalities of each unique individual. To make matters worse, the Internet is rife with "trolls" who delight in destruction, and "fake news" has evolved from a curious cottage industry to a powerful corporate and often state-sponsored weapon.

We need to validate and verify whenever possible, especially since supposed facts are not always black and white. I run into questionable situations all the time in my professional and personal affairs. Perhaps this one sounds familiar: Someone comes to me looking very concerned and says, "Everyone is upset" about something that was said or done. Instead of reacting impulsively to such information, as I may have in the past, I've learned to probe. "What do you mean by 'everyone'?" I generally ask. And, "How upset are they?" I also need to consider the person conveying the message, since individuals react differently to varying types of energy. The point is, I don't want to base decisions on incomplete information, personal biases, or hearsay. No one does.

There is more to data than data. Quality is critical. We have access to so much information that it is easy to get overwhelmed by it all. Knowing what to look for, which needles to pick out of the haystack, and how to interpret the data are skills that are more important than ever. We need data and we need discernment.

Since information can be vetted, formatted, and "framed" to highlight a particular fact or bias, even data-based reports are suspect. Fortunately more and more fact-checking sites are popping up on the Internet to expose urban legends, politicians, product claims, and more. But they are only helpful if they are utilized. My friend Ed Mascioli is a physician who managed various medical research organizations before migrating to the investment world. It's fascinating to watch him respond when someone tells him about some great new product or technique. If his interest is piqued, Ed looks up the associated research. Much of the time he quickly concludes that the study was poorly constructed or the execution was flawed, or the results were misrepresented. However, if he likes what he finds, he will often call the primary researchers to delve deeper into their findings. *That* is listening! But even that may not be enough— experience, common sense, and intuition are not obsolete in the computer age. In fact, they could very well be more crucial now than ever.

Intuition

"The only real valuable thing is intuition."
—Albert Einstein

"Trust yourself. You know more than you think you do."
—Dr. Benjamin Spock

In addition to harnessing supposedly objective data, both big and small, we also have to fine-tune our subjective senses. As Naisbitt observed, "Intuition becomes increasingly valuable in the new information society precisely because there is so much data." That means learning the subtle language of our hearts and our guts, so we can better discern when our intuitive mind is speaking to us, as opposed to falling prey to fear or wishful thinking or past conditioning. It also means getting away from our incessant data-gathering from time to time, to allow the subconscious to process information "offline," and utilizing methods such as mindfulness and meditation to still our hyperactive minds. We know from both the introspective sciences of the East and the rigorous experiments of the West that intuition favors a quiet mind and a stable nervous system.

While most of us don't always pay enough attention to our intuition or trust it to feed us usable insights and inventive solutions, it is also true that we should not trust every feeling and hunch that crops up inside of us. It's very important to discern when our true intuitive mind is speaking to us, and when that inner message is an expression of emotions, historical biases, or some other imposter. How can we know the difference? There is no guaranteed, one-size-fits-all formula. But each of us, once we start paying attention to our inner experience, can increase our sensitivity and selectivity over time—we can learn to listen better.

We can learn through observation and experience to recognize our own personal hallmarks of genuine intuition. They might come with a particular feeling in the belly, or the heart, or some part of the head. Other common clues are whether the delivery arrives with extra clarity, whether it is particularly strong, or whether it nags you or persists over time, even when you doubt it and try to contradict it. One thing is certain: Methods of cultivating a quiet mind greatly improve our odds of being attuned to true intuition.

There is also the matter of external verification. After all, we developed the scientific method and codified the rules of logic to give us the means to verify our hunches—to put those intuitive feelings to the test, to submit them to rigorous analysis, to look for supportive evidence, to try to disprove them. And if, as often happens, you can't validate your hunch, and you can't write it off as bogus either, return to your inner experience and listen to what your heart has to say.

One rule of conduct that has served me well is this: I don't make an important decision until my heart (intuition) and my head (intellect) are both in agreement. When they are not in agreement, it's not necessarily a bad thing. It simply means that I'm either missing or misunderstanding something, and I count myself lucky for having caught it. This practice has saved me from making costly mistakes on countless occasions.

What Keeps You from Listening?

"No one is as deaf as the man who will not listen."

—Jewish proverb

Growing in the art of listening is not necessarily a hard or tedious process. While there are many fine points involved in improving the skill, keeping some basic principles in mind is essential:

Establish your intent. It's your choice. Listening is the conscious act of paying attention. Do you really want to listen more effectively? If so, establishing that intention and letting your brain know you're serious about it is an important first step.

Adjust your state. Be present. Our ability to listen—to an individual, to data, to a myriad of media, to ourselves—depends in large part on our state of awareness at any given moment. Active listening favors a combination of calm and alertness: a quiet and attuned mind, a centered emotional state, and a non-agitated physiology. Breathe, relax, focus—whatever it takes to achieve that receptive state.

Open. Let go and let in. When we avoid prejudging our sources of information, we become more receptive to what they have to offer. If we come to listening with a blank slate, our environment can write on it what we need to hear. Similarly, if our mental and sensory channels are open, there's more room to import energy and information.

Validate. Being open does not mean being gullible. Skilled listeners don't believe everything they take in, and they don't accept as gospel whatever is presented as truth. A certain healthy skepticism enhances the process, as long as it doesn't go to such an extreme that we close down.

Enjoy. Don't make listening a chore. It doesn't have to be hard work. Make it fun. Make it a game. Make it a treasure hunt. What could be more interesting than discovering new things and increasing our powers of perception? *Listening is a never-ending journey along an ever-improving road.* Celebrate it.

Poke and prod. We all have points of resistance. We all have blind spots. We all have fears and desires. And we all need to recognize and overcome those and every other obstacle that gets in the way of seeing the world for what it really is. Listening is one of many powerful techniques that help us learn and grow. Are you taking full advantage of that skill? Here are some sample questions to ask yourself in that regard. Remember: After each question, you can open the door behind it by also asking "Why?"

- Do I lose focus when others are speaking?

- Instead of listening, am I planning what I'll say next?

- Do I have a vested interest in specific outcomes that keeps me from listening to alternative views?

- Am I afraid to look weak, indecisive, or ill informed to others?

- Is winning an argument or being right more important than getting to the truth?

- Am I too attached to doing things my way?

- Am I making decisions that I know are illogical?

If you pay close attention to your own inner responses, these questions will help you become a better listener. And listening is the first step in programming, which is the subject of our next chapter.

PROGRAM and Take Control

"The first step toward maintaining autonomy in any programmed environment is to be aware that there's programming going on."

—Douglas Rushkoff

When I was a little boy, probably in first or second grade, I was in a school play that required me to sing. And sing I did. That is until a teacher told me I had a voice like a frog and shouldn't sing. So I stopped. Ever since that moment, I've been self-conscious and stilted when singing in front of others.

—

When my son Matt was a baby, we tried our best to put him to bed as soon as he started getting tired so we could catch that wave. We would always tell him, "You're the best sleeper in the world. You can fall asleep anywhere."

His fact-based mind took that as gospel, because we consistently told him he could, and he almost always fell fast asleep when we put him down. Today, Matt can fall asleep virtually anytime and anywhere.

—

Would you like to better understand the programming language that governs your brain and, therefore, governs you? Other people understand it, and they take advantage of that knowledge—and not always in ways that serve you well. Would you like to assert more control over your own life?

It's actually easier than you think. The biological supercomputer we discussed earlier is our greatest asset, and it comes bundled with all the necessary hardware and software we need. But as powerful as it is, it still needs to be told what to do. It still has to be programmed, just like a mechanical computer does; and I think you will agree that it's far better to consciously and skillfully program our own brains and bodies than it is to relinquish that power to subconscious conditioning or external forces.

Unfortunately, we often give up the opportunity to better direct our lives because we aren't aware of the dynamics at work. We don't know how to create our own programs or how to neutralize the efforts of others to program us. You may not realize it, but you are both programming yourself and being programmed, all day long. The way we see the world and ourselves, the thoughts we think, the goals we set, the decisions we make, and the actions we take— all that and more—is influenced by our DNA, our upbringing, our environment, and our affiliations, not to mention the powerful impact of our fears and desires. You'll find ample evidence of this truth if you pay attention to your internal dialogue. However, it might not be quite so obvious at first because much of this process is subconscious.

As a starting point, pay close attention to your thoughts throughout the day. Just witness what arises mentally as you go about your business, especially when you think your mind is disengaged—like when you're walking, or driving, or showering, or brushing your teeth—and take note of your self-talk. You might be surprised by how much of it consists of programming "instructions," and you may be shocked at the percentage of it that's negative and counterproductive.

While you're at it, pay attention to the onslaught of programming messages you receive from the outside. Most of us don't appreciate it, but we are being programmed—both intentionally and inadvertently—by the key people in our lives, as well as by impersonal social forces such as politicians, advertisers, marketing experts, and just about anyone else with an agenda. The novelist Tom Robbins compared the brain to an educational toy. "The problem with possessing such an engaging toy," he said, "is that other people want to play with it, too. Sometimes they'd rather play with yours than theirs."

Do they ever! We're bombarded by both blatant and subliminal messages through technologies that were unimaginable back in 1957 when Vance Packard's provocative book, *The Hidden Persuaders*, revealed how advertisers used the techniques of motivational psychology to get us to buy specific products and vote for particular political candidates. So take another step in declaring your independence by realizing that you're being programmed, and then identify the agents and objectives of that programming.

If you don't take charge of your own programming, you'll invite one problem after another—at work, at home, on the playing field, and everywhere else. Ah, but we can turn garbage into gold by seizing control of the programming process. For that, we need to better understand how it works.

Programming 101: Watch Your Language

"Words are singularly the most powerful force available to humanity. We can choose to use this force constructively with words of encouragement, or destructively using words of despair. Words have energy and power with the ability to help, to heal, to hinder, to hurt, to harm, to humiliate and to humble."

—Yehuda Berg

If you're going to program yourself, you have to know the programming language. Fortunately, unlike mechanical computers, the primary language that governs our thoughts and actions is both simple and familiar: It's our own spoken tongue. Those thoughts of ours—some of which we repeat over and over—constitute programming instructions and have a huge impact on our lives. Granted, we're also impacted by our feelings, but even those get translated into language as we attempt to interpret and sort all that is going on and decide what actions to take.

As mentioned in part one of the book, if you have chronic difficulty sleeping, phrases such as "I can't sleep," "I don't sleep well," and "I have trouble sleeping" probably reverberate in your mind many times throughout the day. You may even speak them out loud to others. Inwardly and aloud, every time you articulate those words, thoughts, and feelings, your brain is being instructed and encoded. What's the result? In this example, you reinforce the very problem you wish you didn't have, undermining your ability to discover and implement any solutions that might be available.

The same is true of other self-defeating and counterproductive instructions we feed our brains, such as "I can't lose weight," "I'll never find a better job," "I'm not good at math . . . or relationships." Or even worse, "I'm not worthy." When you think such thoughts repetitively, as many people do, no good can come of it. This is because those messages train the brain to do exactly that: nothing helpful. Phrases like "I can't," "I'll never," and "I'm not" are very simple and powerful negative programming directives. Fortunately, "I can," "I will," and "I am" are also enormously effective instructions, only they're infinitely more positive and productive.

Earlier, I told the story of George Gurdjieff, who was trained from a young age to see challenges as puzzles rather than problems. It's a wonderful example of the enormous difference a single concept, or even one word, can make! One small switch like that can literally change our perception and our programming. Instead of feeling helpless in the face of unknown, outside forces, we adopt a healthy attitude and gain a positive perspective. This gives us a firmer sense of control and far more strength. In a sense, it's like exploring which routes to take when traveling. Instead of being paralyzed by thinking, *I don't know how to go there because I've never been there before*, we rephrase the problem as a type of puzzle that we've solved before, and perhaps even an adventure. This simple form of empowering perspective has served people enormously well in all areas of life.

Observe your own thoughts and your own speech, and notice how much of the language you employ is negative as opposed to positive, undermining instead of empowering. Notice how often you frame situations as "problems" or "obstacles" rather than as interesting puzzles, enjoyable challenges, or exciting opportunities.

It's also instructive to pay close attention to friends, family, and colleagues, because we can often perceive something in others better than we can in ourselves. Notice how they reveal assimilated themes—both positive and negative—in their thoughts, words, and actions. And notice how many of those patterns can be traced back to either their formative years or to social conditioning. Well, guess what? We are all subject to programming; sometimes recognizing it in others can help us see similar patterns in ourselves.

This can be revolutionary. It's also the essence of awareness. I know of few more exciting things in life than opening the doors and parting the veils that define and confine us, or inspire or diminish us. And the more we look, the more we can observe, the more we can understand, and the deeper we can go. Prepare to be amazed!

As you pay closer attention, you'll realize that these internal conversations are not always limited to words. Feelings are just as prevalent, and their impact is just as powerful—maybe even more so. Scientists may differ about which come first, the feelings or the thoughts, but we need not worry about that. Suffice it to say there is an abundance of developmental gold beneath the surface, and it's ours for the taking. One psychologist I know referred to feelings as "the F-word," because they exist in an area where many of us are uncomfortable and fear to tread.

But if you do decide to look under the hood, don't be surprised to discover that deep-seated fears fuel many of our actions, or lack of action as the case may be. Of course, so do positive feelings, since we're also driven to seek success and love and connection. There are plenty of carrots and sticks to choose from. After all, we're hard-wired to survive, procreate, and evolve; we seek safety and pleasure and avoid danger and pain. The trick is to understand our coding— both innate and acquired—and then to modify or leverage it as we deem appropriate.

The process of self-discovery and growth go hand in hand, fueled by our desire to know the truth and break free of unnecessary or artificial constraints. As it says in the Bible, "The truth will set you free." At the very least, it will expose the underlying programming that influences the direction of our lives. There is no single answer that applies to everyone. Rather, the journey is forever unfolding. It's an iterative process and a life-long practice; and with each step forward we get closer to the light.

Our State of Mind and Body

"Things do not change; we change."

—Henry David Thoreau

We often talk about being in a good or bad "state" of mind. What we're referring to is our mood and how we're feeling at that time. Most people see themselves as being at the mercy of external influences. Thus, if we're having a good day, it means that things "out there" are going well; people are treating us well, our assets and activities are progressing the way we want them to, and we're feeling pretty good about it all. Conversely, when we say we're having a bad day or we're in a bad mood, we mean that things (people, luck, circumstances, what have you) seem to be working against us. *But what if we have it backward?* As discussed in Insight 2, what if the world out there is really a reflection of the world within us? What if *we* can determine our state, our mood, and our outlook? What if *we* can take charge of the script?

Our perceived state of being usually refers to two primary mechanisms and their related manifestations: how we feel psychologically and how we feel physiologically. To illustrate how this mind/body programming works, let's try an experiment I often conduct with groups. You can do this by yourself or with friends or coworkers. It's a two-step process that creates profound contrasts. Begin by dimming the lights or closing your eyes. Then sit and slump a bit, as if you are weary. Now think of something decidedly unpleasant and upsetting. Dwell on it for a moment. Note how you slip into a heavy, gloomy, or even depressed state as your mind focuses on unhappy thoughts and your body reinforces the mood with the related physical orientation. When you're finished, consider how you feel on a one to ten continuum from sad to happy.

Now let's change things around. Turn the lights up bright. Stand up tall and proud, and think about someone or something you adore—maybe people you love or your favorite activities. Better yet, combine the two: Think of doing something you love with people you love. Now engage your body some more and smile. That's right—Smile. Even if you're all alone and no one can see the grin spread across your face. Make it a big smile. A big, silly, happy, ecstatic smile. Now let's take it further: Raise your arms high in the air and strike a triumphant pose. Finally, yell the word YES as loud as you can. If you are doing this with a group, do it together. Shout YES! Yell as loud as you can, with your arms way up in the air, like you're the happiest bunch of kids on the planet!

Then, rate yourself again on the sad-to-happy energy scale. Admit it: You went from somber to exhilarated, didn't you? And the difference was enormous. And it was all because you focused on happy thoughts and feelings instead of sinking into a depressed frame of mind, and your body communicated positive physical signals. When you assume a powerful, confident, exuberant pose, you begin to actually feel that way. It's virtually impossible to feel down in the dumps and low in energy when everything in your brain and body is pointing up. This is why salespeople are often trained to stand up when making phone calls to potential customers.

This is basic programming. Behind the scenes, the body and brain modify chemical and electrical impulses to achieve the desired effect. But we don't have to understand the biological mechanisms that are at work, just as we don't have to be able to build a computer in order to use one. We just have to know which buttons to push.

Orchestrating our mind and mood works so easily that we tend to underestimate the power of that process. Not only can you reconfigure your own state of being, you can also impact the minds and moods of other people. If someone is sad and stuck and stubborn, get them to stand up and physically move (this literally unsticks them and makes further adjustments easier). Then get them to focus on something or someone they love—or both. Ask about their children, their spouse, a beloved parent or mentor, their favorite pastime, or the best part of their recent vacation—anything that's positive and upbeat. (And yes, you can ask about positive things first and get them to move afterward.) Then observe how their energy and state of being improved.

Here's a bonus: They will associate the pleasurable experience with you, which might very well enhance your relationship. If you feel good when you're with someone, you look forward to being with that person again. You'll speak more kindly of such people too, and you're more likely to go the extra mile for them. In fact, this type of associative programming is so powerful that I know a number of people who are not especially productive or even dependable, but they're extremely enjoyable, and they get to keep their positions and relationships because everyone loves being around them. Perhaps you know someone like that as well.

Nonverbal Cues and Dancing with the Stars

"What you do speaks so loud that I cannot hear what you say."
—Ralph Waldo Emerson

Much has been written about the various ways that humans communicate. We ascribe meaning to specific words, tones, body language, facial expressions, and energy imprints. Many of these vary according to community and culture, but some signals seem to be universal. Not only can we learn to discern nonverbal messages such as smiles, crossed arms, and slumped postures, *we can also learn to direct the other person.* The basic techniques are quite straightforward. Plus, when we realize that we have enormous influence over ourselves and others, we don't have to go through life feeling powerless.

Think of slow dancing with a partner. Before we can lead, we must align. While this can occur in many ways, the common approach is to signal that we are in tune with our partner's feelings and energy. We are sympathetic and empathetic. We are a friend. That's when one person allows another to enter . . . and lead. That's when they relax and yield to direction. A related approach is to exude strength and capability. Whether they are dance partners, teammates, business associates, or family members, people tend to follow when they decide that the other person is worthy of leading. In both examples, they agree to align and follow.

Here's one of my favorite stories to demonstrate the empathetic approach in action. One summer, years ago, a teenage friend of my son worked as a waiter at a local country club where some of the members were notoriously demanding. One woman in particular had a reputation of becoming belligerent when she was dissatisfied. Although nothing had even happened yet, the young waiter was already intimidated and afraid he would disappoint her or wither under her barrage. So I gave him the following formula to use in case he found himself in the situation he dreaded.

First, allow the person to vent her frustration. Don't argue or struggle. As new parents are often coached, "If you struggle, you lose." Let her express her feelings and release her negative energy. Next, align with her. Let her know that you too have been frustrated when similar things happened to you. Granted, if the waiter's customer was angry because her meal was a few minutes late, the young man couldn't say he had suffered something similar at his own country club. But he could appreciate that her angst came from being frustrated and disappointed, and he could certainly share how hard it is for him when other people let him down. By allowing her to vent, and by empathizing and sharing a related story, he signals that he understands and respects where she's coming from; that he's a friend. At that point, he can much more easily lead. I encouraged him to take advantage of that moment and offer to assist her.

Two days later, he called to say that my advice worked. In fact, it worked too well—because now the difficult woman wanted to be served by him whenever she was at the club!

These steps can be applied in any number of situations. Allowing someone to open up, sincerely aligning with them, and then leading is essentially the three-step process of listening, empathizing, and directing, i.e., programming. When we get in lockstep with someone, they will instinctively follow along with our energy and direction . . . just like when dancing.

Going Deeper

> "The quieter you become, the more you can hear."
> —**Ram Dass**

We have learned from research on hypnosis, autosuggestion, neuroscience, and psychology that self-programming (either self-directed or directed by someone else) is most effective when the body is relaxed and the mind is clear and available—when we're present. That is when we are most receptive. Conversely when we're jittery or anxious and our minds are cluttered by a thousand thoughts, it's like trying to have a conversation across a crowded room. Calming our nerves, relaxing our muscles, and dissolving our usual mental chatter create space to allow the desired message to get in and take root in fertile soil.

This is why regular meditation and mindfulness training produce practical results. When the distractions melt away and our awareness grows, we're less likely to be unwittingly led astray. When we become centered and clear, it's easier to see and hear clearly.

That's why hypnotists place subjects in a relaxed alpha state, named for the brain waves emitted during deep relaxation. It makes them more susceptible to suggestion. The variable in both situations is *awareness*. Therefore, if we want to program either ourselves or someone else, the first step is to relax the person's mind and body and then direct their attention.

Of course, we can be influenced when we're active as well, and later we'll explore techniques for motivating people in a variety of situations. However, if you want to modify your mindset, implant new programs, or disarm pre-existing programs that are getting in your way, it helps to be present and accessible.

Neutralize Negative Programs and Insert New Instructions

> "If you think you can do a thing or think you can't do a thing, you're right."
> **—Henry Ford**

Once you become aware of your internal dialogue and the dynamics of programming, you will more easily notice the negative programs that reside and repeat in your mind, continually reinforcing themselves and virtually taking on lives of their own. Those negative programs are obstacles to achieving your goals. They are roadblocks and sinkholes on the path to a fulfilling life. Most of us have many pre-existing negative programs, often acquired in early childhood, that persist despite our efforts to suppress them. They keep bubbling up in our brains. And, like air pockets under a carpet, they pop back up soon after you push them down—sometimes in the same place and often elsewhere too. Most people ignore or try to suppress the various negative programs that taunt and tug at us. However, ignoring the problem doesn't make it go away. Trying to suppress it doesn't really work either, since it requires ongoing energy and constant vigilance as well. It's much more effective to neutralize those unwanted messages and then insert new and improved instructions.

IDENTIFY AND UNDERSTAND

The first step is to learn to recognize negative programs, and to better understand why and how they came to be. When in doubt, ask yourself, or consult with others who may have knowledge of your situation. As our awareness and understanding increase, the subversive power of undesirable programming diminishes commensurately because we see the truth and often come to realize that, once again, "the emperor has no clothes."

For example, most of us carry painful childhood memories and old wounds into our adult lives. But those early hurts are frequently rooted in events we misunderstood at the time, and the children we were didn't know how to deal with the powerful feelings that were triggered. Cognition in children is limited. Our young brains are not yet fully formed, and brain growth continues into our twenties. We are more apt to understand a story as being about us and then process accordingly, even if that distorts the more complex truth. Or the child will accept and absorb the story spun for them by an adult. That story and its associated sensations take root and become a potentially enduring truth. That is another way false memories occur, and why we believe them.

A classic example is the many children who feel responsible for their parents' divorce. Another common situation is the child who takes on the anxiety or anger of her parents, thinking their feelings are actually her own, or that she's responsible for them, since we easily absorb the energy of those closest to us. A related dynamic is called "repetition compulsion," a common situation where we feel compelled to repeat or re-establish some powerful situation or behavior—it's like a deep groove in our psyche that keeps luring us in.

MODIFY EXISITING NEGATIVE PROGRAMS

While many feelings can dissipate when the truth is unveiled, some self-destructive thoughts are deeply rooted and, like pesky weeds, they keep coming back. Fortunately, there are ways to deal with this. In addition to understanding the underlying causes, we can also graft new instructions onto old negative images. This approach is used extensively by behavioral psychologists, sports psychologists, public speaking coaches, and other professionals. Note that behavioral psychologists have found that merely telling ourselves or others to *stop doing* something doesn't work very well. Strategies that employ positive action are much more effective. (This is explained in greater detail in Skill 4 under the "Dead Man Rule.")

For example, let's say you notice that you have a recurring image of yourself failing at something. Rather than telling yourself to not fail, you can instruct your mind (while relaxed and attentive) to turn the image from color to black and white (thus dampening its power), and affix a big white X onto the unwanted image every time it appears. In doing this, you are creating a new, modified program that automatically gets launched whenever the original destructive program is initiated. And note that you don't have to waste any mental energy trying to suppress your thoughts. As with any new program, these instructions need to be properly inserted and reinforced in order to take root.

At first, this will take a few focused minutes of programming throughout the day; eventually the process can take just a few seconds. As you get better at it, you can simply stop, slow down your breathing, relax your muscles, return to the calm state you have experienced in longer sessions, and reinforce the desired image. As with anything else, we improve with practice.

Now watch for the magic. Pretty soon you'll begin to notice that the old negative program starts appearing with the X already attached. And it gets even better. If you pay close attention, you'll become aware that the process starts to work subconsciously. The new program has taken root and is working for you on its own!

CREATE MACROS AND ALL-PURPOSE RESCUE PROGRAMS

I was shown how to take this relaxation procedure one step further by creating a "macro," similar to the condensed commands that software engineers create for our computer programs. For example, I long ago programmed myself to quickly slip into a relaxed alpha state whenever I touch the thumb of each hand to the first two fingers of that hand. With continued reinforcement, I was able to achieve a tranquil and fully present state almost instantly. And so can you.

Here's another all-purpose macro command I use for neutralizing potentially dangerous imagery. It's something like an emergency rescue program. Whenever a destructive thought or vision enters my mind, I automatically issue the command "Cancel, Cancel," thereby overriding and neutralizing the negative thought, nipping it in the bud before it takes root. This is different from dealing with a long-standing, specific issue in my psyche. I have programmed the "Cancel, Cancel" command to immediately jump to the rescue whenever some dangerous *new* thought or image appears. I also pair it with an all-purpose picture of me happy and healthy.

For example, suppose someone starts talking about car accidents and my mind attaches to that thought and suddenly conjures up an image of me or a loved one suffering a terrible injury. Before I begin to dwell on this vision, unwittingly breathe life into it, and unconsciously move in its direction, my rescue command will leap into action. We can do the same with less life-threatening visions, such as those involving failure or rejection. Whatever the case, "Cancel, Cancel" (along with the associated generic "happy and healthy" image) is a powerful neutralizer; it has become like a guardian angel to me.

Our minds are much more powerful than we realize. We are designed to move toward that which we envision, essentially manifesting our intent. Therefore, if the image is negative, it is important to assume control early on. You'll find that, at first, the "Cancel, Cancel" command has to be summoned up intentionally in the moment. With repetition, however, it will work its way deep into your subconscious and eventually become automatic. As you might imagine, this technique can make a huge difference in your life, as it has in the lives of others. Plus, it's thrilling to watch your helpful programs doing precisely what they were designed to do.

If "Cancel, Cancel" doesn't resonate for you, and you prefer some other command, be my guest. It's your computer. My friend Les uses "Let it go, let it go," which he originally heard in a song from the animated movie *Frozen*. It triggers him to relax and be more open and allows him to feel more in control and empowered in the face of unwanted forces. I've started to use it myself in situations that create anxiety as opposed to danger.

INSERT NEW INSTRUCTIONS

Now that you know how to neutralize, or at least weaken, pre-existing programs that have been hurting you and holding you back, turn your attention to creating new programs that can propel you toward your goals. The guidelines are the same: Calm and center yourself so that your mind and body are receptive; then employ the applicable programming and other cues to clearly communicate what you desire (e.g., what you want to be, where you want to go, or when you want to arrive at your ideal destination).

FOCUS ON THE END RESULTS

You don't have to worry about the *how* of it at first. Once you really know where you want to go in life, be it flying to London, or getting to a specific restaurant at a specific time, or reaching a business goal, or virtually anything else, your brain is remarkably well equipped and resourceful at figuring out how to get there. Granted, you need to manage the process. However, most people are hampered primarily because they don't know, or can't admit to themselves, what they really want. But when you do, your innate creativity and internal guidance systems jump into action. Plus, with the powerful skills discussed in this book, the trip becomes that much easier.

BE REALISTIC

You can't easily fool the brain . . . at least not for long. Unless you are blinded by desires or crippled by fears or pre-existing prejudices, your brain is essentially evidence-driven. For example, if the message you send your brain is consistent with its previous programming and perceived reality, it will respond affirmatively. But if you issue a command that contradicts previously stored information and beliefs, you'll get an error message essentially saying, "Does not compute."

This explains why the use of extravagant affirmations promulgated by many self-help teachers and motivational speakers seldom works as advertised. Positive thinking is great, but it works only if the positive programming language is consistent with the facts and beliefs. Tell your brain you're going to win the next Wimbledon tennis championship, and, unless you're a ranked player in your prime, your brain immediately calculates that your premise is ridiculous. As Byron Katie put it, *I am a lover of what is, not because I'm a spiritual person, but because it hurts when I argue with reality.*

So, what *do* you tell your brain if you want to upgrade your tennis game? You could try something like this: "I'm going to take some intelligent steps to become a better tennis player." That's a realistic statement. Your brain's response will be, "Sounds reasonable. I'm all for it. Let's make a plan." You can then reinforce your program with proven techniques for improvement, such as joining a league, getting a coach, etc.

Reality-based programming is not only logical, but it also translates into positive behavioral changes. The new behaviors will trigger positive results, and the desired outcomes will further reinforce the program and an elevated self-image. This is the opposite of what happens when people end up spiraling downward because they set unattainable goals and inevitably fail to reach them.

Do you want to double the rate of production in your business or your team? If you've never done anything like that before, don't tell your brain that you're going to accomplish this in one month: That's setting yourself up for failure. Instead, set yourself up for success. Create realistic stretch goals that are achievable but initially out of reach. Then celebrate and reinforce each achievement along the way.

Many incredibly accomplished people exhort us to push the envelope more aggressively. They say we must reach for the stars and embark on the grand adventure if we are to break free of our constraints and become the hero that dwells within. Noble words indeed, and such champions are extolled in songs and stories. But what about all those who push too hard and don't, or can't, make it? Who writes their stories of "almost" and "such a shame"?

Reaching for the stars is glorious. It ignites our passions and fuels our quests. But we should go about it intelligently.

The Stairway of Success

> "The greatest discovery of any generation is that a human can alter his life by altering his attitude."
>
> **—William James**

I've discussed this crucial concept before, and it deserves some elaboration in the context of programming. When you meet or exceed your goals once, then twice, and then again, you change your internal database and the underlying program that equates to your self-image. What happens next is fundamental and spectacular: Your brain is now primed to make bigger and faster improvements. As your achievements mount, higher aspirations become reasonable and even expected. Eventually, you achieve goals that your brain would have rejected earlier as unrealistic. At that point, you'll be well oriented to surpass those accomplishments as well.

This is how reality-based programming can be a booster rocket for self-esteem. Our goals, choices, and actions are determined in large part by how we see ourselves. If we think of ourselves as courageous, we tend to act courageously. If we think we're good athletes, we perform accordingly. If we think we're funny, we're more apt to do things that make people laugh. If we think we're outstanding at a particular activity, we don't shrink from opportunities, and we confidently do what's required to perform that task with excellence. And, of course, the opposite is also true. If we think we can't sing, we probably won't.

Therefore, it is essential to shape and maintain a positive self-image. And we can do this with a combination of realistic programming and incremental achievements. That series of mutually reinforcing steps powers our potential instead of undermining it. With each genuine improvement we make, the brain acknowledges, *I've gotten better at this. I can do it!* This affirmation strengthens the validity and value of the positive programming, which in turn makes the next step of improvement easier to conceive, believe, and achieve. Eventually, a light bulb goes off as we realize we can climb as high as we want. This is a huge breakthrough.

As the process continues, at some point the brain realizes that we can use the same principles to get better at other things. And when that proves to be true, a life-changing epiphany is primed: We realize—logically, experientially, and psychologically—that "I can get better at anything," and "I can go as far as I want to!"

Based on evidence and conscious actions, a positive and powerful self-image arises, grows, and gets progressively reinforced and reconfigured until it permeates all aspects of our lives.

Visualization—The Picture of Success

> "If you can dream it, you can do it."
> **—Walt Disney**

World-class athletes practice visualization as faithfully as they do stretching or strength training. To many entertainers, it's as essential as memorizing their lines. Executives and salespeople do it before a speech, a meeting, or a sales call. Although the power of visualization techniques is now well established in numerous walks of life, there is more to the practice than most people realize. Many are still only vaguely aware of it, or wrongly dismiss it as a new fad; while some who try the technique fail to get the most out of it, because they don't implement it properly or consistently.

The basic process is essentially the same as for other programming, whether your goal is to improve your athletic prowess, wow an audience, land a deal, improve a relationship, or accomplish virtually anything else that matters to you. The fundamental principles of programming apply: the crucial role of language, the importance of neutralizing and overwriting negative or counterproductive programs, and the value of establishing a receptive state of inner calm in which to plant these new seeds. However, with visualization we add a vital ingredient: We enlist our other senses to strengthen the basic programming process, multiply the neural connections, and make the technique as powerful as possible.

Public speakers have long known that spoken words are not nearly as powerful as visual aids and emotional triggers. Nor are they as memorable. In fact, some researchers maintain that we retain only 10% of what we hear but 90% of what we see and feel. Therefore, the essence of installing a more motivating, more memorable, and more effective program is to employ a visual component supplemented by our other senses. Bringing color, sound, smell, touch, and *especially* feelings to our imagined scenarios enlists more areas of the brain, which deepens, activates, and integrates the new programming.

Try this: After becoming calm and centered, choose an image in your mind that represents the desired goal. Make sure the scenario resonates with you and has personal meaning. Typically, the guts of a great vision will pop into your head at the outset because, when you're looking to focus on whatever it is you truly want, its essence is already within you. Neuroscientists recognize this initial vision as generally the clearest path and most accessible circuit. Take advantage of these pre-existing neural pathways. The goal now is to refine the image, add to it, and make it richer in detail and meaning.

Let's say you want to give a great speech at the company meeting, or you want to totally delight your spouse on her birthday. Instead of worrying about the mechanics or the required steps, focus first on the outcome. For example, what will it look and feel like when you're standing on stage and everyone is captivated by your every word? How will the audience respond when you've made a persuasive, elegant, and thoroughly enjoyable presentation? What will it look and feel like when your spouse is so happy that she's almost crying with joy because you've made her day, her week, her year, and she remembers why you were the one she chose to marry? What will that look like? What will it *feel* like?

Paint a picture in your mind of the desired result. Give it color, sound, smell, and feeling. Take your time. This should be a magical and thoroughly enjoyable exercise. Choose images that make you feel good and that feel right. Now just sit with this vision and let it sink in. Let yourself know that this is where you want to go, where you should go, and where you are *going* to go. As for the mechanics of specifically how you're going to achieve the objective, while that certainly needs to be addressed at some point, it's infinitely easier when you have clarity about where you're going, and all areas of your being are aligned and energized.

Once the vision is firmly established in your mind, reinforce the desired objective and picture periodically. I recommend doing this a few times per day at the beginning, then every now and again. Just pause, relax, and bring up the image in all its glory. Smile. This is what you want, and now you have a much greater chance of getting it. Enjoy the vision and enjoy the process.

We already imagine and visualize countless things, big and small. When we're going to work or the supermarket or to visit friends, we automatically have a picture in our heads of what we're going to do, and we proceed to actualize that vision as we move closer and closer to it. Visualization is a powerful programming technique, and now we're going to learn how to take advantage of rest and relaxation to get what we want.

Off-line Programming

> "When I am traveling in a carriage, or walking after a good meal, or during the night when I cannot sleep; it is on such occasions that ideas flow best and most abundantly."
>
> **—Wolfgang Amadeus Mozart**

We may appear to be doing nothing during sleep, but a great deal of mental processing takes place during those seemingly unconscious hours. That's why we often wake up with terrific new ideas, insights, and answers to daunting questions. Those gifts of subconscious problem-solving and intuitive imagination may seem to be random, but they're not. They're a response to specific stimuli. That makes every night a fertile field for programming and problem-solving. The same often holds true for daydreaming during relaxed activities when our mind can wander. So why not take advantage and direct the process?

As we've said, you can instruct your subconscious mind to explore specific questions, challenges, and opportunities, dramatically increasing the chances of waking up to a relevant and revelatory solution. Like a farmer planting seeds, you can also insert new instructions that direct your subconscious to address your needs and desires in a more positive, productive, and targeted process. The basic guidelines remain: Calm the mind, then insert the program, question, or vision.

Note that we are especially calm and susceptible to suggestion and targeted energies during the twilight time when we transition between waking and sleeping. Therefore it's important to be aware of unintended and undesirable programming when we are preparing to sleep. Are we watching murder and mayhem on the evening news? Obsessing about bad feelings or unfortunate events that we can't change? Or are we engaged in positive activities like reading something funny, happy, spiritual, or inspirational? Are we hugging a loved one or fanning the flames of anger? Are we programming ourselves for success or reinforcing negative programs? The time and mental space will be filled by something. The critical issues are what they will be filled by and who will make that decision. We should be conscientious about everything we feed our own minds before we go to sleep—and upon awakening.

Programming Others

> "Words—so innocent and powerless as they are, as standing in a dictionary, how potent for good and evil they become in the hands of one who knows how to combine them."
>
> **—Nathaniel Hawthorne**

Does programming others sound malevolent? Selfish? Machiavellian? Well, it depends on how you use your programming skills. Sure, those skills can be misused to manipulate or take advantage of people, as anyone who's seen a TV commercial or listened to a politician knows. But, the fact is we're programming one another all the time, whether intentionally or unintentionally. So why not do it with greater awareness? The process simply entails using good, effective communication for the mutual benefit of those we wish to influence, including ourselves.

I've found this to be extremely valuable in all types of relationships. Let me share some examples from the realm of parenting, where the job description calls for positive programming of impressionable children.

When it was time for our son to go to sleep, we often read bedtime stories to him. We also made up lots of entertaining tales. We chose those stories quite consciously because we understood how influential they could be. I'm sure most parents are just as careful.

There were certainly times when Matt had trouble falling asleep. However, as I mentioned earlier, his primary self-image was of someone who slept easily. So what did we do on those occasions when he was too anxious or excited to sleep? We took those opportunities to not only relax him for better sleep (thereby reinforcing his super sleeper self-image) but also to embed deeply in his subconscious the knowledge that he was loved. We would have him take some deep breaths to relax, give him a warm hug, and whisper, "Mommy loves you, and Daddy loves you." Then we'd take it further and have him close his eyes and picture various people in his life, one at a time, and feel them hugging him while we said softly, "Nana loves you" and "Grandpa loves you," and so on through the list of every relative, friend, teacher, and even his favorite stuffed animals, until he fell contentedly asleep. Not only did it help our son to sleep and feel loved, it also created a beautiful vision that worked its way deep into his subconscious. I'm convinced that Matt's self-assuredness as a young man has a lot to do with that bedtime programming.

Later, when Matt was eleven or twelve, we created an annual game called the "I Can Do It-a-Thon." (I had started to compete in triathlons, and the Boston Marathon passed close to our house, so there was a natural tie-in.) The idea was to build his self-esteem by presenting him with challenges that appeared to be difficult at first but that we knew to be easily attainable. And to increase the odds of success, we linked the challenges to appropriate rewards. For example, that first year we challenged Matt to do push-ups. At first, he could only do a couple, but I knew that an eleven-year-old body could quickly go from two to twenty, so we offered a reward if he could do twenty push-ups in three months' time.

To Matt, the idea of doing ten times as many push-ups sounded intimidating. But I knew it would be easy if he built a Stairway of Success, taking it one step at a time. Sure enough, when he achieved four and then five push-ups, he was extremely proud, positive, and eager to proceed. When he got to ten he was even prouder. More important, he was acquiring confidence along the way, and his brain knew without a doubt that he could improve incrementally and eventually reach the twenty mark.

As our I Can Do It-a-Thon tradition continued over the years, we created challenges that would not only raise Matt's self-esteem but also improve his well-being and teach him crucial life lessons. When he was sixteen, for instance, we challenged him to do an Olympic-distance triathlon, a challenging three-hour event that involves swimming, cycling, and running in succession. Granted, a triathlon requires endurance and mastering specific athletic skills, but we also wanted Matt to learn how to take on that task successfully and enjoyably, and to appreciate the subsidiary requirements involved, such as maintaining a proper diet, finding and working with the right coaches, understanding the use of suitable equipment, mastering strategy, and designing the right training methods and sticking to them. If you do all of these things properly, the triathlon is relatively easy. If you neglect them, on the other hand, you set yourself up for a lot of frustration and probable failure. These were universal life skills that could be applied to many other endeavors.

When trying to influence others, the same basic rules apply as when we program ourselves. First we need the person's full attention. Then we have to appeal to their fact-based intelligence. Thus, one of the reasons the "best sleeper" programming worked with Matt is that we did it when he was calm and in bed. Plus, he continually proved it to be true. As for the I Can Do It-a-Thons, we designed them specifically for him to succeed. Every time he accomplished his goal, he proved to his own mind that he could do these remarkable things.

We also know that programming is not limited to language. We can use and influence all of our senses, or anyone else's. Thus, we can paint mental images, communicate through body language, use emotional cues, and project energy. We can also influence others with clear and specific instructions and by establishing consequences for their actions, both negative and positive. We'll go into this in more detail in the next chapter when we explore the science of behavioral psychology.

Clarity and Consensus

> "A genuine leader is not a searcher for consensus but a molder of consensus."
> **—Martin Luther King Jr.**

Whether it's a family, a team, or a large organization, it is vital for everyone to be in sync with respect to the primary purpose, values, and goals. For collective programming, clarity and consensus are essential. They are the foundation for coordinated action and ultimate success.

What happens when one person wants to do X and the other prefers Y? Whether it occurs in a marriage, a business, or a sporting event, the answer is the same: nothing good. This is because the conflicting programs tend to cancel each other out. Worse, they can create antagonism or heated conflict. Not exactly a recipe for success and happiness.

The next time you are faced with *conflict*, try the following all-purpose recipe to achieve *consensus* instead:

1. Get agreement that a shared goal is the only one that can succeed.

2. Come to an understanding regarding the primary objective (a satisfying marriage for both spouses, a successful business, a winning team, etc.).

3. Identify other areas of agreement to establish even more common ground.

4. Consider differences, but evaluate them in terms of their impact on the primary objective. Note that in the process of exploring differences, people may come to better understand their true desires and, as a result, modify their primary directive accordingly.

5. Review and refine. It's an ongoing process.

Not only does this methodology enhance the prospects for success, it also makes the entire interaction much more enjoyable. By first agreeing on a logical approach and then identifying common ground, you've created a solid foundation on which to build.

Internal Consensus

> "To thine own self be true."
> **—William Shakespeare**

In our own lives, just as with groups and relationships, our various desires and fears commonly pull us in different directions. This creates internal conditions that resemble a car filled with squabbling backseat drivers. It can be disorienting and confusing: What do we really want to do? Where should we go? How should we get there? It's vital to our inner peace and productivity to make sure all aspects of our mind, body, and soul are in sync.

It is just as critical to be clear about our individual purpose and plans as it is within larger organizations. Otherwise, programs can be contradictory and cancel each other out. Often, however, we're not just arguing within ourselves; we're also conflicted about what we think others want us to do or be. Our parents, friends, colleagues, and society as a whole all weigh in on what's right or wrong, what works best, and what we should do. On the one hand, it's important to take advice seriously—after all, other people have experience, knowledge, and perspectives that we may not have. Ultimately however, if we want to live harmoniously, we have to be clear, consistent, and true to ourselves. I've found the following approach to be extremely practical:

- If you're not sure of something, ask questions of yourself and others. Gather information. Sleep on it. And give yourself sufficient time. An open mind and an open heart go a long way toward finding your truth.

- Listen to your intuition. Allow your intuitive mind (what many call their heart) to explore as deeply as is needed. Try to get to the root issues.

- If possible, postpone decisions until both your head and your heart are in agreement. Disparity between the two is not necessarily a bad thing. It just signals that you need to understand more before the tension can be resolved.

Only when we achieve internal clarity and consensus can we move with confidence in the right direction. Now let's turn our attention to influencing the specific behaviors that will get us what we want.

MOTIVATE and Get What You Want

"Motivation is the art of getting people to do what you want them to do because they want to do it."

—Dwight D. Eisenhower

When I was in high school, I had a job doing construction work one summer. It was okay. It was a job. My boss was probably okay as well; I can't say that I remember him. Then one day I got assigned to another project, and apparently the new supervisor was supposed to be . . . super. I wasn't quite sure what that meant since I had never experienced such a thing. I heard that he had a reputation for always getting things built ahead of schedule and under budget, and that his crew adored him and would do anything for him. And then I got to experience working for him. People were right! I immediately liked and respected this guy. He was hardworking and demanding, but always fair and clear and funny and bighearted. I would have done anything he asked me to. Happily.

—

To achieve what we want, we're constantly trying to motivate people—to act (or not act) a certain way, to get something done, to get it done better, to adhere to a particular schedule, or follow a certain code of conduct. The list includes virtually all actions big and small. Motivation is not only the essence of business, advertising, and sales, it's also a primary focus of politics, philanthropy, sports, romance, child-rearing, and just about every human endeavor. In addition to our innate desire to influence others, we are also constantly trying to motivate ourselves—consciously and unconsciously. Our internal dialogue is full of instructions, rationales, and potential rewards or punishments.

The art and science of motivation is as old as the first human family, but we now know a whole lot more about it than our ancestors did. Thanks to gains in psychology, organizational development, and other disciplines, motivation has been, and continues to be, studied, measured, scientifically implemented, and refined.

We're all being motivated all the time. However, we're not always the ones who are pushing the buttons and pulling the levers. We may exert the primary influence on our own actions, but we are, to varying degrees, greatly influenced by outside forces. That's why it's crucial to understand the process and take more control of the mechanisms that drive us, so we get the results we desire more easily and more enjoyably. Along the way, you'll discover some surprising facts about what works and what doesn't work, and why.

It's as Easy as ABC

The template for the art and science of motivation is as simple as ABC. I'm referring to the basic ABC model used by behavioral psychologists:

A = Antecedents
B = Behavior
C = Consequences

Let's start in the middle with "B" since *behavior* is what we want to influence. Whether we want to initiate, terminate, modify, or totally transform the behavior of an individual, a group, or ourselves, this is the focal point. Therefore, after determining what the desired behavior is, the next question is "How do we make it happen?"

"A" and "C" are the two categories that drive behavior. *Antecedents* are the specific instructions, circumstances, and environmental factors that precede the behavior. They provide the information and conditions necessary to facilitate whatever behavior we're looking to cultivate.

Consequences are the sticks and carrots of the equation. They comprise all the things, both positive and negative, that will happen as a result of, or absence of, a specific behavior. The antecedents and consequences work together to inform, influence, and motivate behavior.

This is all extremely straightforward, and yet most people fail to follow this simple and successful approach. Fortunately, it's easy to make the necessary changes and better motivate the behaviors we want and demotivate the behaviors we want to lessen or eliminate. Now let's take a closer look at the mechanics.

It All Begins with B

"If you don't know where you are going, any road will get you there."
—Lewis Carroll

The behavior you want to motivate is a function of the results you wish to achieve. For example, if you want to complete a marathon, you have to run twenty-six miles. To do that, you have to get into excellent physical shape. To get into shape, you have to work out intelligently and diligently.

Likewise, if you want to find a mate, it helps to meet people. But not just any people. The more you can interact with your desired target market, the greater the likelihood of finding a suitable prospect and consummating the deal. Pardon the business reference, but I just want to point out that it's essentially the same process, and the required behavior is much the same.

This may sound obvious, but determining exactly what you want of yourself and others can be elusive, as well as complicated and confusing. We don't always know what we want, or why. Plus, we feel pulled in multiple or even opposite directions. This is where it all begins. When you have clarity about what you really want, everything else is much more straightforward.

Sometimes however, we fail to achieve clarity because facing the truth can be scary, especially if we're afraid of failure, or of disappointing others, or a host of other factors. We're also creatures of habit. The result is that most people go through much of their lives on autopilot. They don't necessarily pause to question where they're going and why they're going there. If they did, they might get some interesting answers. Then again, maybe they're not questioning themselves because they don't want to confront the truth, such as what they really want, what they think of their job, how they feel about their relationships, or about the direction of their lives, or even about themselves. The truth can be frightening. But it can also open up a world of possibility, achievement, and satisfaction.

As with most things in life, the process of determining what we want is improved with targeted questions and deeper awareness. The more we ask and the more we listen—with both our heads and our hearts—the better the answers we receive. And every step we take is an opportunity to get feedback and make refinements.

Antecedents: Communicate Clearly and Create the Right Conditions

> "The single biggest problem in communication is the illusion that it has taken place."
> **—George Bernard Shaw**

Once you know what behavior you're looking for, you have to make sure the right antecedents are in place so that everyone involved, including you, understands precisely what needs to be done and why. Don't expect people to read your mind. The more specific your instructions—and the rationale behind them—the greater the likelihood they will be followed. For example, there's a world of difference between telling an assistant "Please create these slides for me" versus "Please create these slides by 3:00 because I need them for my big presentation tonight."

Now think about when you give that presentation, and you want to motivate the audience to stay awake and listen attentively to you. Ideally, you consider all the relevant environmental factors that influence behavior: You adjust the lighting and temperature to keep people alert and comfortable (but not too comfortable); you show powerful slides that are engaging and easy to comprehend; you tell stories (which are much easier to remember than a string of facts); and you invite audience participation to keep them involved.

That's *ideally*. In reality however, most people, myself included, don't always do the obvious. So, why don't we give specific instructions? Why do so many speakers drone on when they could easily do a few simple things to engage and energize their audience? Well, sometimes we literally forget, and sometimes we just don't know how to do things better. We're unaware, but not blissfully so.

Skillfully employing antecedents is the essence of what is commonly referred to as communication skills. The benefit of thinking in terms of antecedents and the ABC model is that it takes away the mystery and exposes the recipe for enhanced communication and effective motivation. When we stop assuming that some people are born with a silver tongue, and the rest of us are doomed to mediocre attempts at motivation, we can better understand the architecture of the process and proceed purposefully to upgrade our skills.

One of my management axioms is *The quality of the behavior depends on the quality of the instructions.* I've seen too many managers assign projects by saying, essentially, "Please do such and such." End of story. But it's not just *what* to do that matters; it's also why, when, and how to do it. Plus, it's vital to explain your priorities clearly, so everyone knows what's most important and therefore the order in which to do all of their assignments.

The classic example of unnecessary disappointment is the manager who makes a new request but doesn't assign it any priority. Then, when the task isn't done when he expects it to be, he's angry and frustrated. He might conclude that the employee is lazy, neglectful, incompetent, or even spiteful, when in fact he or she just didn't know the manager's time frame or its relative importance. This is common not only in business, but also between spouses, parents and children, teachers and students, and other relationships where requests and instructions are part of the norm.

Since our to-do lists are always long and constantly expanding, we rarely get everything done. So people feel terrible when they work hard at some task only to get criticized for what they *didn't do*, instead of praised for what they *did* accomplish. It's a classic lose-lose scenario. But, in most cases, it could easily have been a win-win. The solution is to communicate priorities, expectations, available resources, time frames, consequences, and anything else that is relevant. A few extra minutes of communication can literally change your world and that of the people around you.

To enhance your communication with others, strive for these attributes (the explanations follow):

- Wait until you have their full attention.

- Speak their language.

- Remember, it's not just your words that matter.

- Realize communication is a two-way street.

- Get in sync before you attempt to lead.

- Broadcast on everyone's personal radio station, WIIFM (What's in it for me?).

- Beware the Dead Man Rule.

- Leave nothing to chance.

WAIT UNTIL YOU HAVE THEIR FULL ATTENTION

Giving instructions or expressing your desires while someone is watching television or is otherwise engaged is a recipe for failure. Your message will at best be diluted and most likely misunderstood and not remembered. Wait until you have their attention, whether then and there or at a time that's more convenient for both of you.

SPEAK THEIR LANGUAGE

If someone speaks only French, explaining something in English would be of limited benefit. Similarly, people from dissimilar backgrounds and orientations may respond differently to certain words, emotions, and rationales. A three-year-old is not a thirty-year-old, and a teenager can't see the world through the eyes of a parent. Similarly, an artist and an engineer might experience a situation in radically different ways, and each of them may see it differently from a business executive or a pastor. Plus, we process what we hear through a filter of personal fears, desires, and biases. So speak the other person's language if you want to communicate more effectively.

REMEMBER, IT'S NOT JUST YOUR WORDS THAT MATTER

You also motivate—or demotivate as the case may be—through positive and negative visual cues, such as facial gestures, grooming, and body language, as well as nuances of speech like volume, cadence, and emphasis. Your appearance and energy are vitally important because we remember so much more of what we see and feel compared to what we hear.

REALIZE COMMUNICATION IS A TWO-WAY STREET

By paying attention to the other person's words, body language, tone, and other cues, we can better understand who they are and *where* they are. Then we can adjust our own messages accordingly, based on how that person reacts. I always used to wonder why Broadway actors and professional speakers didn't get bored giving the same performance over and over. Then I came to appreciate firsthand that the speech or role is never the same, because the audience and the environment are always different, and therefore the energy and the interaction are always unique. The best communicators are those who are fully present and engaged with their audience.

GET IN SYNC BEFORE YOU ATTEMPT TO LEAD

Granted, if you're in a position of authority, you can simply pull rank and intimidate people into acquiescence. But, as we'll discuss in a moment, that negative approach has limited appeal and even less long-term efficacy. Instead, first establish trust. Once you do that, it's much easier to lead, and you'll do it with the implicit agreement of the other person.

In her moving book about Alzheimer's disease, *Still Alice*, the author and neuroscientist Lisa Genova portrays the ailment from the patient's point of view. We learn dramatically from that book, and the movie based on it, that if we want to connect with people we have to meet them where *they* are. For example, if your octogenarian aunt believes she's thirty years old and you're her sister, you can try correcting her or you can meet her lovingly where she is. Professional caregivers will tell you that the latter option is far better for the patient and for your ongoing interaction. Well, it's not only people with brain disorders who have trouble agreeing on the facts. We all do at times, but we are generally pretty good at discerning the true emotions of the people we interact with.

Empathy is the key. If you understand why someone thinks and feels the way they do, and if you can identify with them on some level and communicate your understanding earnestly, you can get in sync with them more naturally and more completely. Then the other person is more likely to listen with an open mind and an open heart. That's when it's easiest to lead and to motivate.

BROADCAST ON EVERYONE'S PERSONAL RADIO STATION, WIIFM

"What's In It For Me?" (i.e., "How will this affect me?") is on everyone's mind, whether we admit it or not. The best motivators are aware of this at all times and communicate with people on this important channel. Therefore, deliver your message in a manner consistent with what the others care about. We'll cover this in more detail when we focus on consequences. And, in case you're wondering, communicating consequences is an antecedent as well since it conveys important information in the service of the desired behavior.

BEWARE THE DEAD MAN RULE

Studies have repeatedly shown that action is more actionable than abstinence. Asking someone to do something that a dead man could do (e.g., abstaining from something) just doesn't work as well as asking someone to do something proactive. For example, suppose you're concerned about a loved one's eating habits. You could say, "Don't eat junk food." But, not eating junk food is something a dead man can accomplish; and the results of such admonitions tend to be pretty lackluster. On the other hand, you could try, "If you want to lose ten pounds and have more energy, switch to a healthier diet." Now that's something dead people can't do. Directives like this are far more actionable than the first option.

Likewise, "Don't make any mistakes" could be accomplished by a dead man. Plus, it creates a mistake-oriented vision in the person's mind, and people tend to move toward the indicated image. (If you doubt that, see what happens if you try not to think of a juicy hamburger with ketchup spilling onto your clothes.) So, instead of saying "Don't make any mistakes with this memo," try "Please make sure to proofread this memo and have someone else check it as well." The second statement is much more positive, specific, and actionable, and therefore a better harbinger of success.

LEAVE NOTHING TO CHANCE

Everything has an effect. So, whether you're explaining the fine points of your instructions (priorities, importance, resources, and so on) or preparing a space for a presentation (the temperature of the room, lighting, engaging slides, sound system, and seating arrangements), make sure to stack the deck in your favor!

The Truth About Consequences

> "Typically, if you reward something, you get more of it. You punish something, you get less of it."
> —**Daniel H. Pink**

When we think about consequences, the positive vs. negative equation gets most of the attention, but other elements are also crucial—like timing and dependability. It boils down to this: PIC vs. NFU. PIC (Positive, Immediate, and Certain) consequences tend to be far more effective than NFU (Negative, Future, and Uncertain) consequences. To understand this more fully, let's look at each attribute and its opposite:

Positive	vs.	**N**egative
Immediate	vs.	**F**uture
Certain	vs.	**U**ncertain

Starting at the top, both *positive and negative* consequences can be powerful motivators. As my mother always said, "You can attract more people with honey than with vinegar." That may be true, but threatening to hurt someone, or fire them, or even dislike them, can be powerful motivators as well. We all need carrots and sticks in our toolkit. And, in most circumstances, the best strategy is a combination of the two.

Research reveals significant differences between these two forms of consequences. Generally speaking, the threat of negative consequences effectively promotes the minimum behavior required to avoid the punishment, but little more. If, for example, you're concerned about an employee's absenteeism or general poor performance, the right message and motivation might be "If you don't show up for work and do what you were hired to do, you'll be let go." But when you want to get more out of people—when you want them to go the extra mile, reach for the stars, and succeed beyond their basic desires or perceived limitations—positive motivators work best. Knowing that high-level performance will be amply rewarded inspires people to go above and beyond.

What about *immediate vs. future* rewards? Well, would you rather get your well-earned recompense as soon as you've fulfilled your end of the bargain, or would you rather wait a few weeks, months, or years? The anticipation of immediate benefits generates much more interest and energy than contemplating a long wait time before you get to celebrate. Obviously, long-term rewards often motivate people as well, and studies show that a child's ability to delay gratification can be an indicator of future success. But in most cases, sooner is more appealing than later. If you give people a choice between $1,000 today or $2,000 ten years from now, most would take the bird in the hand even though the long-term return may be greater. And if it's $1,000 today or $1,000 ten years from now, there's no contest.

Which brings us to *certain vs. uncertain*. All other things being equal, we assign greater value to outcomes that are definite vs. may-or-may-not-happen. While this might seem too obvious to mention, it's actually an important and much-overlooked factor in crafting consequences.

Let's consider how it all plays out when we see it in context. With PIC vs. NFU as a conceptual foundation, we can now understand why some plans and programs motivate people better than others. Take diets, for example. Is depriving yourself of food positive or negative? Obviously, it's negative. It's unpleasant, and it's hard. Are the consequences immediate or future? Dieters have to struggle for weeks or months before they come close to their weight-loss goals. As for certainty, anyone who says the odds are in the dieter's favor is probably selling a diet book.

Conversely, the pleasure of eating something delicious is positive, immediate, and certain; and that almost always tops a regimen of deprivation and unsatisfying food whose benefits won't be seen for a while—if ever. A hot fudge sundae is a PIC; a stalk of celery, not so much, for most people.

That said, we diet for some very positive reasons, including health, beauty, self-image, and attracting a mate. The problem is that while the desired benefits may be positive and powerful enough to get us to start a diet, those benefits are not going to show up until well into the future, and they are uncertain even then. This is one reason why so many diets fail.

Fortunately, our model also tells us how to stack the weight-loss deck in our favor. A successful regimen should be structured around PICs such as tasty, nutritious food, with immediate and certain rewards. And, as we'll discuss later in this section, we can create and reward intermediate goals to make the benefits more timely. We can also customize rewards to better suit the individual.

If you want to see some of the best examples of the ABC model in operation with crystal clarity and predictable results, watch competitive team sports. You will notice the following:

Antecedents are firmly in place. Information is clear, precise, detailed, and it is shared with players, coaches, and fans. Scoreboards, announcers, and officials combine to make sure everyone knows what's going on. And if you want even more information, the Internet and the person next to you are at your service.

Desired behavior is specific. Players are trained to know exactly what they're supposed to do in every conceivable situation, and also when and how they're supposed to do it. In baseball, for example, the infielders position themselves differently depending on whether a righty or lefty batter is at the plate, whether there are base runners, how many outs there are, and various other factors.

Consequences are clear, precise, targeted, desirable, and dependable. Little is left to chance, and everyone knows the score—literally and figuratively. This doesn't guarantee success, but it definitely increases the probability that the desired behavior will be energetically and enthusiastically attempted and achieved.

Feedback is virtually instantaneous. Whether it's the scoreboard or the reaction of the coaches or the fans cheering and jeering, consequences are about as immediate as can be. As a result, the players know exactly what is effective, and refinements and improvements can occur in real time.

A Matter of Art and Science

> "Every art should become science, and every
> science should become art."
> **—Friedrich von Schlegel**

Crafting compelling reasons to behave in a desired manner is both an art and a science. While experience and research provide guidelines, there is always room for innovation and improvement. The "wild card" concept in sports, for instance, is a brilliant example: Keeping more teams in the running for the playoffs ensures that passion will still run high late in the season, motivating players and fans alike. This in turn boosts stadium attendance and TV ratings.

Other such revolutionary innovations appear in virtually all areas of human endeavor. You need only look around your home to see that almost every appliance you own has benefited from breakthrough improvements in pleasing you. Our smartphones are loaded with applications that provide what we want, when we want it. When we order merchandise online, we get instant gratification, competitive pricing, and easy return policies. Our home entertainment systems are likewise powerful, personal, and priced right. And in all of these examples, the vendors who provide the best PICs get our business.

Positive, Immediate, and Certain is the ideal to aim for. When people know they'll definitely receive a desirable reward soon after they perform the requisite behavior, they are far more motivated versus *maybe* getting some *lackluster* reward sometime in the *future*. It gets a bit more challenging, of course, when you're unable to put PIC together as perfectly as you'd like. If that's the case, two out of three of these ingredients—or even one out of three—is a whole lot better than none. Likewise, when you determine that it's appropriate to use negative consequences as a motivator, such as penalizing someone or giving them critical feedback, try to do it immediately and with certainty. And if possible, look for positive side benefits that don't undermine the power of the negative consequences. For example, it's one thing to tell someone that he made a big mistake, but simultaneously framing the setback as a potential opportunity to learn and grow could be much better.

Give Them What They Want

"Rule #1: The customer is always right. Rule #2: If the customer is wrong, please refer to rule #1."

— Ann Brashares

Together, the ABC model and PIC/NFU constitute a simple structure for understanding, remembering, and executing the best motivational practices. Now let's look at some refinements that can help turn good motivators into great ones.

CUSTOM DESIGN

One person might work day and night to earn a $1,000 bonus or to win a contest because he is extremely competitive and relishes the limelight, while his coworker couldn't care less about any of those things but would go all out to attain a secure employment contract or more vacation time for her family. Some people would love to go to a football game and sit outside and drink beer on a wintry Sunday afternoon, while others would see that as punishment. We're all unique. And because people are turned on or off by different things, consequences should be customized accordingly.

It usually doesn't take much effort to find out what people want or cherish or need the most. A little research pays big dividends. How do you discover what people want? Start by asking them. If they don't provide a specific answer to such a general question, or if you want to test their response, then suggest some potential rewards and ask which one is most desirable and motivating. Keep presenting comparisons and, little by little, you'll discover what strikes their fancy and what doesn't. You can also query their friends and coworkers. The key is to ask.

You can also pay attention to how people behave. When and why do they get excited, and when do they get turned off? Do their actions substantiate their previous assertions regarding what they desire most? Do they validate your own opinions about what they deem important? Ultimately, you'll come to your own conclusions. After that, it's all about refinements.

A LITTLE LEVERAGE GOES A LONG WAY

Some of the most powerful incentives center on achieving benefits for others—in a sense, leveraging the rewards to serve an even greater good. Altruism is in our DNA. While we may be self-absorbed in many ways, we're also part of couples and families and communities. You might be surprised how motivated people become by the opportunity to help others. In some cases, this may inspire them far more than the prospect of personal gain.

If you want to motivate a person or a group to help you achieve a goal, consider linking the reward to a benefit for others. For example, a sales executive I know told his team, "If I reach my goal of an additional X dollars of revenue this month, I will share half of that increase with the entire team and the charity of your choice." That deal not only gave him highly motivated workers, but enthusiastic cheerleaders.

There are many ways to leverage our resources and our rewards. Now that you're aware of the concept, you'll begin to notice examples throughout your life such as charitable matching gifts, "two for one" sales, frequent flyer miles, and innumerable "specials" designed to get someone in the door and keep them there. We're only limited by our creativity. And if we can't think of a great way to leverage our resources, we can always ask others for their ideas.

USE MILESTONES

Eventually, people tend to become desensitized to the usual incentives, such as money (especially if the incremental amount won't change their lives) and various perks that they no longer cherish or need as much. At such times, when ordinary rewards fail to inspire, introducing performance milestones can generate a surge of energy in individuals, teams, and entire organizations. The opportunity to make it to the next level, along with the attendant recognition, self-satisfaction, and special rewards or prizes can be extremely motivating.

I learned this early on in business. Predictably, the prospect of earning substantial fees and commissions motivated most salespeople considerably. But after a point, another client or additional sale wasn't going to make a noticeable difference to their well-being. That extra business stopped becoming as big a positive in their minds. So we, like many organizations, started adding milestones. For example, if someone performed at a certain level by a specific date, they got a special bonus or qualified for an incentive conference or some type of a significant award, prize, or honor. In other words, we made the entire journey interesting, challenging, fun, and, most important, desirable.

Don't underestimate the power of recognition and achievement. We all want to feel good about ourselves. So if rising to the next level of performance will satisfy that objective, people will give it their all. In addition, moving up the ladder generally means associating with others who have likewise excelled, and that also becomes an extremely potent enticement.

In driving toward major goals, we can measure, acknowledge, and celebrate subsidiary achievements. Once again, organized sports serve as the poster child for how to do it well. A player's stats not only indicate all manner of achievements, they also show whether he or she is on track for a record, an award, the ability to stay in the majors in baseball, or on the tour in golf. But this isn't just specific to sports. Milestones and mini opportunities to celebrate abound in all fields of endeavor.

The logic of milestones applies especially well to fundraising. Suppose you're running an annual campaign and using volunteers to raise money for a worthy charity. Can those workers stay consistently motivated and energized while putting off gratification for an entire year? Probably not. One solution is intermediary goals: For example, in addition to acknowledging those individuals who raise X dollars at certain intervals (monthly, weekly, or even daily), the entire team gets to celebrate and reinforce every achievement. Researchers have found that a minor reward when an interim goal is reached can not only help people persevere in their efforts, it can also increase energy and enjoyment. Think of the symbolic thermometer that shows the progress of a fundraising drive or other campaigns. This image provides immediate feedback as it inspires everyone to get the total up to the next level.

Such milestones also motivate the donors. While an annual fund drive or a big capital campaign may be programmed to run for a year or longer, contributors are often asked to help achieve a more immediate subsidiary goal. Just as sports fans celebrate all manner of victories, big and small, so can donors, workers, and families.

This is the essence of the "star chart" that parents have successfully used with their children for generations. Little kids rarely have the ability to focus on long-term goals, hence the star chart, which awards recognition when the child does something desirable along the way, usually daily. The star gets posted on a chart, which is visible and prominent, making each new star an achievement in itself and a constant reminder of the positive consequences of success. When the number of stars reaches certain thresholds (typically daily or weekly with young children), milestone prizes are awarded, all ultimately leading up to a big prize.

Note that stars can also be taken away for bad behavior, which is also a powerful motivator.

There's a long list of things we can do to divide long-term goals (and their associated rewards and celebrations) into incremental steps. Identifying and celebrating each segment of the journey creates ongoing reinforcement of the desired behavior. It's PIC in action.

Milestones can work magnificently as *self-motivators* as well. By dividing up large goals into smaller-sized stepping stones, we get to focus on more attainable goals and celebrate more often—and that's more motivating! Consider swimming champion John Naber, who won four gold medals at the 1976 Summer Olympics, breaking a world record with each victory. I had the pleasure of meeting John many years later at the Atlanta Olympics. He explained that when he was a teenager, he dreamed of winning Olympic gold. Unfortunately, he was only an average swimmer at the time. He was good enough to excel at the high school level, but there was a huge distance between where he was and where he had to be to reach the medal platform. Knowing he had a ton of work to do, he had to motivate himself to go back to the pool every day and work out instead of doing something that was more immediately satisfying. In addition, the ultimate reward was well into the future and decidedly uncertain.

So what was John's solution? He made a series of calculations and broke down his ultimate goal into interim milestones and time frames. At the end of one year, he determined, he'd have to swim distance A in time B. At the end of two years, it had to be distance X in Y time. Then, he broke it down further: Where did he have to be in each month? Finally, he asked himself, *To reach my one-month goal, what exactly do I have to do? What skills, training, and practice will be required?* He picked the brains of his coaches and structured a system of interim goals, training techniques, and associated rewards. He didn't know about antecedents or the acronym PIC, but he sure understood the concepts. The consequences he designed were positive, immediate, and certain.

Day after day, week after week, month after month, John's system kept him on track, informed, and motivated. Eventually, he went to USC, where he led the swim team to four consecutive NCAA championships. At the Montreal Olympics in 1976, his dream came true four times over.

Sometimes, however, the objective isn't to train for some big medal, but rather to literally survive an extended ordeal. Rob O'Neill, the Navy SEAL from the elite SEAL Team 6 who is credited with shooting Osama bin Laden, has shared his story of the remarkably demanding eight-month training that all candidates must endure to qualify for the basic SEAL program. This intensive training is followed by another nine-month ordeal for those who succeed and want to apply for SEAL Team 6. The majority of them don't make it. Frankly, I can barely imagine lasting an hour, let alone eight months. According to Rob, he and the rest of the candidates were very anxious (although they probably worried about lasting a day as opposed to an hour), but when he told us the lesson the lead instructor taught the recruits, I immediately understood why it worked. In addition to creating attainable milestones, he was also teaching a variation of the Stairway of Success.

The trainer said they would likely fail if they focused on lasting eight months. That goal would be overwhelming. But if, instead, they were focused on lasting until the next meal, they had a much better chance of succeeding. He encouraged them to take it one step at a time. Each step completed counted as one victory. Three victories per day would feed them and keep them going. And each victory provided increasing proof that it could be done.

We can do the same in less demanding arenas. When I teach someone to windsurf, for example, I break down the process into small manageable steps and milestone achievements. Otherwise, most people are easily discouraged when they first give it a try because they underestimate its complexity and difficulty. They assume that they will soon be standing on the board, sailing along, and easily moving the sail to take them where they want to go.

They don't realize they have to learn a lot of subsidiary skills to get to that point. And since they don't know that going in, they soon begin to see themselves as failures each time they lose control and fall into the water. As they get more fatigued, they conclude, and prove, that they can't do it. Of course this is no fun, and most of them quit.

But, when I divide what they perceive as the first step into five subsidiary steps, all of a sudden they're having some successes—admittedly small ones, but achievements nonetheless. With milestones to celebrate, the process becomes much more enjoyable as they experience an elevated self-image and the boost of energy that comes with it.

TANGIBLE AND SOCIAL REWARDS

Studies show that money is not necessarily the biggest or best motivator. Tangible rewards such as money and valuable prizes certainly work well when they're truly needed and valued by the recipient. But in most circumstances, social rewards can be far more powerful. These include things like public recognition, an award ceremony, a big trophy (or even just a little blue ribbon), the admiration of others, congratulations from peers, a pledge to a favorite charity, or most commonly—a sincere thank you. Social rewards are great for getting people to go the extra mile, because the benefits touch the heart in ways that money and merchandise alone cannot.

I've found that the simple act of telling people how much they're appreciated is a tremendous way to motivate them, not to mention make me feel wonderful as well. Tracy, an employee who had been a smiling and luminous presence in our office for years, did her work with unflagging dedication and excellence. I'd always appreciated those qualities but never shared it with her. Then, one day when I was teaching a class on motivation and was describing this concept of tangible and social rewards, I looked at Tracy's big smile and realized that I'd never actually told her how much her presence and her participation meant to me. Like many people, I imagined that because I'd thought it many times, I must have expressed it. But I hadn't, so right then and there, in front of a large group of her coworkers, I said, "Tracy, this is something I've never told you. Whenever I see your smiling face, I smile too. I see you in the office, running your department, and I think of how you climbed the ladder here and what an incredible job you do, and how important you are to our company. I am enormously appreciative. I never told you that, so I'm telling you now."

That fifteen-second, straight-from-the-heart recognition didn't add a dime to Tracy's bank account, or take away anything from mine, but it touched her deeply, and I think she'll remember it longer than any bonus she's received. I believe it motivates her to this day. I've seen similar reactions when I've told the parents of an employee how wonderful their son or daughter is. Mom and Dad beam, and the employee looks like a kid with a straight-A report card.

Most social rewards are quick, free, and available 24/7. They're always in your back pocket, ready to be distributed, utilized, and leveraged. They're pixie dust, and you're the fantastic person who makes others happy by inspiring love and loyalty. The only caveat is that your rewards have to be sincere.

You might wonder whether compliments can be overused and thereby diminished in value. I certainly thought they could. However, my experience has suggested otherwise. People much prefer to be valued than to be taken for granted. As long as the appreciation is sincere, and the delivery is appropriate, it works wonders for them and you. I know a few individuals who really excel at making people feel valued, and it's usually one of their greatest attributes.

Of course, tangible rewards like cash, gift certificates, and expensive gifts also work, and they work best when they're targeted to the recipient. Many researchers suggest a ratio of 4:1 as a guideline (four social rewards to every tangible reward), but there's no hard and fast rule. A big part of the art of motivation is determining the right proportion of the various consequences, based on the specific circumstances and individuals involved.

The Law of Reciprocity

> "Kind words can be short and easy to speak,
> but their echoes are truly endless."
>
> **—Mother Teresa**

It's human nature for people to respond in kind. We're instinctively moved to give back in a way that seems commensurate with what we've been given. For example, if we offer our hand to someone to shake, they instinctively extend theirs in response. It follows that one way to motivate people to act in a particular way is to bestow the desired behavior on them. Treat your sales staff with respect, and they're likely to treat you and your customers the same way. The same goes for your friends and family: If you're kind and considerate, you'll get kindness and consideration back. Plus, there's a ripple effect that can benefit others who come in contact with this elevated energy. Conversely, it also stands to reason that if you take advantage of people and disrespect or offend them, they will define your relationship in those terms, and that's usually not very productive.

Addiction Theory

Do you know why slot machines are so addictive? Because of something called a "variable ratio, variable reward response"—players never know when they're going to win or how big the payoff might be. The jackpot can always come with the very next press of a button, or not. That's why it's so hard to walk away. But perhaps the more appropriate example these days is our digital devices, coupled with social media and the various apps we use. They're so addictive that overuse has become a major problem—but not for the companies that get you to press those buttons.

This same principle can be used benevolently to motivate others at home, at work, on the ball field, anywhere. If everything is predictable, activities can become dull and energies can drift. On the other hand, surprise celebrations and rewards at unpredictable times keep people energized and alert. The objective is to keep your audience interested and involved, and the benefits can far outweigh the costs. It's like Vegas, except that you're in control and everyone's a winner. We're only limited by our creativity. And if you hit the limit of yours, just ask others for their ideas.

The New Science of Gamification

Gamification is a game-changer. It involves the use of game thinking and game mechanics (e.g., point-scoring, competition with others, rules, and rewards) in traditionally non-game contexts to engage users in solving problems and behaving in a desired manner. Basically, it's about turning work and problem-solving into a game. When a task becomes more engaging, people invest more energy *and* derive greater pleasure.

Its practical implications are enormous, especially now that it has been merged with Big Data. All of a sudden, we can follow a huge sampling of people in real time and organize the information in a thousand different ways from countless angles. Online marketing is one of the most visible applications and biggest beneficiaries. Gamification also allows us to see on a large scale how modifying specific variables in society creates different results. Incentives can be tweaked, and results can be quickly measured, tested, and refined.

The concept of gamification can be applied to everything from families and small businesses to giant industries. One well-known application was the result of a Volkswagen contest to find ways to make obeying the speed limit fun and effective. The winning entry was a system in which motorists were awarded a lottery ticket for driving at or below the speed limit. The prizes were funded by the fines charged to drivers who exceeded the speed limit. This very system is now successfully in use in Sweden.

Observe, Test, Measure, and Refine

Let's harken back to the first two skills, "Ask" and "Listen." It's critical to question your assumptions, gather feedback, and continuously modify your motivational techniques. The first step is always to be clear about what you really want and why. There's no sense going fast in the wrong direction. As you get clearer about your true purpose, your passion will increase. So will your ability to enlist, motivate, and leverage others.

You can use the ABC model to craft campaigns and gauge results. Observe what happens when you change the antecedent circumstances or establish different consequences. Does behavior change in the desired direction? Whenever possible, gather hard data: Quantified results will give you an accurate reading of the actual impact of your procedures. Subjective impressions, personal observations, and the reports of others can be extremely valuable, but sometimes numbers tell a vastly different story. That said, don't underestimate the power of intuition. At first your hunches may seem subjective, fuzzy, and unreliable, but the more you pay attention, the clearer the intuitive signals become. For best results, listen to your head *and* your heart.

The Primary Objective: Motivate Yourself

"Control your own destiny or someone else will."
—Jack Welch

Since you are the center of your own universe, no one is more important to motivate than you. This cannot be overstated. So whether you work under supervision or you're the boss, whether you live alone or with others, and whether you enjoy solitary pastimes or group activities, you need to know how to motivate yourself to achieve your desired objectives. The protocols for motivating yourself are the same as for motivating others. The recipes work, but they must first be implemented. This is an important choice, and it's yours to make. You can design your own motivational programs or relinquish control to outside forces. After all, something is going to move you to act, so why not take charge of the process and usher in a new era of achievement and well-being?

STRUCTURE and
Win by Design

"By failing to prepare, you are preparing to fail."
—Benjamin Franklin

We celebrated New Year's Eve 2003 in Rio de Janeiro. The tradition in Rio is that everyone wears white that night to welcome the New Year with hopes for peace and prosperity. Millions of people flock to the beach at Copacabana, and we were right in the middle of it all. An incredible night to remember.

The next morning, my wife went for her first swim of 2004 in the hotel pool. She usually swam with the same ease as most people walked. But that morning she felt a bit tired after only a quarter of a mile (she normally swam for a mile), and then noticed that she was a little out of breath climbing the main staircase in the hotel.

When we returned home a few days later, Robbie's energy was still somewhat off, so she went to see our doctor. He detected some fluid in her lungs and suggested that it might be pneumonia. Just in case, he ran a number of tests. When the results came in, it wasn't pneumonia. It was ovarian cancer. Stage four.

"Stage four out of five?" we both asked.

"No. Stage four out of four." Curse words were invented for moments like that, and they filled the air.

The survival rate for advanced ovarian cancer was not good, but we learned that certain things help your odds: underlying good health, a strong support network of friends and family, proper medical care, and a positive attitude. We were in great shape in all respects, and we were determined to do whatever it took to increase the odds further. The other part of our game plan was to hang in there long enough for medical research to find a cure.

But the most important part of the plan appeared a few hours later when we visited with the oncologist to discuss treatment. In the waiting room, I read a headline on a magazine cover that I will never forget: "Cancer was the best thing that ever happened to me." That was exactly what we needed to hear, and we vowed that we would make this next journey the best thing that ever happened to us!

In addition to pursuing treatment with resolve and a positive attitude, we looked for ways to turn every single minute and mile on that journey into something wonderful. For example, chemo treatments: On our first visit to the oncologist we came face to face with the devastating impact of chemotherapy. His office was filled with sad and sick people who were injecting poisons into their bodies and experiencing the ravages of both the disease and the treatment.

I had no intention of letting my wife suffer like that, so we invented "The Chemo Party." We asked for an empty room where the therapy could be administered and invited all of Robbie's friends to come hang out with her. I catered the first party and then they all took over. For three hours every few weeks, there was laughter and love and loads of support. In fact, the chemo parties took on a life of their own as many of Robbie's friends were from different spheres and had never met before. New friendships were formed *that persist to this day. And as strange as this may sound, everyone looked forward to the chemo parties—including Robbie.*

From the start we vowed that cancer would not define, confine, or control us, and we planned accordingly. We continued to conduct our lives much as we always had, only we were much more aware and appreciative of every precious moment and every ray of sunshine.

Eventually, however, the damage took its toll and Robbie's body began to shut down; just prior to Thanksgiving 2006, we were told that she only had a week or two left. We waited until after our traditional Thanksgiving dinner to let people know (Robbie didn't want to dampen their festivities). Then we decided to party. In the Jewish tradition, like many others, someone's passing is followed by a celebration of their life, as friends and family gather to mourn together and support each other. But Robbie loved a good party, and it seemed so unfair for her to miss what might be the biggest one of her time on earth. So we alerted one and all and told everyone what was happening. We invited them to come to our house whenever they could to say goodbye, raise a toast, laugh, and cry—with Robbie instead of after her.

While no one wants to die of cancer, or lose a loved one, we had vowed to make that odyssey "the best thing that ever happened to us," and that's exactly how we structured it. Those three years were the most loving, and in many ways, the most productive of our twenty-five years together.

—

The word *structure* functions as both a noun and a verb. We build structures, and we also structure everything from romantic evenings to corporate take-overs, tennis games, careers, and battles with cancer. And while every structure is different, the act of structuring always has the same purpose: to create something that functions well and supports the fulfillment of what we aspire to achieve. That's where we find the similarities.

Without proper structure, good ideas and intentions seldom come to fruition, and worthy endeavors commonly fail or fall apart. While it seems perfectly logical that creating a solid structure would be crucial in all endeavors, actually doing so is often overlooked.

There are many reasons people don't appreciate the importance of structure and therefore fail to optimize its potential. Sometimes we take basic concepts for granted, like proper planning and the efficient flow of information, because they seem so obvious. Unfortunately, the cost of that assumption can be high. Another reason for our avoidance is that creating a truly dependable structure requires detailed analysis and conscientious implementation. That not only takes time, but it also goes against the grain of our short attention spans and our craving for immediate gratification. We tend to focus on immediate problems and putting out fires rather than planning for the big picture or the long haul, which would, ironically, prevent many of those fires.

Many people resist the very notion of structure in day-to-day life because they equate it with rigidity, conformity, and unnecessary and unwanted limitations. They may also believe that formal structure is excessive in many areas, thinking that a couple, a family, or a small organization should be able to get by just fine without the time-consuming and constricting rules, measurements, and discipline that "structure" implies. Or they sense that the extra scrutiny inherent in most structures would clash with their personal style or agenda. Whatever the reason, we end up paying a big price for ignoring or neglecting the need for structure in our lives. So why not reverse that tendency and stack the deck in our favor?

Great by Design: The Ingredients of a Successful Structure

"Planning is bringing the future into the present so that you can do something about it now."

—Alan Lakein

No aspect of structure is more important than proper planning. The very process of identifying and articulating our objectives, resources, challenges, and solutions forces us to confront where we want to go and how we're going to get there. It prompts questions, leads to answers, and creates pathways to success.

All structures exist in the service of a specific purpose. The ultimate achievement of that objective depends on the ability to perform well consistently over a period of time. The following elements are usually found, in varying degrees, in the planning of both enduring edifices and successful ventures:

CLARITY AND CONSENSUS ABOUT THE PRIME OBJECTIVE

First things first: We have to know what we want to achieve. A great structure starts with an end goal in mind—that's the prime directive. Being crystal clear about *what* we want and *why* we want it allows us to move efficiently and effectively in the right direction. Therefore, it's essential to step back and get in touch with our critical needs as well as our underlying desires.

If we aren't clear about what we truly want, let alone the reasons we want or need it, our initiatives generally take a circuitous and costly path to completion. That's one reason the construction of custom homes often involves an expensive series of change orders. The same fate befalls relationships and careers; only the regrets are even more rampant in those areas because the stakes are much higher.

Clarity is the key: clarity of purpose and clarity about the task at hand. Purpose should be our North Star, as it reflects what we care about most. When true purpose plugs into true passion, we get charged with all the energy we'll ever need. And if we are fortunate enough to join our talents, energies, and desires with those of like-minded people who are equally purposeful and passionate, we have pretty much found the Holy Grail.

On the other hand, when we don't have consensus and people are pulling in different directions, the opposing goals and desires cancel each other out. Worse, they can conflict with one another, leading to disastrous consequences. Sadly, this is more often the norm than the exception. Just think of couples with competing desires who never pause to reconcile them properly. The result is two people struggling with one another, and that's not especially romantic or nourishing. Consider businesses in which individuals or departments have conflicting objectives. Instead of having a clear and firm foundation to build upon, the organization is now divided and weakened, which can result in wasted energy and unnecessary expense and aggravation.

Note that conflicting desires are not always a problem in and of themselves. Often, the tension can stimulate exploration, innovation, and improvement. The problems arise when the incompatible issues are neither explored nor resolved. So, regardless of the endeavor you're engaged in, before creating any kind of structure, make sure you're clear about your purpose and that the other stakeholders are in accord with you.

Unfortunately, clarity and consensus can be illusory. We may think we know where we're going and why, and we may think that others are on the same page, only to discover otherwise. Unless there is a dependable process in place to explore, understand, and verify our sense of direction, we are susceptible to structural flaws and the problems that follow.

Midway into my business career, I assumed that everyone else in my company understood my vision and agreed with it. I believed that our primary purpose was so obvious that it didn't need a detailed explanation. However, after reading a business case study on this very topic, I decided to test my hypothesis. Much to my surprise, while there was a certain amount of consistency about most of the company's general initiatives, we were not totally in sync. Important issues like quality and community were acknowledged but not clearly defined. People were interpreting and prioritizing matters based on their individual needs and desires, which is generally our default mechanism. To make matters worse, our employees were confused whenever they heard inconsistent comments from any of the principals.

The solution was simple: Senior management needed to get on the same page. We needed to speak with one voice regarding our vision, mission, and strategy. So, over the ensuing three months, we engaged in individual and group discussions around our primary purpose and major objectives, exploring where we agreed and where we differed, and why. The end result was a written document that was enthusiastically agreed upon by everyone. We wanted to grow much bigger; but we also ardently wanted to retain our boutique feel and avoid devolving into a bureaucracy. We declared our true north to be a passionate pursuit of both quality and community. More specifically, we agreed that we were committed to being the best in our industry in everything we do ("quality"), and we also chose to foster a supportive environment where everyone can thrive ("community"). After that, it was a relatively simple matter to communicate our vision and goals to the rest of the firm and to all of our customers and industry partners.

Combining purpose, passion, and people is a recipe for enormous satisfaction and true success in all we do and aspire to. That three-month exercise has stood the test of time and has successfully guided us for fifteen years and counting.

KNOW YOUR AUDIENCE

There are many stakeholders and participants in any enterprise. If you're looking to impact the behavior of others—whether theater audiences, coworkers, consumers, children, a spouse, or even your-self—then you must understand who they are, what makes them tick, and why, and then address them on their own terms.

I remember reading years ago how Frito-Lay, the chip and snack food giant, produced over 150 different flavors to appeal to the different tastes and cultures of their customers. Frito-Lay is that targeted in their planning and that rigorously structured in their design and distribution. No doubt that's part of why they're so successful.

Earlier, I shared the story of Professor Louis Agassiz, the legendary teacher of natural history who had his students study a pickled fish for endless hours until they knew that fish in minute detail. When you know your audience that well, your resultant structure will be that much more effective. The reverse is also true. Stories abound about businesses that took successful products to other countries and eventually had to totally retool because the cultures were so different.

Human beings are generally the single biggest component of any undertaking. They comprise the target market. They also deliver the service or product. Therefore, their concerns and desires must be taken into account. As discussed in the previous chapter, most people mistakenly assume that others see the world as they do and are motivated as they are. How many times have you been disappointed by this unrealistic belief and suffered as a result?

If a plan is to be successful, it must align with the needs and desires of the people involved, and it must do this continually as circumstances evolve. This approach works wonders, but it has to be designed, implemented, and updated for each situation.

BLUEPRINTS, RECIPES, AND CHECKLISTS

> "God is in the details."
> **—Anonymous**

Every business, activity, and relationship can benefit from capturing and codifying repeatable practices with proven value. We can replicate successful designs and convert valuable lessons into blueprints, recipes, and checklists. Without such aids, we end up reinventing the wheel and taking on unnecessary risks.

A great example is the pre-flight checklist that all airline pilots use. It's universally employed because it has been shown to reduce avoidable risk to almost zero, sparing the world an enormous loss of life. As a result, the likelihood of dying in a commercial airliner is less than one in ten million travelers. And the last fatal crash of a commercial plane in the United States or Canada occurred over ten years ago. (Unfortunately, private pilots are not always as thorough.) Likewise, studies show that hospitals utilizing basic checklists dramatically reduce unnecessary pain, suffering, and loss of life.

It may seem strange in our high-tech world that something as simple as a checklist could be so critical. But it is, and the same rigorous process of codifying best practices can apply to every form of structure. Most of us have stories about things that went awry because we didn't do what logic, common sense, and past experience dictated. That's why maxims such as "Look before you leap" and "Measure twice, cut once" have stood the test of time, and why standard operating procedures (SOPs) can be a building block for success, rather than an impediment to creativity.

One of my favorite business recipes is the twelve-point list that the Gallup Organization compiled for cultivating satisfied employees, which you can read about on their website. Gallup interviewed hundreds of thousands of workers in a variety of industries to come up with a list of consistent ways to keep employees engaged and motivated. While we at Commonwealth were already doing much of what Gallup recommended, we immediately set out to improve in areas where we were weak. As a result, we have won almost forty awards for Best Place to Work, both locally and nationally. And since happy, motivated employees tend to provide great service and consistently good performance, we've also won tremendous praise from clients and customers. The result has been enormous satisfaction from all parties, fewer mistakes, and more predictable profits. And essentially, all we did was follow a recipe.

Recipes and blueprints also provide a foundation for further advancements. Once we have an established baseline, we can more easily identify weak links and find creative opportunities to improve.

INFORMATION, EXPERIENCE, AND EXPERTISE

Reliable information, proven experience, and targeted expertise are every bit as critical as bricks and mortar. In designing a building, the need for architectural and engineering advice is obvious. Similarly, we know that experienced coaches will hasten our progress in sports with proven techniques and tips. But not all engineers, architects, or coaches are equally knowledgeable or best suited for a particular project. Finding the right match for each situation can make a huge difference. Quality begets quality, whether you're designing a building, starting a new business, or managing a baseball team.

One of the most interesting considerations when sorting through these factors is the expense differential among various choices. For example, in businesses where productivity can be measured, superior employees may cost 20 or 30% more than their counterparts, but they often turn out to be 100 or 200% more productive when we calculate the quantity and quality of their work, the creativity they bring to the improvement process, their infectious enthusiasm, and their ability to free up managers to focus on bigger issues. Then there are things that are not as easy to measure: Knowledgeable, seasoned, and diligent people regularly help to avoid mistakes, both big and small. Dodging bullets and averting disasters may not show up in balance sheets, and people don't often talk about their blunders that were fixed by someone else, but expertise can make a big difference in every important aspect of life.

Yet even with all the obvious benefits that expertise can confer in fields like sports, business, and medicine, many people avoid it like the plague in personal and interpersonal relationships. Couples suffer needlessly because they won't work with a counselor. Professional managers sacrifice bottom-line results because they won't get coached on how to improve their communication and interpersonal skills. *Ironically, people often avoid experts where they feel weakest and most vulnerable, when it is precisely in such areas that they can benefit the most from them.*

Depending on the needs of the project or the person, getting the knowledge and skills we require might mean taking on a partner, a full-time employee, a part-time consultant, a coach, or maybe just bouncing some ideas off friends from time to time. Think about the important areas of your life where you want to have more success. Then ask yourself whether your results might be significantly improved if you had a bona fide expert in your corner—one who also knows and cares about you. Chances are you said yes. Well, why not get such a person (or organization) and reap the rewards? If, while contemplating this, you realize that you're probably *not* going to do it, then you've discovered a valuable opportunity for personal exploration. Either way, you win.

TRUST AND TEAMWORK

Many years ago, I learned an important lesson working with an interior designer: The parts are in the service of the whole. Whether you're decorating a home or an office building, every choice of fixtures, furniture, or paint color should fit the overall look, feel, and function of the whole project. Likewise, whether you're dealing with a business or a basketball team, success depends on how everyone functions together as a unit. A team is a structure, and each member is an individual element in the service of that entity.

However, as we know from professional sports, the best team isn't necessarily comprised of the most talented and experienced people in every position. Teams made up of individual superstars don't always win. Great teams have chemistry, complementary skills, camaraderie, and players who are willing to subordinate their egos for the good of the whole. These attributes are a direct result of clarity, consensus, and communication around a shared vision. You can have the most talented professionals in the world, but if they don't trust one another or function well as a team, you won't come close to realizing your potential.

Unlike nuts and bolts, people and the circumstances they create are never standardized. We are all multifaceted and more changeable than the weather. For all these reasons and more, trust and teamwork are vital in crafting a structure for success in any group effort. They are the essential ingredients that enable the group to be open and honest and consistently improving.

STRENGTH

"That which yields is not always weak."
—Jacqueline Carey

Exactly what constitutes strength varies from one structure to another, and it is not necessarily obvious. As Malcolm Gladwell points out in his book *David and Goliath*, the common wisdom about strength and weakness is often way off base. The biblical David, for example, is regarded as one of history's great underdogs because he was so much smaller and physically weaker than Goliath. But David prevailed because his combination of assets added up to a far greater force than Goliath's brute strength. David had intelligence, advanced weaponry (the slingshot), and agility in his favor. He also had an enormous sense of passion and purpose.

There are many types of strength, and their relative merits depend on the needs of the particular structure. Any resource, skill, or attribute that can be put to good use is a strength. Examples include physical power, technology, knowledge, analytics, people skills, durability, leadership, task-specific skills, organizational efficiencies, access to money and other relevant resources, and agility. Pretty much anything can be a strength if it is used skillfully in the service of the desired goal. The trick is to know what you need, where to get it, and how to deploy it.

Certain strengths can be converted into others. When we go to work, we are trading our energy, time, and skills for money; that money can be converted not only to food and shelter but also to the tools and ingredients we require to achieve other goals.

Unfortunately, people often forget the true purpose of money; that it's merely a medium of exchange. We get in the habit of thinking that accumulating dollars is the actual goal, and that our net worth defines us and bestows happiness. If that were the case, the richest people in society would be the most fulfilled. But health, happiness, and gratitude far outweigh money. Keep your focus on the real goals and they will guide you to the strengths you need.

FLEXIBILITY AND ADAPTABILITY

"The willow which bends to the tempest, often escapes better than the oak which resists it; and so in great calamities, it sometimes happens that light and frivolous spirits recover their elasticity and presence of mind sooner than those of a loftier character."
—Albert Schweitzer

The Taoists say we should aspire to be like a stalk of bamboo. It is incredibly strong and hard to break; yet it is also flexible enough to bend with the wind and be used for multiple purposes. Those qualities make bamboo a useful metaphor for structuring any organization or venture. Or relationship. Or even ourselves for that matter. Being strong and true to ourselves is essential in life, and so is keeping an open mind and offering a forgiving heart.

Flexibility bestows options. It allows us to seize opportunities and evolve with changes in the environment. The opposite of flexibility is rigidity, which can render objects, people, and organizations susceptible to unnecessary damage and destruction.

While the benefits of flexibility may appear obvious, many people are stuck psychologically, emotionally, or intellectually. Some consider it a great virtue to stick to their beliefs. Phrases like "a man of conviction" evoke dependability and fortitude. But what appears to be strength of character may often be a disguised form of rigidity based on fear, lack of understanding, or intellectual cowardice.

Perhaps you prefer the term adaptability to flexibility. Either way, imagine how increased flexibility and adaptability can improve your athletic performance, your investment performance, your career, your relationships with others, and even your relationship with yourself.

Since change is a constant, our structures must be practical, versatile, and ultimately adaptable. We may know this in principle, but we don't always execute accordingly. And that's a problem. People can get fixated on one way of looking at things, one way of doing things, and one way of projecting how things will play out. They become entrenched. They hold on too long. They don't adjust in time, or at all, and they suffer the consequences. I have learned time and again the importance of being open-minded and having multiple backup plans.

The happiest people I know are adaptable in mind and spirit. Being steadfast and firm is important, and it works quite well in many situations. But those qualities don't always serve us well, especially when steadfast morphs into stubborn. Our assumptions should not be mistaken for reality. Understanding this is essential because, as the Greek philosopher Heraclitus observed, "Change is the only constant in life."

MULTIPLE FOUNDATIONS

The success of every endeavor depends on the strength and integrity of the foundation that supports it. Therefore, it's imperative to determine what constitutes a sturdy foundation in each particular context. Then we must make that foundation as durable, robust, and resilient as possible, and keep it strong and functional as circumstances evolve.

But what constitutes a foundation is not always apparent. With buildings, we have only to look at the bottom. However, with other types of structures, identifying the supporting elements can be tricky. With physical activities, for example, a strong footing, or "root," is certainly foundational. We may also know that the strength of our core is a critical foundation in most athletic pursuits. However, most of us have not devoted sufficient attention to our abdominal strength, and a weak core not only leads to poor performance, it can also make us more susceptible to mishaps and injuries.

Further complicating matters is the fact that an entity can have *many* foundations, and each one can evolve as time and circumstances change. However, we don't always realize what constitutes a foundation, and that's a major reason many ventures falter. I have found that defining a foundation as *that structural element we rely upon to succeed and grow* enables us to better appreciate what we need to strengthen and protect. You may think, for instance, that you're well positioned for success because you have strong financial resources. But if you don't have the right people or product or pricing, your deep pockets will soon be empty. Leadership is another supporting determinant. Leadership can be weak or strong, united or divided—with varying results. Similarly, in a marriage, compassion, trust, respect, and shared purpose are foundational. In fact, when you think about it, aren't those qualities foundational for *any* group venture to prosper and endure?

Granted, it can be confusing to think in terms of multiple foundations, but that's why life often feels so perplexing: It's multifaceted. The most practical approach is to identify the factors we rely on most, prioritize and improve them, and give special attention to potential weak links.

NECESSARY AND SUFFICIENT

> "Simplicity is the ultimate sophistication."
> **—attributed to Leonardo da Vinci**

Take a lesson from nature. Natural structures, whether bodies, plants, or ecosystems, generally expend just the amount of energy required to accomplish a task and no more. My favorite example from daily life is picking up a suitcase. If we don't use enough energy, the suitcase barely leaves the ground. But if we exert too much force, we risk tossing it high in the air. So what do we do? We employ "just enough" energy to achieve the desired result. In the process of feeling and lifting, we engage in a series of micro adjustments so that we allocate just the right amount of energy. We do this type of thing so often, in so many different ways, we don't even notice it: walking up and down steps, dancing with a partner, eating with a fork, and countless other examples day in and day out.

A corollary in life and business is the concept of *necessary and sufficient*. When we're trying to decide which resources to allocate to a particular venture—be it a project at work, cooking dinner for our family, or swinging a golf club—the best approach is usually to identify what we absolutely need for success and not pile on additional resources. If what we have in hand is sufficient, we can stop right there. Going overboard may not do any good. In fact, too much of any one thing cannot only backfire, it can create unnecessary work, unhealthy stress, and additional and costly management time.

While this may seem like a minor issue at first glance, the fact is that the most precious resources in today's world may be time and attention. We constantly grapple with getting everything done and done well. We want to be consummate professionals, loving parents, and good friends, all while continuing to evolve and somehow enjoying life to the fullest. Something has to give. That's why understanding priorities and employing *necessary and sufficient* is so important in structuring our life and all of its subsidiary endeavors.

ALIGNMENT AND DYNAMIC INTEGRATION

> "Knee bone connected to the thigh bone . . .
> Thigh bone connected to the hip bone . . .
> Hip bone connected to the back bone . . . "
>
> **—"Dem Bones" by James Weldon Johnson
> and J. Rosamund Johnson**

In the end, all aspects of a structure are connected, so if one thing is deficient, damaged, or misaligned, every other part—and the entire entity—will be affected. Proper alignment fosters optimal functioning and reduces wear, tear, and unnecessary risk.

When we injure or weaken one part of the body, we typically compensate by using other parts in a new way, only to end up creating problems elsewhere as a result. For example, we compensate for foot pain by walking differently and thereby trigger hip, knee, or lower back issues.

All types of structures function according to this same logic. Whether you want to improve your business, your golf swing, your marriage, or all three, make sure the structure is strong, balanced, and flexible, with all parts in proper alignment.

When a structure is properly aligned and integrated, a dynamic tension connects all the parts, making the flow of energy strong, constant, and virtually instantaneous. Think of a garden hose: If the structure is sound, and there are no kinks or leaks to disrupt the flow of water, once the faucet is turned on and the hose fills up, a dynamic tension is created, and water enters at one end while an equal amount flows out the other. Similarly, in a well-integrated human structure such as a team, a business, or a family, information and energy move smoothly when all communication channels are lined up properly and are free of kinks, leaks, and blockages.

When there is alignment of purpose coupled with trust and teamwork, energy flows effortlessly among people and departments.

When communication is so quick and clear that the entity moves as a unified whole, it's a thing of beauty—like watching a massive flock of birds perform aerial acrobatics as a single integrated unit. It's seemingly miraculous and is totally attainable.

Conversely, if there are gaps, leaks, and misalignments, the flow of energy and information is undependable and easily disrupted. In business, team sports, communities, and couples, misalignment of purpose and corruption of communication among the constituent parts can be deadly. It's also quite common, as most of us have no doubt experienced. As Martin Luther King Jr. observed, "Whatever affects one directly, affects all indirectly. I can never be what I ought to be until you are what you ought to be. This is the interrelated structure of reality."

WEAK LINKS AND RISK MANAGEMENT

"To be prepared is half the victory."
—Miguel de Cervantes

The old adage that something is only as strong as its weakest link is right on point. Be it faulty wiring, undetected arterial plaque, a discourteous employee, or the classic "communication gap," one problem area can bring down the whole house. What good is all that planning and all those strengths if your dream falls apart because of one overlooked weakness? Whether the building catches on fire, you have a massive heart attack, your customers run to your competitors, or your marriage falls apart, weak links can be disastrous.

When we identify and deal with our weak links, we can achieve enormous structural improvement in the entire system with minimal effort. Experts abound in all areas, and they can help. Looking back, I could have avoided a great deal of unnecessary cost, pain, and suffering if I'd hired the right specialists in the first place to help me find and fix my weaknesses. While it's often said that we learn from our mistakes, and I have, part of the solution to any problem is almost always to get good advice ... and to listen to it.

As a young boy, I was a Boy Scout. In addition to learning how to tie knots (the square knot, bowline, and half hitches have served me well ever since), I always appreciated the Boy Scout motto, *Be Prepared*, because it prompted me to avoid unnecessary problems. It mitigated risk. Like so many things in life, proper preparation and actual readiness is something that most people pay too little attention to. Which is why we so often hear the phrase, "I wish I had (fill in the blank)."

In love and war, health and wealth, and other circumstances where damage can be devastating, formal risk-management protocols need to be considered and built into the design process. Stress testing and taking something for a "test drive" is simply an indispensable part of design and due diligence. At least it is for professionals. But sometimes, people get so excited and so focused on getting their projects off the ground that they don't take enough time to think about what could possibly go wrong. Sometimes, they don't even see why they should bother. Their attention is on growing, not slowing down to consider all the possible potholes on the road ahead and the unintended consequences of their actions.

Similarly, when people in business or family life are struggling to keep their heads above water, they're even less likely to concentrate on protecting themselves against a potential calamity—because they're already in a real one.

Financial advisors know from experience that people and organizations typically go through a growth and accumulation phase before they start focusing sufficiently on safety. But risk management needs to be built into the design process from day one. It doesn't guarantee success, but like everything else in this book, it greatly increases the odds of ultimately realizing our objectives.

In my own life and business, I have made numerous mistakes because of poor risk assessment. It was generally the result of being unaware, impetuous, inexperienced, unwilling to listen, fearful, greedy, afraid . . . it's a long list. And I suffered the consequences: insolvency, intestinal ailments, unnecessary fights with my wife, and a lot more. And I'm not alone. Fortunately, I was able to recover both physically and financially. But oh did I learn many valuable lessons along the way—one of which is that the school of hard knocks is the most expensive way to go . . . and the riskiest.

In retrospect, one of the most interesting things about this odyssey is how many years actually passed before I finally created a formal risk-management process in my business. When I eventually realized the need for it, we started by creating a team with representatives from our major departments. We asked them to brainstorm every possible thing that could go wrong, then prioritize the list based on potential damage, and either plug the holes or develop procedures to minimize the potential risks. That was twenty years ago, and we're still meeting, finding, and fixing on a regular basis. Risk management is now a part of our corporate DNA.

We all make mistakes. We grow too fast, or too slow, or the wrong way. Granted, we can't realistically spend all our time worrying about what might go wrong when we're focusing on making things go right. But we do have to consider risk if we are to survive and thrive.

The Key Ingredient

"The buck stops here."

—popularized by Harry Truman

What is the single most important ingredient in structuring our lives, our businesses, our families, and our future? It's ourselves. We are at the center of all and everything. We perceive and filter information, and we set the course and command the expedition. The structures we create and implement are reflections of our strengths and weaknesses, our knowledge and ignorance, our insights and misperceptions, and everything else about us. *If we want to improve results, we need to improve ourselves.*

Since our perception of the world shapes how we interact with it, it's critical to understand what that outlook is, how it came to be, and how it may be helping or hindering the structures we create and depend on. It's often said that we are our own worst enemies. It's often said because it's often true. As we've seen throughout the book, a critical part of becoming what and who we want to be is to elevate our awareness—to notice when we are being counterproductive and utilize the necessary techniques to make things better.

This was the understanding that sent me back to business school. I realized that I was the analyst, designer, builder, and operator of my life all rolled into one; and if I wanted to improve my business, my life, and the world I lived in, I needed to upgrade the most important and impactful structure of all: me.

This is the core issue. Not only is the world we create a reflection of our inner reality, but it's also a dynamic process. We change structures, and structures change us. Thus, as we create more flexible structures, we become more flexible. As we appreciate what works and codify effective procedures, we become more organized and effective. And the reverse is also true: As we become stronger and more versatile, so do the structures we create. But first and foremost, the structures we most need to tend to are our own minds, bodies, and spirits.

To drive this skill to its maximum effect, you need to access energy, which we'll explore next.

ENERGIZE and
Fuel the Machine

"Energy and persistence conquer all things."
—Benjamin Franklin

We all need energy to function, and the higher we set our sights, the more energy we require. This is especially true in the case of professional athletes where being prepared, alert, and invigorated makes the difference between winners and losers. I will often watch two competitors, either individuals or teams, start out strong, and then see one run out of gas. The final score tells the story.

But energy isn't just a measure of BTUs. There are other factors at play, such as the power of the mind and spirit. One of the most memorable examples for me was watching the women's world soccer finals in 1999, when the USA beat China 1–0 after double overtime. Both teams rose through the tournament, constantly using as much energy as they could possibly muster. They were both resolute, and they gave it their all and then some.

In that final game, no team let the other get a single goal. In overtime, they were theoretically depleted, but somehow they all kept going. And then, in an instant, it was over. The American team scored and won. They were jubilant, ecstatic, jumping and hugging each other. In the TV interviews that followed, they remained joyous, full of energy and more. In stark contrast, the beaten Chinese players were defeated and worn out. It looked like they could barely trudge off the field.

—

Energy is the proverbial goose that lays the golden egg. Without it, little is possible. On the other hand, with an ample supply of energy, virtually anything is attainable. It's the fuel that sustains all the engines that nourish our health, well-being, and achievement—not just physical strength and endurance; not just mental alertness and creativity; but also vital personal and emotional traits, such as ambition, confidence, courage, and love.

As the legendary football coach Vince Lombardi said, "Fatigue makes cowards of us all." It is, therefore, extremely important to empower all of our engines and activities with the requisite energy for both short-term impact and long-term sustainability.

Increasing our energy, personally and organizationally, can be both amazingly simple and overwhelmingly complex. We all know that we benefit from optimal sleep, nutrition, exercise, and other lifestyle choices. We also know that fueling our bodies and minds for maximum efficiency is not only essential for good health, but also for productivity and achievement. And with energy, note that the Multiplier Effect also kicks in: When one aspect of the mind or body starts to get stronger and more energetic, the impact is felt across all the other areas. Conversely, if one component is weakened or depleted, the others falter more readily.

It's important to appreciate that in the realm of health, a single bad decision can have disastrous results. Just as a faulty wire can burn down a building and bad legal advice can leave us exposed to substantial risk, taking the wrong medications or not taking the right ones can be crippling. Allowing pain or injury to go untended can turn a minor problem into a debilitating condition. Eating or drinking too much of X or not enough of Y, can cause our energy levels to plummet. The list of significant repercussions from individual error or neglect is extensive.

The converse is also true. Individual decisions can have beneficial life-changing results. A well-timed medical exam can uncover and potentially avert a life-threatening condition. Cutting back on alcohol, leaving a destructive relationship, or learning to meditate can fundamentally change our perception of the world and how we live our lives. Taking up an exercise regimen or shifting to a nutritious diet can usher in a new era of health and happiness. The point is that one critical decision can change everything. So, choose carefully and consciously.

Most of us understand this, in theory, yet we don't always do what we know to be good for our health and well-being. It's really quite interesting. We would never consider sabotaging our cars or computers or any other machinery we rely on; nor would we neglect them in the countless ways we neglect our bodies and minds. So what's going on? Why do we regularly mismanage our greatest resource? I would divide the answers into two categories:

1. *We really don't know as much about personal health and energy management as we think we do.* Many areas of medicine, physiology, and psychology are complicated and contentious, making it hard even for professionals to agree on the best practices.

2. *We're human.* And as mere mortals, we're subject to

conflicting desires, destructive programming, fears, fantasies, and fatigue. As a result, we don't always do what we know we should.

Fortunately, this is an area where it's relatively easy to make a big difference if you are so inclined. And if you're not? Well, that raises some interesting questions about your priorities and programming, doesn't it?

What follows is an overview of some primary pathways to vitality. While neither exhaustive nor definitive, nor intended to substitute for medical advice, this guide represents a wonderful opportunity to implement and experiment with many of the insights and skills we've already discussed. Toward that end, you'll find it helpful to direct your awareness to what you're doing (and not doing) and why. Ask questions. Listen. Program a plan for improvement. Create a structure with appropriate incentives. Make it a party. Build a Stairway of Success and celebrate each step along the way.

Be Your Own Best Advocate

"Learn to value yourself, which means: fight for your happiness."
—Ayn Rand

No one cares more about you than you do. Therefore, when it comes to the care of our bodies and minds, it's up to each of us to be our own best advocate. To do that well, we need to be well informed and willing to take charge. That means being thorough and objective when it comes to uncovering information and evaluating what we find. It also means being assertive when dealing with health care professionals, insurance providers, our families, and ourselves.

Not all doctors and health care advisors are specialists, and not all specialists are equal. They vary widely in knowledge, experience, skill, motivation, and empathy. There's also the issue of professional bias. That's why psychologists instinctively look for psychological causes, surgeons lean toward operations, acupuncturists check meridians and reach for needles, nutritionists evaluate what's being eaten, and so forth. For these reasons, and because they typically have a more holistic perspective, general practitioners are usually the best place to start. But even GPs vary greatly in terms of their backgrounds and their openness and understanding of newer technologies and so-called complementary modalities.

Fortunately, we have an abundance of easy-to-access information about health, wellness, and personal energy at our disposal now. Unfortunately, there is also an abundance of easy-to-access *mis*information. Unfounded theories, fads, and hucksters are all over the Internet, and controversy rages even within scientific circles. Everyone has a voice today, but not all voices are knowledgeable or benevolent. Plus, ours is a society that likes quick fixes rather than thorough analysis or long-term solutions that require patience and effort. We gamble unnecessarily with our precious health because we get lazy, greedy, and anxious; we deceive ourselves, we allow others to deceive us, and we simply make mistakes.

Each of us is a unique organism. Even identical twins are different in significant ways due to various environmental factors and individual experiences. And because we each have a particular makeup, history, biochemistry, and psychology, optimal health solutions will be specific to each of us.

In the end, you are the center of your universe, and you succeed or suffer based on the choices you make. No one else has as much at stake. No one else can feel what your body feels or think what your mind thinks. It's up to you! To find resources you trust, initiate discussions, ask penetrating questions, push for thorough answers, process all the information, filter all the advice, and ultimately make your own decisions. Your energy, your health, and your life depend on it.

The State of Your State

"If you do not change direction, you may
end up where you are heading."

—Lao Tzu

Earlier we explored the concept of "state" and saw that our physiological and psychological positioning is a powerful aspect of programming. The techniques we learned can be used to immediately boost our energy. It's all a function of how we choose to orient ourselves to the world.

People can view identical situations through vastly different mindsets, and therefore ascribe divergent meaning to what they see and experience. One powerful example is when we focus on the bounty we have instead of bemoaning what we lack. The impact of that difference in perspective is tremendous, and it translates directly into our state and our energy. Focus on the negative, and we inhabit a negative world. Focus on what we love and appreciate, and our state resonates with a more positive energy.

The old tale of the three bricklayers is a perfect illustration of this: Once there were three bricklayers, and each one was asked what he was doing. The first man answered, weary and unhappily, "I'm laying bricks." The second replied, "I'm building a wall." But the third man said, enthusiastically and with pride, his eyes and mind bright and alive, "I'm building a cathedral." We choose how we define the world and our place in it. We should also note that we can serve others well by helping them to see the cathedrals they're building in their own lives.

Likewise, our physiological orientation can communicate health and vitality or disease and despair, and each of those states will produce vastly different results in our lives. One fundamental physical modification we might pay special attention to is posture. As we saw earlier, our mental state affects how we hold our body—and how we hold our body affects our mind and emotions—all of which impact our energy in an up or down direction. For example, studies show that depressed people, and those who feel powerless or afraid, tend to slouch. But that's just half the story. When non-depressed people are asked to slouch, they display more negativity, worse moods, lower self-esteem, lower productivity, and more fear than those who are told to sit upright. No wonder traditions such as yoga, meditation, and martial arts always train students to keep their backs straight and their heads upright. In addition to enhancing one's mental state, a properly supported head and back take advantage of "gravity stacking" and minimize the energy required to hold ourselves in a position of strength. This position also lowers stress on joints and muscles, thereby reducing potential injuries. You might want to keep that in mind when you're working at your desk or reading.

Another simple recipe for increased energy and happiness? Smiling! Not only does it work, it's infectious—even to ourselves. So is enthusiasm. It's actually so contagious that even if we don't feel enthusiastic, if we imitate the mood by assuming the physical manifestations of enthusiasm, we will actually catch it. This is similar to the exercise where we smiled, held our arms up triumphantly, and screamed YES. Smiling changes our state and increases our energy. And with increased energy, we have the power to do more.

Food and Nutrition

"Life expectancy would grow by leaps and bounds if green vegetables smelled as good as bacon."

—Doug Larson

It's hard to think of an area as important—and as misunderstood and abused—as what we should eat. Over time, a parade of "experts" have prescribed this or that regimen, only to have us find out later they were wrong. As recently as the 1960s, the US government published a food pyramid whose foundation was a preponderance of grains and carbohydrates. Not only has this recommendation changed dramatically over the years, but some experts now believe the old standard actually contributed to obesity and heart disease. Likewise, the invention of margarine as a substitute for butter was followed by the discovery that such trans saturated fats were worse than what they replaced. Even artificially sweetened soft drinks were initially touted as a good thing, just like cigarettes. Nor does it help that product manufacturers deluge us with advertising designed to entice us emotionally and convince us with half-truths.

The following are some basic protocols that have generally proven helpful to many. While you may find most of them familiar, it's our individual choices that really make the difference:

A balanced and healthy diet. While the precise definition of "balanced" may be disputed, the concept is helpful. We benefit from a diet of fruit, vegetables, grains, healthy fat, and protein to survive and thrive. Generally, "all things in moderation" seems to be sound advice. It's when we wander off into extremes of either excess or abstinence that most of our problems arise.

Quality, not just quantity. Terms like organic, local, and natural may get misused and abused, but the basic point is that quality counts. Much of today's food supply is tainted with pesticides, herbicides, antibiotics, and various carcinogens. That's why the organic, unprocessed, local, and whole food movements have become so popular.

Preparation is also a factor. Fresh or frozen? Cooked or raw? Deep-fried? Drenched in oil? Processed? It all matters. Fried food and saturated fats are less healthy than non-fried food and nutritious fats like olive oil. But "less desirable" doesn't begin to convey the danger that some processed junk foods pose when they become a significant portion of our diet. Yes, they're convenient. But how convenient is having chronically low energy or a serious illness?

Pacing and portions. The general objective is to better match our intake with our energy needs. Do what works best for you and your lifestyle. And think smaller portions. In the United States, over one-third of adults are currently considered obese. That is nearly three times the rate of the early 1960s and more than double what it was as recently as 1990 (based on data from the US Department of Health and Human Services). The result, in addition to the reduction in energy and functionality, is increased death and disability from heart attacks, strokes, type 2 diabetes, and certain types of cancer.

Slow down and pay attention. It takes time for your brain to tell your body that it's had enough to eat. That's why we generally eat too much before we realize we've overloaded our system. And, needless to say, the more delicious the food, the harder it is to stop.

Sugar highs and lows. A problem occurs when we get a sugar high from consuming too much sugar (or from refined carbohydrates, which are transformed by the body into glucose, the major type of sugar in the body). This triggers the body to release insulin, which can drive the sugar too low, causing lethargy and irritability—this is the well-known "sugar crash," where the body then secretes adrenalin to release emergency sugar. And so the cycle continues.

If your daily routine relies on boosts of energy from caffeine and carbs, then one obvious way to smooth out the pace is to spread the intake throughout the day. You might also want to focus more on foods that are low on the glycemic index. They metabolize more slowly and don't exacerbate the problem of energy highs and lows.

Read labels. In addition to educating ourselves as to what is actually in our food before we buy or eat it, reading the labels on packages fosters greater awareness of the entire process of food production and consumption. It's illuminating to say the least. And, as we've seen, awareness impacts action.

A customized diet. Not all bodies are alike, and we hardly lead identical lives. Eskimos in the Arctic require more fat than people in warmer climes, and a triathlete or a construction worker needs more caloric intake than a couch potato or a desk worker. Seasonal changes, heredity, muscle mass, and other individualizing factors create differences within the broader categories. Therefore, an optimal food plan should be adjusted and customized to each individual. Experimentation and testing, along with expert advice, can provide the personal guidance you need.

Proper hydration. Unlike most of what we ingest, water and its associated electrolytes are necessities for which there is no substitute. In that regard, it's more like oxygen than spinach or meat. Our bodies are approximately 60% water, and just about every organ and every function requires it. Unfortunately, many people fail to drink enough water. As a result, they become dehydrated to varying degrees, and dehydration is an energy drain that affects most of our biological systems. Signs can include lethargy, headaches, muscle pain, cramps, dry skin, and a general sense of confusion.

Make a habit of drinking water throughout the day. In fact, one of the added benefits of increasing your water consumption might be that you cut out less healthy fluids and the sugar, caffeine, acid, and alcohol many of them contain. You simply won't have enough room for king-size soft drinks if you drink a proper amount of water.

As with all foods, the quality of water is also important. Most water today, even in remote locations, is contaminated with bacteria, as well as with chemicals such as pesticides, herbicides, and antibiotics that leach into the supply from land, sea, and air. That's why municipalities add chlorine and other purification methods to their systems. However, water is still likely to travel through old pipes that might leach contaminants into what pours out of your faucets.

Bottled water isn't always the best answer either. Aside from the increased cost and environmental concerns, we don't necessarily know how healthy the water is because the quality varies from source to source. Plus, chemicals can leach from many of the plastic bottles into the water, especially when they heat up in transit. The solution is to know what you're drinking and purify your water if necessary. Inexpensive purification systems are available for drinking water, and industrial solutions can be integrated with the water main to bring cleaner water to your home or building.

Drugs: Use vs. Abuse

"Even the humblest creature has to know how to react to the difference between food and toxin if it's to survive."

—David Darling

Research clearly shows that toxic substances deplete energy and can cause significant damage to our health. That would seem obvious if your definition of a toxin is limited to substances like poisons and pollutants. But it gets more interesting when you consider that some toxins are okay in limited doses, and some are more destructive over time than others. Then, of course, there's the issue of social usage and personal preferences. Exactly where to draw the line depends on a host of factors, and the toxic effects are likely to vary from one individual to the next. Think of alcoholic beverages: In limited amounts, they may not only be harmless, but research suggests they can be good for your health. Unless, of course, you're an alcoholic, or pregnant, or just very sensitive to the effects of alcohol.

Then there are substances we actually call "drugs." The word conjures up images ranging from helpful medicines to dangerous experimentation and opiate addiction. I suggest that it's not always the drug per se that's either good or bad, but how it's being used—and by whom. Alcohol, sugar, and caffeine can be beneficial, but they can also exacerbate disease and deplete energy if used inappropriately.

The point is that anything we put in our bodies is a chemical, and every chemical is a drug in the sense that it affects our biochemistry. What matters is how it is being used or abused—and the line between the two can be both vague and highly variable. Unfortunately, when it comes to foods and drugs that make us feel good, we have an extraordinary ability to rationalize. Alarms are sounded when a few people die from tainted food from a supermarket or restaurant—and they should be sounded to warn other consumers—but the fact that almost half a million people die annually in the United States from tobacco-related illnesses after fifty years of anti-smoking campaigns is mind-boggling. Alcohol also continues to wreak havoc, aided by marketing tactics that romanticize its consumption. In the end, whether it's caffeine, alcohol, marijuana, fatty foods, or the fad du jour, it always comes back to *use vs. abuse*, and to decisions each of us has to make.

Sleep

"Without enough sleep, we all become tall two-year-olds."
—JoJo Jensen

We need sleep, and most of us simply don't get enough of it. Few things deliver so many benefits with so little effort. The amount and quality of sleep directly affect mental acuity, physical vitality, productivity, emotional balance, and creativity.

Scientists say that seven and a half to nine hours is best for most adults, and teenagers require nine hours or even more. But those are averages: Many people thrive on less, and others need more. If you're often tired throughout the day, there's a good chance you're not getting enough sleep; conversely, craving too much sleep can be a sign that something is awry—physically or psychologically.

As with many other areas of our lives, we ignore and rationalize the disconnect between the sleep we need and the sleep we get—and what we do or don't do about it. Many of us also sabotage our ability to get the sleep we need by eating or drinking too much before going to bed. Again, there are wide individual differences: Some people can drink coffee or alcohol late at night and sleep like babies, while others are kept awake by a few sips with dinner. The first step is to observe and document our lifestyle practices to see how they affect our sleep. After that, we can experiment by adding, reducing, or eliminating specific elements.

Another practice that is not questioned enough is engaging in exciting and/or negative activities right before bedtime. Whether it's an argument, an action/adventure movie, or even the nightly news, filling our mind with murder and mayhem before laying our heads down for the night produces a very different mental, emotional, and physical state than when we nourish it with love, joy, and encouragement. Here are some other considerations:

Power naps. Many people find that a quick snooze is a remarkably effective way to get recharged during the day. This is not surprising, considering most of us are sleep deprived and the vast majority of mammals sleep more than once per day. How can a ten- to thirty-minute nap be so recuperative? One answer is that daytime respites are almost entirely REM (rapid eye movement) in nature. It would seem that our body innately knows what it's lacking and responds accordingly (note that naps longer than thirty minutes tend to lapse into a more traditional deep sleep and create the familiar groggy feeling that takes a while to shake off). My naps are almost always twenty minutes, and they work like a charm. In addition to feeling much more alert and energized when I wake up, I almost always feel more centered. Emerging science confirms that short midday naps not only repair and restore mental functions, they are also beneficial to numerous biological processes. Like a meditation session, a good nap allows the mind to release the accumulated tensions of the day and the body to restore its balance.

Some of history's great nappers include Thomas Edison, Leonardo da Vinci, Winston Churchill, Napoleon Bonaparte, Eleanor Roosevelt, and a number of US presidents. In fact, brief midday naps have proven to be so beneficial to health and productivity that many businesses have added designated napping areas.

Unfortunately, many people have convinced themselves they *can't* nap, and their language and self-talk reinforces this self-imposed reality. But napping is just a programmed habit, and it's relatively easy to create an enjoyable new habit. If you have trouble napping, focus on resting rather than falling asleep. Get comfortable, close your eyes, slow your breathing, and relax your body with each breath. Your body knows what to do. Give it time. Give it an opportunity.

Sleep disorders. Common sleep disorders such as excessive snoring, sleep apnea, restless leg syndrome, and different forms of insomnia have been well studied, and medical science now offers protocols for systematic diagnosis and treatment. If you have trouble sleeping, or sleeping well, or if you are generally tired throughout the day even though you seem to get enough sleep, it's best to consult your doctor or contact a sleep clinic.

Medications and natural remedies. Sleeping pills can be so powerful, their interactions with other substances so complex, and individual reactions so diverse, that it is unwise to use them without consulting an expert. Dependence on drugs for both waking and sleeping can be a vicious cycle; there are consequences to tampering with our equilibrium. Furthermore, side effects are compounded when a second medication is added to modify the effects of the first one.

Fortunately, there is plenty of good advice about how to improve sleep without drugs. Experiment first with safe, natural options: exercise regimens; herbal, vitamin, and mineral supplements; traditional Chinese medicine (acupuncture, herbs, and the gentle exercise forms of Tai Chi and Chi Gong); Ayurveda, the ancient Indian medical system; yoga; breathing exercises; and various types of meditation. These natural practices are mainly aimed at correcting physiological or biochemical imbalances and training the mind and body to relax. While most of these methods are safe, it's always wise to consult with professionals. If problems persist, see a sleep specialist. Proper sleep is too important to neglect.

Exercise

> "A sweet life is a sweaty life."
> **—Toni Sorenson**

Proper exercise is a great investment: We expend energy and get more energy in return. I'm always surprised when I meet people who only exercise begrudgingly in order to lose weight or stay in shape. Exercise is, and can be, so much more. Our bodies were made to function and move, and the expression "Use it or lose it" applies. Exercise keeps the machinery lubricated and humming. It builds muscles and enhances our capacities and capabilities. It increases strength, flexibility, coordination, and responsiveness. It helps keep us young and vital. Plus, it generates the neurotransmitter serotonin and various other feel-good hormones that can frame and reinforce a positive worldview.

It's never too late to exercise or start a routine. Studies consistently show that both strength and cardiovascular training are beneficial regardless of one's age. The same holds true for flexibility and coordination. In fact, the older you are, the more important it can be to stay in shape. Likewise, if someone is incapacitated in some manner, it can be critical to find ways to exercise so that the rest of the body doesn't atrophy—the Multiplier Effect works both up and down.

Exercise taken to an extreme can be harmful, and stressing the system can cause overexertion and injury. But few things can match the benefits of a reasonable amount of exercise that's right for the individual and performed correctly. As for enjoyment, we can make almost anything enjoyable if we really want to. But we have to want to.

Now let's consider various subcategories of exercise with their associated benefits and protocols:

Strength training (aka resistance training). Aside from the obvious benefits of being stronger and more capable of negotiating daily life, strong muscles protect our frame and enable us to function properly. As biomechanical machines, we are subject to the laws of nature and physics. Often, the remedy for physical stress is physical strength. Our weakest links (e.g., lower back, rotator cuff, neck, and knees) are quite vulnerable, but strengthening the surrounding muscles protects those areas and promotes overall balance and stability, which fortifies the entire physical structure. This enhances the generation and maintenance of energy. The weaker we are, the more we have to labor to do things, and the more susceptible we are to fatigue and injury.

In addition to strength and functionality, resistance training also improves metabolic rate, reduces harmful fats, and increases bone density, thus slowing the onset of osteoporosis. Regular training also increases our anaerobic capacity. The greater our anaerobic capacity, the better we function at high-intensity, low-duration activities such as weight lifting, isometrics, walking up a hill, or sprinting. Granted we can choose to avoid lifting heavy weights or sprinting up hills in daily life, but we can't always avoid emergency situations and unforeseen needs, one of the major reasons that people end up in hospitals. Anaerobic capacity allows us to deal with increased demands without unnecessary injury.

Aerobic capacity. This refers to the maximum amount of oxygen consumed by the body as it undergoes intense exercise during a given time frame. It is a function of both cardiorespiratory performance and the ability to remove and utilize oxygen from circulating blood. The heart muscle is responsible for pumping the oxygenated blood that every bodily system needs to perform its functions. Blood circulation also carries away many of the toxins and harmful byproducts that our body generates. Because aerobic exercise strengthens the heart muscle and improves its pumping efficiency, it bestows a host of measurable benefits. It enhances the flow of air into and out of the lungs; improves blood circulation; reduces blood pressure; facilitates the transport of oxygen by increasing red blood cell count; reduces stress, anxiety, and depression; and lowers the risk of diabetes and other weight-related conditions.

Clearly, those benefits improve overall health and wellness. By logical extension, they would naturally be energy enhancing, and research on performance reinforces that logic. Exercise improves the storage of energy molecules in the muscles, thereby increasing endurance; increases blood flow through the muscles; helps muscles use fats more efficiently during exertion; increases the rate of muscle recovery from intense exercise; and supports cognitive functioning.

Cross-training and muscle-confusion training. Habits keep us going, but they can also keep us stuck in old unproductive patterns, and research shows that growth accelerates with new and different activities. When it comes to exercise, we tend to keep on doing what's known and comfortable. This can limit the benefits we hope to achieve.

Cross-training is one great way to make sure the entire body is being attended to, and that we are using our bodies in a variety of ways. "Muscle-confusion" training is another term that is commonly used. It recognizes that our bodies have the ability to adapt to repetitive motion and activities, causing us to plateau. When it comes to working our muscles, mixing it up has proven to be extremely valuable.

Breathing

> "In this very breath that we now take lies the secret that all great teachers try to tell us."
>
> **—Peter Matthiessen**

In Eastern traditions, our breath is linked to the primal energy of life, called *prana* in India and *chi* in China. Those countries' ancient medical systems describe elaborate networks through which that energy flows throughout the body. Mindful, purposeful breathing is integrated into the performance of every martial art and every system of yoga to not only facilitate physical action in the moment, but also to improve the flow of breath and energy in the context of *all* activity. Many variations of yogic breathing exercises (called *pranayama*) serve to help the body access, build, and move energy. Taking breath-oriented yoga classes is a great way to improve the quality and consistency of your energy.

The key point is that there is a direct correlation between our body, our brain, and our breath. Growing up, when we got agitated, we were told to take a deep breath, or even three deep breaths, and count to ten. Now psychologists and stress management experts have experimental proof of what our parents knew: Our emotions are linked to our breath. So is the quality and quantity of our energy. Breathe deeply, breathe slowly, breathe consciously, breathe lovingly.

Flow and Flexibility

> "Be water, my friend."
>
> **—Bruce Lee**

What good are strength, power, and endurance if our range of motion is impeded and we can't move our bodies properly? Numerous practices have evolved over the millennia to achieve flexibility and increase the flow of energy through the body, including yoga, which has become enormously popular in the West in recent years.

There are also flexibility practices where you don't move; instead, practitioners move you. Massage is one of them, and there are many variations under that heading. With some methods, like Thai massage, the therapist moves and stretches your body into positions similar to certain yoga poses.

You might also want to consider *structural integration*, such as Rolfing, a type of bodywork that focuses on the fascia. Fascia is a sheath of connective tissue that surrounds muscles and various organs and nerves, binding some structures together while permitting others to slide smoothly over one another. Fascia should be elastic and move freely with muscles and bones. But injury and stress (both physical and psychological), repetitive movements, and the effects of aging can cause fascia to lose its elasticity and become shorter, tighter, and more dense. When this happens, the muscles and skeleton are pulled out of proper alignment, which can lead to pain, discomfort, and fatigue. My favorite analogy is wearing a tight jacket for years after it has shrunk and become a few sizes too small. As a result, the full range of movement is impeded and actually atrophies over time. Practitioners are trained to stretch the fascia, which allows the body to achieve its inherent capacity.

It's important to remember that true flow and flexibility also include the mind and the emotions. Making the body more flexible helps free the mind and emotions from constrictions, and the opposite is also true: Psychological constriction can manifest physically. By working on one area, we can relax and release the other.

In every area of life, not just with our bodies, it is wise to identify mental, physical, emotional, environmental, and interpersonal sources of energey obstacles. Once identified, you can remove those obstacles or adjust to get the energy flowing properly. Expressions like "Go with the flow" and "Being in the flow" suggest an effortless and maximized movement of energy, a concept that applies to individuals and groups, to athletes, artists, armies, families, and all other human units. Finding the sweet spot where energy flows effortlessly and efficiently throughout the system is highly productive as well as immensely satisfying.

Environmental Energies

> "The enviroment is everything that isn't me."
> —**Albert Einstein**

We influence our environment, and our environment has a huge impact on us. One way to maximize our personal energy is to plug into all the positive energy we can access while eliminating or reducing the negative. Basically, it's a two-pronged approach of addition and subtraction: Add joyful, positive, healing energies to your life and subtract the negative forces that drain you. The end result is increasingly liberating. Consider the following examples:

Climate control. A cold day has a different effect on our mental, emotional, and physical functions than a warm or hot day. But it's not just about temperature. When we feel uplifting energy after a bracing rain shower or when we're in the vicinity of a waterfall or a river, it's due to the negative ions that fill the air around flowing water, which are quite different from the positive ions that make us feel sluggish on a humid day.

Plus, we're all different. Some people are more energized by sunshine and warmth, while others sag in the heat and get exhilarated by chilly winds. Psychologists even have a term for the deep depression that debilitates some people in the dark days of winter when they can't access the energy of the sun. It's called SAD, which stands for Seasonal Affective Disorder. Once again, awareness is the beginning point: Knowing how your energy is affected by climatic changes is the first step to adapting to different conditions (e.g., using special light bulbs to counteract SAD) and positioning yourself for maximum gains.

Subtle energies. We don't consciously hear the ambient noise from appliances, electronic gadgets, telephone wires, radio and TV signals, vibrations of cars and trucks on nearby streets, and other sources, but they can affect the electromagnetic and chemical conditions in our nervous systems. So can the energy of other people. As mentioned before, we are all essentially tuning forks. The energy we emit contains information that penetrates and affects others. It passes from them to others and ever onward. Similarly, we receive and absorb the energy emitted by other people. That's why we feel great when we enter certain places and diminished when we walk through others. And why being around some people lifts us up and being around others brings us down. Be aware of the locations you place yourself in and the energies that inhabit them.

Energizing associations. We can exert more control over who we choose to interact with, when we interact with them, and how the exchange of energy proceeds than we might realize. With the skills in this book, we can energize our colleagues, teammates, and families and be energized by them. We can also protect ourselves from being depleted by the negative energies and intents of others.

It all begins by raising our awareness of our own energy, the energy of the people and places around us, and the ways in which those energies interact. Little by little, we can learn how to activate the most beneficial pulleys and levers in ourselves and others. Basically, the more you energetically nurture the people in your environment, the more energy you will have to draw upon. If you cultivate relationships with people who energize you with support, encouragement, creativity, and humor, you will have more energy. And the more you can *be* those things to others, the more you will energize them and the more uplifting energy you'll get back.

Defense Mechanisms: Dismantling the Walls

"Neurotics complain of their illness, but they make the most of it, and when it comes to talking it away from them, they will defend it like a lioness her young."

—Sigmund Freud

Most of us have held on to psychological defense mechanisms that evolved in our childhood and continue to live in our subconscious minds, accompanied by various irrational fears and biases. We may have needed those mechanisms when we were small and vulnerable and ill prepared for the world, but they have probably outlived their usefulness and might even be damaging in adulthood.

Many years ago, my wife explained this concept of defense mechanisms to me, but I resisted fully accepting what she was trying to say. I argued that my success in life was partially a result of the walls and psychological reflexes I had built up over time. She looked at me with love and compassion and told me I was a wonderful man. Then she said those walls I referred to were meant to protect my younger self from the dangers of my childhood environment, and I no longer needed them. If I let go of those unnecessary defenses, she added, I would free up all the energy that was being used to uphold them. Not only that, I would be better able to let in more love to nourish me.

She was right. When we cut through the clutter and get in touch with who we really are, and when we connect with our true purpose and passion, the generators within us ignite and the energy flows freely. To live authentically, aligned with our true nature, is to experience the beauty and fullness and vitality of life itself. Oh, and by the way, we're generally much more enjoyable to be around, and certainly more productive, when we do so.

Defense mechanisms can manifest both emotionally and physically. Being the integrated mind-body machines that we are, we can deal with unconscious defenses and energetic walls through psychological exploration as well as physiological and spiritual practices. When we open ourselves up physically, for example with bodywork such as acupuncture or Rolfing, the release can activate related psychological openings. In a similar manner, targeted meditation, prayer, and spiritual regimens can also open psychological and physical pathways.

We have a lot going on behind the scenes and beneath the surface. Focusing attention on areas of vulnerability, or fear, or even shame, can be sensitive work. We have to feel comfortable and safe enough to relax and open up; but when we do, enormous gains can be realized. Fortunately, many have explored these paths before us and are available to serve as guides and teachers when we are ready. As the Chinese philosopher Lao Tzu said over 2,500 years ago, "A journey of a thousand miles begins with a single step."

Boundless Energy: Opening the Energy Gates

"We are part of the universe; we are in this universe, but perhaps more important than both of those facts, is that the universe is in us."

—Neil deGrasse Tyson

The universe pulsates with energy that is traveling across inconceivable distances at unimaginable speeds, and we are connected to all of it. This is the realm where ancient spiritual insights mingle with quantum physics.

Without getting trapped in religious dogma or confused by spiritual or scientific nomenclature, it makes a lot of sense to become more aware of the energy within and beyond us, and to utilize methods of tapping into it.

Over the course of millennia, various Eastern traditions and lineages focused on becoming more attuned to these subtle and not-so-subtle energies. Knowledge has been gained, expanded, and passed on to subsequent generations. Those advances parallel a lot of the progress the Western world has made in understanding the external realm through ongoing scientific exploration. People from all walks of life have found benefit in these insights and the practices that derive from them.

This is the domain of meditation, prayer, precise physical movements, breathing exercises, acupuncture, martial arts, giving and receiving love, connecting to nature, service to others, and more. Each of these practices is a world unto itself, with a variety of philosophies, traditions, techniques, and teachers upholding and propagating them. But what they all have in common is that they expand awareness and open the energy gates.

It's all about letting go and letting in. Letting go of obstacles and energetic constrictions frees us to take in the pulsating, ever-present, inexhaustible, positive energy around us. When we open our minds and hearts, the energy of the universe floods in.

Eastern terms such as *prana* and *chi*, chakras, and meridians have become more mainstream in the West, thanks to globalization and their demonstrated efficacy. And yet, most Western people don't quite know what to make of these concepts, which lay at the heart of traditional Indian and Chinese medicine as well as numerous spiritual practices.

An in-depth description of these ideas and their associated disciplines is well beyond the scope of this book, but the following exercises will help you understand and work with your internal energy flow to better sense where and how it's moving and how you can take steps to improve it:

Sit or lie down comfortably and close your eyes. Begin by taking some slow deep breaths. On every inhale, imagine the healing oxygen and the loving, nourishing energy of the universe coming into your body and making its way throughout. Then, on every exhale, feel your body relax. Each breath brings more love and nourishment, and then more relaxation. After a while, allow your body to breathe on its own, but instruct it to continue nourishing and relaxing.

Now, tighten one hand like a fist. Hold this position for a few seconds, then relax it. Notice how the hand felt when both clenched and relaxed as well as the associated energy flow. And note that it did both because you directed it to do so.

Next, relax every part of your body sequentially: Begin with your feet and work your way up to your hips, abdomen, shoulders, neck and face, feeling and releasing each body part. After your entire body is relaxed, you can then let go of the tension in your mind and emotions. Leave the body on the ground and drift upward to the clouds. Become one with the clouds, with only awareness remaining.

A variation on this exercise can be performed standing upright. Stand up straight and imagine that your body is suspended from an imaginary point on the crown of your head. Allow your spine to relax and hang. Now feel your spine the same way you were feeling your other body parts. Sense the top, middle, and bottom parts of your back in sequence, then feel the spine as a whole, from the back of your skull all the way down to your sacrum. Now, go deeper and see if you can feel the front, back, and sides of your spine as well as your individual vertebrae. Relax and release any tension where you notice it. Keep going as deep as you are able to, dissolving any blockages.

If you do this exercise regularly, you'll start to become more and more sensitive to both the body parts and the flowing energy. You'll sense where there are kinks and blocks and perhaps even bulging discs. When you do this, try to relax the tension and open the energy gates where you find them, just as you relaxed your fist at the beginning. Can you go deeper and deeper into each vertebra? If you continue doing this for a few days or weeks, you'll be amazed at how much more you can sense that you had been oblivious to. Eventually, in the words of one instructor, "each individual vertebra reveals itself like a detailed map of a neighborhood." And the possibilities are not limited to the spine. You can survey and explore your entire body in ways you never imagined.

$$\infty$$

As with any skill, the more you pay attention and the more you practice, the better you'll get. Now that we've identified ways to increase our energy, let's explore how to leverage it.

LEVERAGE and Lead

"Give me a lever long enough and a fulcrum on which
to place it, and I shall move the world."

—Archimedes

In my martial arts training, I learned how to push over another person with just one finger. Once you know how to accomplish this, you can do it to almost anyone, no matter how big they are—and no matter how small, frail, or out of shape you are. In my classes and seminars, it's fun to demonstrate this skill on the biggest person in the group. Then I teach it to someone who is among the smallest and therefore likely to think of himself or herself as mismatched and underpowered. The audience is always astounded to see them easily dislodge a much bigger person with only one finger.

—

How does it work? Physicists would explain it with the technical term *vectors*. Basically we identify the energy flow inherent in the stance of the person we're trying to move (their "magnitude" and "direction"), and then leverage that energy to push them off balance by applying pressure at a precise point. It essentially gives us a handle.

Don't worry if that makes no sense to you. This technique is much easier to understand by visualizing it, and even easier to appreciate by doing it: Begin by asking someone to assume a solid stance that he feels can resist force. He will usually crouch a bit and plant his weight firmly. You then mentally draw a line connecting the tips of the big toe on each foot, and focus on a point midway between the two feet. Then imagine a line running straight up from that midway spot and locate the point at which the imaginary line first touches his body— usually somewhere on the chest. This is the leverage point. Just push on that spot with one finger. Then enjoy the amazement on his face (and everyone else's) as he tips backward.

Or, if he realizes what you're about to do and tries to thwart you by leaning forward to exert a counterforce to your finger, simply move around to his back and push him forward off his stance. It takes little more than a touch. Try it. You'll be astonished at how easy it is.

Why do I do this demonstration, and what does it have to do with leadership? For one thing, it captures people's attention, and you can't lead people until you have that. More important, it's a simple, vivid way of proving that we're much more powerful than we think we are. We can do much more than we realize if we become sensitive to the forces and energy flows in our environment and know how to move and manipulate them. As soon as people see this presentation, they think, "Wow, I can do that too." Then, consciously or subconsciously, they also realize there are probably many other fantastic things they can also do.

Note that in performing this exercise, I'm using leverage in various ways, not just in the physical act of pushing someone out of position. First, I command the group's attention by claiming to possess special powers. Then, I increase my credibility by performing an amazing feat, which expands their minds as they process all the possibilities. They would probably understand the principles involved if I just explained vectors on a whiteboard, but the demonstration brings the points home dramatically.

One of my favorite things is to teach this skill to children. They're still at the stage where they perceive the world as filled with big powerful adults and weak little kids. As works in progress, they're also incredibly impressionable. Teaching children that they can easily move people much bigger than they are expands their minds and nourishes their imaginations at a critical age. Sharing this technique can change a life in five minutes. That's leverage!

$$\infty$$

It is said that managers manage mountains while leaders *move* mountains. It is also said that managers light fires under people, but that leaders ignite a flame *within* them. When we truly plug into the purpose and passion that reside within ourselves and ignite the same in others, we can link our energy to theirs and wield the power of leverage. And that makes just about anything possible. It's basic physics and psychology applied to virtually everything we do and aspire to. In this chapter, we'll look at how we can move our proverbial mountains by leveraging people, time, information, and other resources—and by preventing leverage from being used against us.

What do I mean by leverage? For the purposes of this book, *leverage* is using influence and/or energy to impact a structure, person, or environment in a way that increases output. Taking advantage of leverage is a science and an art form that can be learned by anyone. It enables us to inspire both ourselves and others, infusing everyone with energy we didn't know we had. And it all adds up to a dramatic multiplication of results.

The Mechanics of Force: Combining Physics and Psychology

> "There is a vitality, a life force, an energy, a quickening that is translated through you into action . . . "
>
> **—Martha Graham**

One of Isaac Newton's monumental discoveries was the second law of motion:

$$F = ma \text{ (Force equals mass times acceleration.)}$$

Practically speaking, Newton's law tells us that increasing mass and/or acceleration leads to a *multiplication* in force. This is the principle behind most athletic pursuits, from throwing a baseball to driving a golf ball. For instance, if you throw a ball with just your arm, utilizing only the mass of that one limb, it won't travel very far. But if, like a baseball pitcher or a football quarterback, you access the power of your whole body, with your legs firmly planted and pushing against the ground, the mass multiplies and so does the force.

Similarly, boxers and martial artists don't strike with just their arms. They put their whole body into it. We use this same approach when we try to push a car that won't start or is stuck in snow or mud. We don't slap it with our hands and arms. Rather, we get our entire body into position so all of the necessary components act in unison. Then, with our limbs aligned, we use the ground as a base for our legs to push against. It's basic physics and body mechanics.

But mass is just half the equation. Acceleration is just as important, and it's potentially an even greater multiplier. You've probably seen martial artists break boards with one swift stroke of their hand. You may have thought it was a trick, or perhaps something only a few highly trained, exceptional individuals can do. Well, it's not a trick, and it's not reserved for the gifted few. I know firsthand because someone showed me how to do it, and now I can break boards almost effortlessly. I also teach others to do it, usually to their astonishment and almost always followed by a big smile.

It takes a basic understanding of force and leverage—not just in the physical sense, but the psychological as well. Physically, you need proper alignment. With your feet planted firmly on the ground, you can marshal the mass of your entire body. Then you add speed and acceleration. That's the physical part. But you also need a mindset that combines relaxation (to facilitate movement and acceleration) with conviction and total commitment. Belief is the essential ingredient that allows you to strike your hand swiftly into and *through* the solid board.

The first time this technique was explained to me, I was part of a group at a meeting we were hosting. The instructor told me beforehand that no one usually volunteers to be the first to try it. They're worried they might hurt their hand, or, just as painful, fail in front of others. So I enlisted my wife, all 105 pounds of her, to raise her hand . . . and she made it look easy (and yes, we had practiced previously). After that, the big guys in the room couldn't step up fast enough. The women were likewise emboldened. As boards broke one after another, everyone beamed.

Since then, I've shown hundreds of people how to break boards, and 98% of them succeed. The 2% who fail come up short for the same reason: self-doubt. Doubt leads to hesitation, which translates into deceleration, and therefore much less force as their palm approaches the board.

These demonstrations are a lot of fun, and they offer a great illustration of the Stairway of Success, which itself is another example of leverage. When we realize that we can do something that appears to be difficult, our self-image adjusts accordingly, and that affects how we view ourselves and the entire world—not just pieces of wood. And then, once people realize they can easily break a board, many of them get excited about the possibility of breaking multiple boards—or breaking through other barriers. Yes, it's all about mass and acceleration, but those factors are heavily influenced by our self-image and our strength of commitment.

It's easy to see how these concepts can apply not only to physical activities but also to achievement in all areas of our lives, whether building a business, cultivating a relationship, or breaking free of our perceived limitations. This is where the understanding of psychology meets the science of physics—mental and emotional qualities impact mass, speed, and coordination just as surely as physical properties do. (Note that outside the realm of science, both *acceleration* and *speed* convey the concept equally well to most people. The same can be said of *force* and *power*.)

Anything we can do to increase mass (more resources, more talent, more unified people) and acceleration (conviction, passion, fear, or ambition) will directly multiply results. That's why leaders can achieve seemingly impossible tasks. It's also why we can win games, contests, wars, hearts, customers, and just about everything else we compete for.

Anyone who has worked with groups of people knows the difference between a cohesive team and a chaotic gang. If you go into a game or a campaign—whether business or personal—aligned with shared passion and commitment, you exert greater psychological and emotional mass and speed/acceleration, thereby increasing force/power. On the other hand, if you are ambivalent, indifferent, or divided, you significantly undermine and reduce the amount of force.

One of life's great joys is connecting to that which truly excites us. When that happens, when we have the luxury of connecting our purpose to our passion, the task is no longer a chore but rather an exuberant and fully energized opportunity. We can do that for ourselves and we can do that for others. That's leverage and that's leadership.

Going with the Flow

"You can't stop the waves, but you can learn to surf."
—Jon Kabat-Zinn

It's generally a lot easier to go with the flow, or at least take advantage of it, rather than struggling against it. Consider gravity, for example. When we oppose gravity, we expend energy. When we go with gravity, we access energy. You're watching flow and leverage at work when you see graceful skiers glide downhill, as they ride along with gravity. Watch a brand new skier, however, or even an intermediate skier who hasn't had adequate instruction, and you'll probably see someone with improper form, fighting gravity instead of using it. They'll be skiing with less speed, less control, and a lot of wasted energy.

Flow is central to other physical activities as well. Surfers catch and ride a wave. In martial arts, we utilize our awareness of the opponent's energy flow relative to our own and move accordingly, first pivoting away from their energy and then adding to it to easily move them away. Similarly, in sailing we capture and use the wind instead of struggling against it.

Metaphorically, we see flow operating in investment markets, where seasoned professionals discern a trend and ride along with it. We also see it in the arenas of marketing, politics, and public relations, where the goal is to piggyback on a wave of public sentiment. In fact, the principle applies to just about every endeavor we can think of, including personal interactions, where we want to leverage the flow of the other person's psychological energy and orientation—their purpose and passion. "Go with the flow" may sound like a New Age slogan, but it's worked since the beginning of time.

Once again, it comes back to awareness and action. When we're fully aware of the flow of events and conditions—be it beliefs, desires, power vacuums, zoning laws, or weather conditions—we can exert maximal leverage, essentially placing a fulcrum in just the right place and applying just the right amount of force. To paraphrase a business axiom, we can't control the marketplace, but if we know what the marketplace wants and why, we can position ourselves accordingly to take advantage of opportunities and maximize results.

Getting a Handle on Leverage

> "When you know what a man wants, you know who he is, and how to move him."
>
> **—George R.R. Martin**

What is easier to pick up and move—a thirty-pound suitcase or thirty ounces of spilled maple syrup? Obviously, the suitcase, even though it's a whole lot heavier, because we can easily get a grip on a solid object. Here's another question: Is it easier to pick up and move that thirty-pound suitcase or a twenty-pound rock? Probably the suitcase, even though it's ten pounds heavier. Why? Because it has a handle.

In human terms, the equivalent of a handle is a psychological or emotional trait you can grasp, grip, and maneuver to achieve maximum leverage. Such "handles" include needs, desires, goals, fears, anxieties, allegiances, obligations, attachments, and other motivators.

What if you can't easily locate someone's handle? After all, it's not always obvious. First, we can question either the person directly or ask others in the know. We can also create a handle ourselves, by initiating an action (or suggesting one) that elicits a response. That response is either the handle itself or an indication of what the handle is. I had the honor of working with Tai Chi grandmaster William C. C. Chen. I was amazed at how quickly he could identify an opponent's handle and move him. Even more remarkable was what he did against more experienced opponents who had no easily identifiable handle. In these instances, Master Chen would induce a handle by doing something to startle his opponent, thereby rendering him momentarily rigid or off balance. Almost instantaneously, and seemingly without effort, he would seize the opening and do whatever he wanted to his opponent.

It was extraordinary to watch—and even more amazing to be manipulated in that way myself. This is essentially what is done in every arena where individuals and populations get emotionally influenced and then moved and maneuvered, such as advertising, politics, and sports. Think of all the plot lines in movies, TV dramas, and novels that hinge on the handles of fear, love, sex, money, and power.

The most memorable movie villains are experts at identifying or creating potential handles and employing them for maximum leverage. That's why blackmail works. Of course, handles can also be used for altruistic ends; the same principles can be used to lead others in benevolent ways for everyone's mutual gain. Think of the use of honors and accolades to induce people to help others. Or contests and prizes to motivate people to accomplish more than they otherwise would.

The primary and most effective handles tend to come under the umbrella of purpose and passion. Simply put, purpose is synonymous with the essence of a person's drive. In many respects, it feels as if it is their very reason for being. And passion is the energy associated with great desire. It fuels the process of fulfilling that objective.

Identifying, amplifying, and directing another person's passion or purpose is a skill that comes with paying attention and with experience, and it bestows powerful abilities. For example, a political leader who fans the flames of nationalism can mobilize tremendous energy and action toward a goal—for better or for worse. Similarly, individuals who share a meaningful purpose can be energized by a leader who knows how to connect with that issue and heat up their passion. The more you look around, the more you will see these qualities and principles at work in matters big and small. From an experienced teacher getting a class to shift easily from one activity to another, to a gifted sports coach getting his or her team to devote themselves completely and deliver almost superhuman efforts toward winning.

Leverage and Leadership

"Management is doing things right; leadership is doing the right things."
—Peter Drucker

Much has been written about leadership, but one simple truth is so obvious it is astonishing how frequently it is overlooked. I can still remember when a seminar leader posed this critical question: "What do people want their leaders to do?" We thought and thought, grasping for both simple and sophisticated answers. Eventually, hands went up and qualities were suggested: Be smart, be honorable, be charismatic, be this and that. Then the teacher told us the all-too-obvious answer: "People want their leaders to *lead*."

That is literally what constitutes a leader, and the greatest leaders are masters at leveraging people and their passions. By harnessing flow, discerning handles, and mobilizing whatever energies and resources they can, such leaders constantly amaze and inspire us. Now let's consider some primary skills to increase leverage and become more effective leaders.

Lead Yourself

"No one saves us but ourselves. No one can and no one may. We ourselves must walk the path."
—Buddha

When we hear the words lead, leader, or leadership, we usually think of someone taking charge of others. The reality is, the greatest resource we have is ourselves, and we have more influence over ourselves than we do over anyone else. It follows, therefore, that we can make the biggest impact on our lives, and employ the greatest leverage, by becoming wise self-leaders.

As we explored in Insight 2, if we want to change the world out there, we should start with the world within. In many respects, the ability to lead ourselves is a prerequisite for our leading others successfully. We can't truly lead others effectively until we learn to access and align our own energies.

Leveraging Failure and Success

"I have not failed. I've just found 10,000 ways that won't work."
—Thomas A. Edison

If you employ the principles of leverage with intelligence, purpose, and passion, you can move both people and mountains. But what if the mountains *don't* move?

Most people fail to appreciate that they can leverage mistakes as well as successes. While a great many people in business and other fields pay lip service to the well-known maxim that we can learn much more from our failures than from our successes, how many take full advantage of that opportunity? Do you? Think about it: What, if anything, do you learn when something works just the way you knew it would? Conversely, consider how much we can learn when things don't go as planned, and we have to dissect everything that happened to understand why.

Learning from setbacks is a function of openness and curiosity. Everything we do benefits from an appreciation of experimentation and the enhanced understanding that comes with it. Those who don't embrace this perspective are much more likely to make similar mistakes over and over again. As Mark Twain said, "History doesn't repeat itself, but it does rhyme."

And while we may not learn as much from our successes, they are definitely opportunities to acknowledge and reinforce the people and processes responsible for getting the job done. I always exhort people to celebrate every victory, understand what was done right, reinforce that behavior, and then raise the bar and do it even better next time.

Leveraging Personal Resources

"Progress isn't made by early risers. It's made by lazy men trying to find easier ways to do something."
—Robert Heinlein

The more efficiently we allocate our resources, the more leverage we create. Consider personal energy, one of our most precious resources. By way of analogy, think of airplanes: They use a tremendous amount of energy on takeoff and initial ascent; however once cruising altitude is achieved, they require far less energy to stay aloft, and available energy can then be utilized elsewhere, or at another time. People can do the same when launching a career, starting a business, attaining athletic prowess, or winning someone's heart. It usually takes a large investment of focused energy to get a venture off the ground and running properly, but once it's fully operational and it's reached a sustainable cruising level, much less energy is required to maintain it. At that point, resources can be deployed where they will have the greatest impact.

Unfortunately, people often fail to commit enough energy to the launch phase. If a pilot did that, his plane wouldn't achieve sufficient liftoff and would plummet back to earth—which is basically what happens to a lot of human endeavors. Many people get motivated and moving during the launch phase, but they don't get their projects sufficiently off the ground and firmly established. They end up trying again and again, never achieving cruising altitude and, ironically, expending much more energy over time.

Case in point: I learned to ski late in life. Our family would take off the odd weekend and head to the mountains. My progress was sporadic and slow; and each year, I'd have to relearn some basics before making additional progress. In contrast, I'd periodically hear about someone who jumped into the sport and dedicated a few weeks to work with a great coach. After one month, they were better than I was after ten years.

Yoga was another area where I could have benefitted from this approach and after many years of doing it every now and again, I decided to get serious and do what's called a "thirty-day challenge". So every day for a month, I committed to taking a class. It was transformational! My strength, flexibility, balance, energy, and focus all skyrocketed. And the only thing I had to sacrifice was a little mindless TV. Heck, I even met a lot of new nice people.

But rather than beat myself up for waiting so long, I started thinking about other areas to invest some concentrated energy: Typing was an area that made a lot of sense since I had always been a hunt-and-peck kind of guy. Playing the piano also came to mind. Then there was speaking other languages, becoming a better cook, and elevating my tennis game. And more! Not only was my thirty-day challenge fun, efficient, and effective, it also made me incredibly excited about future possibilities.

Take a moment to think about how you are allocating your energy. Do your expenditures line up with your priorities? Do you invest sufficient resources when and where they are needed? Or do you spread yourself too thin and end up paying more in the long run?

When you think about resource allocation, keep in mind that you have many kinds of bank accounts, not just financial ones. Some of these accounts hold friendships, others family, and still others hold health, love, and experience. These vital assets accrue value just as money does, and they can be invested and leveraged, not just for advantage in achieving tangible goals but also as engines of nourishment and enlightenment in their own right. I've known a lot of people with enormous financial resources, and far too many of them discover late in life—often too late—that their huge pile of money isn't worth much if those other accounts are depleted.

Leveraging Time

> "Time is what we want most, but what we use worst."
> **—William Penn**

Of all your personal resources, your time is certainly the most finite, and it is, unfortunately, non-renewable. If you manage time effectively, and train others to manage theirs, you can ride the Multiplier Effect to extraordinary gains in productivity. The key is to make sure your time allocation is aligned with your goals, values, and priorities.

Have you ever noticed that people are remarkably efficient the day before they leave on vacation? That's because there is much less ambiguity about what needs to get done. There are lessons to be learned from that simple observation, which brings us to two of the most powerful practices I know for using time efficiently.

THE A(B)C'S OF TIME

This exercise is made to order for people who get lost in the weeds, or who get lured into pursuing opportunities that yield less than optimum results. It's a simple way of getting crystal clear on what has to get done and then doing it.

Start by dividing everything on your to-do list into two separate columns or piles. One is the "A" pile. That's where you place everything that's very important. The second column or group is your "C" pile. There, you put everything else.

I know what you're thinking: *What about the "B" pile?* There is no "B" pile, because something is either important or it's not, and having the third choice tends to blur the lines.

Now, once you have the two piles, get to work on the A pile. Don't even bother with the C's until you've taken care of all the A's since those projects are much more important. It's highly likely that you'll never do much with the C pile. In fact, you may never even get started on it. That doesn't matter a whole lot, because if you focus on the A pile, you'll be handling everything that matters the most. I've discovered that most of the C's invariably get taken care of—other people get some of them done; some expire; some resolve themselves; and many never really mattered that much to begin with, and were more of a distraction than a necessity.

The advantage of this simple system is that it eliminates ambiguity by drawing a well-defined line between the important and the unimportant. With that kind of clarity, it's a lot easier to focus on what really has to be done, especially when compared to our usual to-do lists, which consist of a long list of items that appear to be equal in weight because they generally occupy the same amount of space on the page. Plus, without clear protocols, we often do what feels good or easiest instead of what's most important.

THE TEST OF TIME

Here's another deceptively simple but valuable tool I've used effectively for my own time management and in my seminars and coaching sessions. It's a procedure for quickly producing a powerful and revealing analysis in just a few weeks or less. The purpose is to see exactly how you're actually spending your time. And if you're like most people, you may be shocked and embarrassed by the lack of alignment between your stated priorities and how you truly spend your time. But don't let that stop you from finding out the facts.

The first step is to acquire accurate information. Create a spreadsheet and record on it every single thing you do for two or three weeks. I recommend thinking in terms of six-minute segments (one-tenth of an hour). Sort your activities into major categories like business, health, family, sports, and whatever else makes sense in your lifestyle, and then divide those further into subcategories. Don't forget to add social media activities and Internet surfing, distinguishing between productive use of online technology and time-wasters. Our electronic gadgets can be black holes for time and energy. Also include bathroom breaks, swapping pleasantries with coworkers—everything.

Record your use of time diligently; and when you're done examine the results objectively. As I said, you may be stunned by how much time you're now wasting. And that's probably why most people never actually complete this exercise: They quickly see what's really going on. But knowledge is power, so use the revelations on your spreadsheet to start leveraging. Get past the shock and embarrassment and begin to reconsider how to best use your precious time. Make the obvious and desirable changes. It's your life, so do what you want, but at least do it consciously.

The benefits of this exercise go well beyond leverage and efficiency. It also reveals what your passions are, what rewards and distractions are actually motivating you (and perhaps why), and which of your supposed priorities may be suffering from lack of attention. *Efficiency is a powerful tool, but if you're not aligned with your purpose, you may just be going fast in the wrong direction.*

Delegation: Leveraging Human Resources

"Delegating work works, provided the one delegating works, too."
—Robert Half

Delegating work to others allows us to leverage our time and talent by focusing on what we do best. One solution to the inefficient allocation of time that your spreadsheet analysis might reveal is to employ others to carry out less critical functions that you're spending time on and shouldn't be. Let others complete tasks that you haven't been getting to and expand your influence beyond what you can do yourself. Effective delegation has always been a major factor in the success of executives, entrepreneurs, managers, parents, and other leaders. It's something that can benefit anyone who wants to accomplish more or wants to use his or her time more wisely.

Here's a powerful illustration: In the business world, executives may perform many functions over the course of a week. Their work can be valued at vastly differing rates depending on the specific tasks they are engaged in at any given moment. For example, when they are trying to land a new client or convince an existing client to purchase additional products or services, studies show that they're actually worth about $1,000 per hour (this varies by industry).

Conversely, when they are performing other tasks, their per-hour value is generally much less. This is easy to calculate when employees or outside services can be hired for each function. For instance, some financial analysts are normally worth about $100 an hour. But when they are doing administrative work, their per-hour value falls incrementally, all the way down to the ten-dollar-an-hour range, depending on the specific duties.

The point is, people often spend time performing tasks that can be given to others who cost considerably less. Delegating to others frees up the entrepreneur or executive to focus on more productive activities. In my financial business, we have tested the theory with thousands of advisors over the years, and the results have been clear and consistent. The reasons for choosing to be inefficient vary, but the solution to the problem almost always begins by acknowledging it, along with the enormous opportunity it represents.

Delegate to the Best and the Brightest

"Hire the absolute best. Their brilliance will not diminish your reputation; it will make you shine even brighter."
—Lee Cockerell

I exhort all our managers to hire the best and make sure everyone under them does the same thing. While this may sound obvious, the fact is that the vast majority of managers *don't* hire the best people they can. As a result, they drastically limit themselves and their enterprise, and that's neither leverage nor leadership.

I often drive this point home to managers by asking them to recall when they were playing sports during recess in elementary school and all the kids lined up to get picked for teams. "When you were the one doing the choosing," I ask them, "who did you pick, and why did you pick them?" Invariably, they say they picked the best available player in each round. I follow up with, "Did you ever choose a bad player so you would look good by comparison?" No one says yes. They wanted to win the game, so they chose the player who would add the most value to the team.

You've probably already guessed what I ask next. "In business, do you always hire the very best people you can find? And do the people under you hire the best they can find?" The reality is that they often don't, and many businesses end up being diluted with lower-quality team members. As a result, some large organizations end up being renowned as bureaucratic sinkholes. In many places, government agencies can be the poster children for such accusations, but it can happen anywhere if allegiance to the team or organization is weak.

Here are a few reasons why this happens: Let's say we rate employees on a scale of one to five, with five being the best according to whatever criteria you use. Chances are, you'll always want to hire these amazing fives for a particular position. However, sometimes you feel that you can't afford them. Or, since there aren't that many fives out there, and it may take too long to find one who is available and affordable, you may end up with a crew of fours instead. Now, suppose Mr. Four has to hire someone. In addition to the potential time and salary constraints already mentioned, he's concerned about his future in the company, and he doesn't want to be eclipsed by a new person. So he may hire a three instead of a four or a five. It's a trickle-down effect. Add to those factors periodic employee shortages caused by unforeseen events, such as the loss of current staff or a dramatic upsurge in business, and before you know it, your organization is swimming with warm bodies that are threes and maybe even twos.

This is where leadership is essential. Superior employees can dramatically increase your leverage, not just because they do better work, require less supervision, and regularly come up with ideas to improve even more, but because their excellence is contagious and other employees try to emulate them. But that also works in reverse. When you hire mediocre people and let them stay, other workers wonder why they should bother striving to do better when their co-workers are allowed to coast.

That's why I tell the managers at my companies to always hire someone *better* than they are. This involves a certain degree of trust at first, since it's natural for them to fear that such a person might get the next promotion instead of them. But in reality, a manager who creates high-performing teams is generally more valuable than an individual employee who performs one function well. Both are necessary, but the leader who builds exceptional teams is the one who moves mountains.

Be Careful Not to Get Leveraged and Manipulated by Others

> "People generally cannot believe themselves so easily manipulated and controllable. This is precisely why they are so easy to manipulate and control."
>
> **—Wilson Bryan Key**

Think back to our discussion of handles earlier in this chapter. We all have handles, whether we realize it or not, and those handles can and will be used against us. If, under certain conditions, your handle is a psychological trait (anxiety, stubbornness, guilt, greed, neediness, or fear), that makes you vulnerable. You can be manipulated by skilled practitioners—and they're everywhere. Don't think you're so savvy that you're impervious to being influenced and leveraged by others. I often laugh when I notice how susceptible I am to flattery.

This is a bigger deal than most of us care to admit—not the flattery but the pervasive nature of manipulation. People and social forces are trying to move and motivate us all the time. Even when we recognize an obvious attempt to play on our patriotism, our libido, our vanity, our conscience, our fears, or our desires, it doesn't necessarily follow that we're completely unaffected by it.

Here are some ways you can protect yourself and neutralize the self-serving efforts of others:

Know what makes you tick. To be forewarned is to be forearmed. Be aware of your vulnerabilities. Try to identify your historic weak spots, your unhealthy fears, your unbridled cravings, your unreasonable attachments, and your strongest drives, needs, and values. Those are the parts of you that others can more easily leverage for their own ends.

Be fluid, and look before you leap. Develop a repertoire of techniques that make you more centered, more relaxed, more open, and more adaptable. Something as simple as always asking trusted advisors for their opinions can make all the difference in the world. Be wary of people who attempt to pressure you into a rigid position, or maneuver you into an uncomfortable corner. Instead, relax. Take a few deep breaths to center yourself before reacting, or defer your response to another time that will give you the space and time to respond appropriately.

Observe and analyze the manipulators. Watch how people try to leverage and control others. Notice how they try to control you. See how they work to create handles in your psyche and use those handles to direct you. Learn to recognize their techniques and your reactions as well.

Experiment. Try some new responses. How do they affect the other party? How do they make you feel? What did you learn? Keep refining and learning. Remember, the manipulators have their craft, but you can have yours too. The more aware you are, and the more skilled you are at becoming centered, open, and fluid, the better you can retain control.

Leverage and the Art of Negotiation

"Principled negotiation shows you how to obtain what you are entitled to and still be decent. It enables you to be fair while protecting you against those who would take advantage of your fairness."

—Roger Fisher

It was once thought that negotiation was a zero-sum game. We assumed that the parties involved valued the same thing (e.g., money, land, resources, power) and one's gain was counterbalanced by the other's loss, making the sum of gains and losses equal zero. It was assumed that a successful negotiation was one in which no one made a killing and both parties were a little disappointed.

In reality, most negotiations are multifactorial. People rarely want the same things or the same things in equal measure. On the contrary, we typically want different things at different times in varying degrees. Also, the opposing parties in a negotiation are motivated not only by financial factors, such as maximizing short-term profits, but also by individual objectives, both strategic and psychological. That means you're not always dividing up the same pie.

The essence of successful negotiation is understanding, motivation, and communication. Great leaders are great negotiators because they have a solid grasp on the priorities, power dynamics, and personalities involved—on both sides of the negotiating table. As Harvard law professors Roger Fisher and William L. Ury showed in their classic book *Getting to Yes*, it's critical to know exactly what is important to you and to the other side. That's what makes it possible to achieve a win-win.

The better you understand each party's actual circumstances, needs, and preferences, the easier it is to make beneficial tradeoffs. If you're negotiating with a wealthy business mogul, you would do well to remember that he or she may be driven more by vanity, pride, or prestige than money. It's also imperative that you know exactly what you really want—and sometimes that's as hard to discern as the motives of others.

In many respects, life is a series of ongoing negotiations with ourselves and with others. As we move from a mentality of us vs. them, from a paradigm of a zero-sum game to one of mutual benefit, we become much more successful in every sense of the word. And this is a perfect segue to the greatest benefit of all: Love.

LOVE and Be Loved

"All You Need Is Love."

—The Beatles

We were in Calcutta (Kolkata), India, in Mother Teresa's Home for the Dying Destitute, which is now called the Home of the Pure Heart. Located in a very poor area of the city, it was unlike any hospital or hospice any of us Westerners had ever experienced. It was a medium-sized space divided into two primary areas and populated with about forty army cots. A sick and dying person lay on each one. They had come to die with dignity. No air conditioning, no flowers or balloons, and no visible medical equipment. But there was an immense calm.

Attending to these people were volunteers, many of them nurses and most of them affiliated with the Missionaries of Charity. I wandered over to one cot where a woman lay naked except for a loincloth. She was just skin and bones, and barely conscious. The only personal article to be seen was a thin gold band on her ring finger that hinted at a life with a husband and family. I imagined that she was once a happy little girl playing with her friends, moving through life, and ultimately ending up here, naked, with nothing and no one.

Sitting next to the fragile old woman was a nurse from Ireland, one of the volunteers. She was caressing the woman's arm, slowly and lovingly moving her hand up and down. But while it was only the arm that she was physically touching, she was somehow impacting the old lady's whole being. I asked her about the treatment she provides the patients, and this one in particular. I'll never forget her words: "Mother Teresa says that we should just love them." And that's what she was doing. With all of her body and soul, the nurse was channeling her love into this whisper of a woman. And they were both being nourished.

—

But what is love? The precise definition has been the subject of both debate and delight. The word itself, as well as the usage, varies from culture to culture and language to language. Suffice it to say that love is an expression of extremely powerful and positive feelings, well beyond just liking or appreciating, deeper than mere sentiment, and more profound and enduring than lust. In every culture on earth, in every era of history, love has been portrayed as a fundamental, powerful force that generates positive energy, unifies the beings that share it, nourishes those who give and receive it, and produces selflessness, gratitude, and generosity of spirit.

Love could easily be the primary theme of any book that aspires to touch upon the full range of human wisdom and achievement, with all the other topics being subsidiary. Love is primary. It is massively important. To think or act otherwise is to deprive ourselves of true wealth, health, and happiness.

Love may be the closest thing we humans can experience to divinity. The path of love is a path of opening—both to ourselves and to others. These two approaches are interrelated, and one facilitates the other. However, it can take a while to realize this connection, and even then, our appreciation can phase in and out. As with the other insights and skills, practice produces results. And the practice of love is like nothing else!

We all know the power of love. The problem arises when we can't find or feel love. Or when we're feeling the pain of love lost or unrequited. We want more love, but we don't always know how to get it, or how to get it back, or even how to deal with it when we do have it. Are the solutions to that dilemma as straightforward as the other skill sets in this book, or is love something different altogether? Apparently, it's a little of both.

From the moment we come into the world until the day we move on, we need—and crave—the connection, nourishment, energy, and enlightenment of love. Whether we think of it in spiritual or secular terms, the need to love and be loved reflects a primal yearning to reconnect with our essence and nourish our soul. We come from love, and we are constantly, inexorably drawn to love.

Love towers above all else. In its various forms, it is the most common theme in the creative arts. Be it songs, stories, movies, plays, paintings, or any other manifestation of our psyche and culture, nothing else captures human emotions—from longing to joy to despair to ecstasy—with such power and poignancy.

Thanks to curious scientists, we have learned a good deal about the psychology and physiology of love. The findings add up to what we all intuitively know: More love equates to better health, greater well-being, and a longer life; whereas, less love equates to more illness, more unhappiness, and a shorter life. Feel-good neurotransmitters like dopamine and serotonin, and bonding hormones like oxytocin and vasopressin, are released when we feel love, touch someone affectionately, or even think about a loved one.

But science barely scratches the surface of what lies within when we experience the joys of loving and being loved. Philosophers, sages, prophets, and theologians throughout the world have long asserted that there is so much more—suggesting for example, that God is love, or that love is the fundamental force that binds everything in creation. Even philosophically inclined physicists have come close to that position when contemplating the possibility that some force stronger than gravity might be at work in the cosmos.

Love Is at the Heart of All that Is Good

> "Love is why we breathe."
>
> **—Lisa Genova**

While we could argue with the philosophers, artists, and spiritual teachers who call love the most powerful force in the universe, why bother? It is certainly one of the most compelling motivators in human life, and that is what's important. We are all fundamentally driven by the love of something, be it a cause, a belief, an object, a principle, or an activity—or by the love of someone, or many some-ones, in the case of a family, a community, an organization, or a country. It's clear that the happiest and most fulfilled people on the planet are those who love what they do and the person or people with whom, or for whom, they do it.

In business, sports, and other results-driven domains, the quali-ties that love enhances and enables (enthusiasm, dedication, respect, empathy, trust, loyalty, friendliness, fairness) are not merely valued but are considered paramount. There is a massive difference in health, happiness, and productivity between drudgery and whistling while we work.

"When love and skill work together, expect a masterpiece," said the art critic John Ruskin. I would say that is true not only in the arts but also in every endeavor; whether we are building a busi-ness or creating a family, deepening a relationship or pursuing our dreams, love is a critical catalyst. All enterprises are about people, and all people yearn to be nourished by love. Love attracts and love energizes. It binds people to one another. We climb mountains and cross oceans to get love, and we will go just as far to avoid losing it. Do we really need hard data to tell us that love is the principal driver and the common currency in every vital human interaction?

Love Is Both a Path and a Goal

> "The path is the goal."
> **—Mahatma Ghandi**

In both Eastern and Western spiritual traditions, love is a path as well as a goal. While it leads us to psychological rewards, physiological benefits, and spiritual illumination, to attain love we must be loving. We must open ourselves to love, and we must practice love. If we only see love as a goal, we will be continually frustrated. But if we realize that love is the path itself, then we can start to experience and appreciate the journey that is love.

Remarkably, love can benefit the giver even more than the receiver. Love inspires selflessness, but, in truth, it is also selfish. Giving love feels good. It nourishes and enriches our lives immensely. Studies show that being *prosocial* stimulates the reward centers in the brain. When we behave altruistically, the same areas of the brain light up as when we obtain food, money, or sex—and, of course, love. This is the same reward center that addictive drugs activate but without any of the negative effects. And here's something even more remarkable: Love is the ultimate sustainable resource. The more of it you use, the more of it you have.

So, how can we better access love, direct love, and multiply love? This is not a sentimental question. It's an immensely practical and important one. It is the question that resides at our core, the question behind almost everything we do and aspire to.

Let's begin with a fundamental premise: Love is essentially everywhere. It surrounds us and is also within us. We could even say it *is* us. The key to harnessing love's miraculous power is quite straightforward: *We need to do that which opens us to love.* True, that may not always seem easy, especially when past pain has created callouses in our hearts and our defenses have erected walls. But we can dismantle the barriers we place before love. Love itself is never far away, and it seeps through every crack in our armor, like water into fractures in a dyke or light beneath a door.

Fortunately, love and everything related to it have been the subject of enormous investigation and experimentation through the ages. The simple suggestions in this chapter have been found to be remarkably effective catalysts for love. They not only open doors, they also help to open us. While you may notice some common themes from elsewhere in the book, love is different in one important respect: We may think that we're doing love, but love is also doing us.

The practices that follow involve, to varying degrees, cultivating awareness and applying the core competencies we explore elsewhere in the book. Have fun with them—after all, love is joyous—and feel free to experiment.

∞

To quote Miguel Ruiz, "You don't need to justify your love, you don't need to explain your love, you just need to practice your love. Practice creates the master."

Open Yourself to Love

> "No bird can fly without opening its wings, and no one can love without exposing their hearts."
>
> **—Mark Nepo**

The more you open yourself to love, the healthier you become, the more energy you possess, and the more you can love. It's a glorious virtuous cycle! It may sound unromantic to compare love to exercising muscles, but the analogy holds up. The more you exercise your love, the stronger it becomes. And, like exercise, there are practical procedures for strengthening our capacity for and connection to love.

The first step, as with most things in life, is to consciously choose. This is critical. Once you truly choose to increase the love in your life, you will not only increase your awareness as you experiment with these exercises, you will literally *open* yourself to the process. And here's a secret: Love is available all the time, whether you realize it or not. The glass of love is always full.

Becoming awash in love can be a glorious experience, but it can also be a bit frightening. That's normal. After all, while love has the power to open us up and set us free, the perceived vulnerability that follows the opening can be scary, especially if love is knocking on the door of some entrenched defense mechanisms. That's why it's so important to make this a conscious choice and to be aware of what's going on.

Feeling vulnerable is an important part of our psychological communication system. Opening up to love exposes us, but it also informs us. It allows us to better understand why we're afraid and what we're afraid of. It points a finger at previous pains and current concerns. It allows us to better see and understand, and hopefully heal.

Surround Yourself with Love

"When you fish for love, bait with your heart, not your brain."
—Mark Twain

Love is a form of energy. It's a vibration. When we're in its presence, we feel that energy, and we are charged by it. Since we all function as tuning forks, if we surround ourselves with people attuned to the vibration of love, we absorb their energy and are transformed by it. So choose your companions consciously and carefully.

There are many ways to surround yourself with loving energy. For example, you can—

- Set aside ample quality time with your family and your closest friends.

- Spend time with young children, whether your own or others; they tend to be uninhibited masters at expressing love.

- Read spiritual books and inspiring stories (especially before falling asleep at night or arising in the morning).

- Go to a house of worship or any spiritual center that feels loving and nourishes you.

- Expand the size and scope of your connections.

How else can we let more people into our hearts? One suggestion is to step back and observe what type of people you connect with most easily. What is it about them that appeals to you? How did the relationships begin? Who opened up to whom first? Is there something that worked with them that you can apply to others?

The truth is, you already know how to do this. Most of us immediately open up to babies, whether human or animal (who can resist a puppy?). Sure, they're adorable and they present no danger, but the critical component is that we approach them with an open heart and we attempt to communicate with them on their level—and they generally respond in kind. So why not adopt the same attitude to grown-up human strangers? If we want more love in our life, and if we want to expand our circle of care, concern, and connection, we just need to bestow openness and warmth to more people more often. Imagine how much more amazing life could be if we opened up to all people. Imagine how others would respond if we were warm, sincere, and respectful to everyone.

Think It, Say It, Feel It, Be It

> "What you think, you become. What you feel, you attract. What you imagine, you create."
>
> **—Buddha**

Our psychological disposition and physical stance affect how we feel. Thinking sad thoughts makes us sad while thinking happy thoughts elevates us. As previously discussed, slumping evokes a low listless feeling while standing with arms raised high energizes us. We can play this game like a piano: Hit the right notes and the music follows accordingly. It's magical.

Apply this simple approach to feeling love. Fill your thoughts with images of love, and you'll move in that direction. Modify your use of language to emphasize the love of life and that becomes your reality. Adopt the expressions of love, such as open arms, a warm countenance, and a welcoming soul, and inhabit that persona. Whether you're looking to attract the love of your life, or just a lot of nice people, studies have shown that smiles and positive moods are enormously appealing. Experiments with dogs and other animals suggest that smiles communicate something that makes us all want to move toward the smiler. Could it be universal? Could it be love? Could it really be that simple? There's only one way to find out.

Chant and Dance

"You've gotta dance like there's nobody watching . . .
Love like you've never been hurt . . .
Sing like there's nobody listening . . .
And live like it's heaven on earth."
—William W. Purkey

Cultural and spiritual traditions across the globe have developed practices involving ecstatic chanting, singing, and movement. They endure because music gets us moving and affects our mood and more. It has tremendous power and has been used extensively and effectively to stir the soul and transform our state from dark to light.

Examples abound: Sufi dancing and whirling dervishes, Native American drumming, Jewish *davening,* Hindu *kirtan*, sing-alongs (whether in churches or saloons), and Saturday night dancing from ballrooms to rock clubs, nightclubs, and Texas line dances. And yes, hip-hop, tango, and every other way to bust a move—whatever calls to you. Scientists have made interesting discoveries that explain why moving a certain way can be more uplifting than sitting still, and they substantiate what human beings have known for millennia: Moving and grooving is a catalyst for raising our vibrations, lowering our defenses, and opening ourselves to love.

Human Touch and Tantric Sex

"To touch the soul of another human being is to walk on holy ground."
—Stephen R. Covey

From the moment we leave the womb, we literally need human touch. Research has verified what we all understand intuitively: Giving and receiving a loving touch enhances our psychological and physical well-being. This is especially true during our formative years, but grownups and elderly humans also thrive on touch. Sadly, some people are deprived of this important and primary form of nourishment because of unfortunate circumstances. But the remedy is always at hand. A simple hug can be miraculous. Try it: Hug someone and experience the benefits of being hugged in return.

In recent years, hugging has become quite common and acceptable in American culture, but it wasn't always that way. For me, growing up in a tough Boston neighborhood with a father who had not been emotionally or psychologically nourished himself, hugging was simply not a part of my life. Many years later, my wife's business partner, Evan, would try to hug me when we got together. He was a bear of a man, and hugging wasn't the cultural phenomenon then that it is now. So I would just be polite about it . . . until I realized that it actually felt good. When I shared this with Robbie, she looked at me with pride and love. Apparently I was growing up— or getting back to basics. Ever since then, I've been a committed hugger (I have some funny stories about trying to hug people who didn't feel entirely comfortable with the gesture; I've since learned to read them better and be more respectful).

Americans who hail from northern Europe, with its puritanical heritage, seem to be a little late to this party. It's not hard to find other cultures that have centuries, even millennia, of experience with the importance of touch and sensuality. The *Kama Sutra* is perhaps the most widely known of the ancient texts about love, dating back to approximately 200 BCE. While it is thought of as a compendium of sexual positions, it's actually a broad guide to a satisfying life that delves into the nature of love, family, and related issues.

In terms of using human touch and sexuality to cultivate love, much can be learned from the study and practice of tantric sex. One translation of the word *tantra* is "tools for expansion." Like the *Kama Sutra*, the tantric traditions—a body of knowledge in which sexuality is only one small piece—originated in India more than 1,500 years ago. The teachings and practices are designed to help us feel more deeply and to become more aware of energy—our own, others, and that of the cosmos—primarily (but not exclusively) during sexual union.

Most people know the incredible power of sexual orgasm in opening us up as we briefly let go of our egos and join with another person physically, emotionally, and hopefully spiritually. However, the loving connection created during orgasm can be fleeting, especially for men. Wouldn't it be wonderful if that level of energy, awareness, release, and spiritual union could continue for much longer? This is one goal in the study and practice of tantric sex. It involves slowing down, learning to control your muscles and emotions, moving in concert with the other person, and consciously cultivating love. Love for yourself, for one another, and for all and everything. It's literally the practice of love while making love.

Serve and Be Served

"It's not how much we give but how much love we put into giving."
—Mother Teresa

Another proven way to access the love within and to attract the sincere love of others is to perform service work and give of yourself.

In addition to the good you do, you will personally benefit from the company of other loving souls who are serving. Plus, you will put yourself in a position to receive appreciative love from the recipients of your service.

Every spiritual tradition encourages its adherents to devote time and energy to selfless service—to the poor, the needy, and the sick; to a noble social cause; or to a religious or spiritual community. They do this not just because action taken in the spirit of service makes for more harmonious families and communities, but also because service serves the server.

As with love in general, the rewards of service are many and diverse. Religions may emphasize otherworldly benefits, while science offers other motivators: An ample body of research suggests that those who engage in regular acts of service have healthier, happier, and longer lives than their non-serving counterparts. A thirty-year Cornell University study found that people who did volunteer work had a greater sense of purpose and were generally more satisfied with their lives. Other research clearly indicates that the selfish have more stress, a lower immune response, worse sleep, and greater risk of heart disease than those whose attitudes and actions are more service-driven. It seems clear that "look out for number one" is not the best formula for happiness, or for number one. As one spiritual teacher put it, "If you want to be depressed, think about yourself all the time."

Those who make service a regular part of their lives don't need scientific research to convince them of its value. They know how good it makes them feel. Why wouldn't it? Focusing on something or someone outside of ourselves expands our hearts as well as our minds. It reduces our usual preoccupation with personal pleasure and material gain, and it enhances our connection to the greater whole of which we are small parts.

Wherever you live, you can surely find a service opportunity that suits your lifestyle, interests, skills, and temperament. You are needed.

Meditate

"The moment that judgment stops through accpetance of what it is, you are free of the mind. You have made room for love, for joy, for peace."

—Eckhart Tolle

Accessing love involves opening up. When we open up, we let in. And one of the main things that generally comes in is love.

Meditation is a practice of letting go, being present and aware, and opening up. When we meditate, we activate chemicals and cultivate skills and states that naturally inform and affect everything we do. The practice is an all-purpose vitamin of the highest order—a powerful addition to anything we wish to achieve. It increases clarity while diminishing the countless tugs on our consciousness and getting us more centered and grounded. It's a powerful multiplier for all the other paths that cultivate our capacity to give and receive love.

Meditation is generally seen as a solitary and static practice where we sit, get still, and allow the mind to empty. That is certainly one form of meditation, and it is known to provide a foundation for a more compassionate, loving presence in the world. However, the essence of meditation is the cultivation of calm, non-attachment, and awareness; and we can easily add a component of meditation to other activities by simply being more present when we engage in doing something.

For example, "walking meditation" is a popular and easily accessible practice. It's literally the act of walking while bringing our full attention to the experience—the muscles in our body, our interaction with the ground, the wind and warmth and sounds that we sense, our breath, everything. Likewise, we can practice being more present during any activity. By focusing on the moment rather than dwelling in the past or the future, we become more centered, more open, and more available to the love that surrounds and abounds.

Say (or Think) "Namaste"

*"I am another you and you are another me.
And the journey continues. Namaste."*
—TImber Hawkeye

Aside from the fact that most yoga sessions end with everyone saying "Namaste" as they bring their palms together at their hearts, the traditional Indian greeting has caught on in the West because we have no exact equivalent. One translation is "The divine light within me recognizes and honors the light within you." Saying or thinking namaste has a remarkable ability to foster a feeling of connection between you and another soul, even if you don't have an established relationship with that person.

You might want to experiment with a silent and inconspicuous three-step process that I've found to be transformative. Note that it can be practiced either while alone and still or surrounded by a crowd:

1. *Sense and connect with the divinity or light within yourself.* If you don't quite feel as if you're connecting with love or anything sacred or divine, not to worry. The simple act of focusing your energy and intention in that direction initiates a process that is more powerful than you may at first comprehend.

2. *Try to feel, sense, or imagine the divine essence within the other person.* Again, directing your sincere intention works wonders. And with time, the benefits build.

3. *Consciously allow the two sparks of divinity to recognize and honor each other and connect energetically.* At first, you may feel as if you're just imagining the connection, and in a way you are. That's perfectly fine. Over time, that sense will grow into something stronger. And as you begin to experience the effects of this practice, you will be filled with wonder and delight.

You can adapt this technique to your own conception of divinity and the language of your particular tradition—or to secular and scientific concepts that unite humanity. No dogma is required. Non-religious people may prefer a word like "sacred" or "essence" or "light" instead of "divinity." Use terminology you're comfortable with that evokes the humble sense that we are all precious and interconnected parts of a web of energy, being, light, and love. Like any other skill set, this technique takes practice. But in time it can change the way you perceive, experience, and interact with others.

When I do this, I immediately unclench and relax. I open up. I become more perceptive, receptive, and at ease, which makes me better able to help the other person feel at ease. Basically, by focusing on the divinity within each of us, I feel and communicate more love. Even saying namaste silently helps to create a bond of trust, as it prompts my awareness and points my love in that desired direction.

I've had a lot of fun practicing this exercise. In addition to doing it (silently and secretly) with people I may know or have an easy connection with, it's been especially interesting trying it with those who appear to be worlds apart from me in background and nature. For example, when walking around a supermarket I'll try to connect via a silent namaste with people of different ages, genders, nationalities, and so on. There's a lot to be learned and gained from others, *especially* if they appear to be different. As with most things in life though, it's not about them, it's about us. By opening up to others—or at least trying to—we open ourselves more, and that's the critical component. The more we can open, the more we can let in and let love.

Namaste is a wonderful word and concept, however the power of the practice does not depend on the actual word itself, but on our intent. We can adopt whatever words and concepts work best for us. In the end, it's not merely the divine within us that we connect to, but the divine that is us.

Practice Empathy

> "Could a greater miracle take place than for us to look through each other's eye for an instant?"
> **—Henry David Thoreau**

The practice of namaste engenders our ability to connect with other human beings, which brings us to the realm of empathy. The dictionary defines empathy as "the intellectual identification with or vicarious experiencing of the feelings, thoughts, or attitudes of another." What could be more useful? Increasing our capacity for empathy is like improving our search engine capability. It puts us in touch with a broader range of people and information. Empathy is a tremendous aid to communication as well, because it allows us to interact with others with a greater degree of knowledge and intuition of what it's like to be them.

While we are obviously separate from others, we are also connected. Philosophers and scientists may differ somewhat on the precise description and definition of this connection, but why get lost in philosophy or physics? Opening to that connection enhances our capacity for empathy, and empathy informs, elevates, and nourishes us. It's also a gateway to greater love.

Cultivate Compassion

> "If you want others to be happy, practice compassion.
> If you want to be happy, practice compassion."
> **—The Dalai Lama**

One of the most famous and beloved precepts in the Judeo-Christian tradition is what has come to be called *The Golden Rule*. Commonly expressed as "Do unto others as you would have them do unto you," this adage has equivalents in every religious tradition and is valued as an ethical standard by secularists as well. It is the essence of applied compassion. It's also one of the most practical recipes for a healthy, loving life, not to mention a harmonious and loving world. When we model compassion, we initiate a chain reaction that affects ourselves as well as others.

Compassion can be considered a pragmatic, everyday form of love. It has demonstrable power to improve performance, emotional states, brain chemistry, and other factors relevant to achievement and well-being. As the heading of a *Newsweek* article read, "Research says you can be compassionate at work and boost the bottom line." I think that's true no matter how you define your bottom line, whether in business or any other undertaking.

Scientific studies, not to mention centuries of spiritual traditions, indicate that the capacity for compassion can be cultivated. Every religious tradition has methods designed to develop this important trait. One of the best-known Eastern exercises is the Buddhist practice of *metta* ("loving-kindness") meditation, which has been studied by Western psychologists and neuroscientists.

The practice of metta essentially involves inwardly projecting compassion to people in widening circles of care and concern. It begins with the person many of us have trouble feeling compassion for: Ourselves! Here is one of the many variations on metta.

Sit or lie down comfortably. Take some deep breaths and settle into a calm state. Silently and slowly allow the following words to arise in your mind: *May I be happy. May I be free of distress. May I be strong and well. May I be peaceful and at ease.* Rest a few moments in the feeling of loving-kindness for yourself.

Such practices can be adopted inwardly and outwardly. In a sense, it's always both, in that the love we direct toward others is always and instantaneously reflected back to us. Give it a try: Think of someone who is near and dear to you. Silently address the same compassionate thoughts to him or her, modifying the language: *May [name] be happy. May [name] be free of distress. May [name] be strong and well. May [name] be peaceful and at ease.* Rest a few moments in the feeling of loving-kindness for that person.

Then visualize someone farther from your inner circle of loved ones—someone for whom your feelings are neutral, or maybe even someone you dislike, or for whom you harbor anger or hostility, or with whom you've had conflict. Silently think the same series of phrases with that person's name.

Rest a few moments in the feeling of loving-kindness for that person. And don't worry—this is not a test. You're not being evaluated. Results vary, and we always have something to gain and learn by engaging in the practice. What's important is the attempt and the intent.

Finally, try expanding your compassion to all sentient beings: *May all beings be happy. May all beings be free of distress. May all beings be strong and well. May all beings be peaceful and at ease.*

Experiment with the frequency and the duration, and with the language; and invoke different people as you see fit. Get creative if you wish, and observe how regular use produces a shift in your consciousness and your capacity for love and compassion.

Visualize Love

"See Me. Feel Me"
—The Who

While you can make a case that all the exercises in this book represent various forms of programming, it helps to periodically think in those terms and consciously decide what you do and don't want in your life. Once the desired objectives are clear, it's much easier to neutralize unwanted behaviors and associations as well as augment your desired path. You can apply the principles of programming to help yourself become more loving and to attract more love to your life.

Visualization exercises are enriched instructions that focus on a desired end result and engage multiple senses to strengthen the program with added neural connections. The procedure here is the same as discussed earlier: First, relax and clear your mind. Then identify and neutralize any pre-existing negative images or programs that may be undermining your intention to bring more love into your life. Finally, decide on the *who, what, where, and when* of the love you want. Then infuse that vision with a rich sensory image. Periodically bring up that vision as you continually strengthen the program.

The practice works because it takes advantage of our wiring. So why not use this simple technique to invite, generate, and enjoy more love in your life?

Pray for Love

"Prayer does not change God, but it changes him who prays."
—Søren Kierkegaard

Prayer is a traditional form of communication that acts as a powerful program and a proven path to connection with the sacred dimension of life. All spiritual traditions have a repertoire of devotional practices aimed at deepening our intimacy with a higher power, however we conceive of it. Many of those rituals and disciplines—which include private and public prayer, congregational worship, and various forms of chanting and singing—have the effect of cultivating our capacity and orientation for love. That love might be directed to a specific image of God, or to an abstract sense of a supreme being, or to a notion of a universal consciousness that unites us all. Whatever the focus, just as with namaste and similar practices, when we pray sincerely we are calming our minds, declaring our intent, directing our attention, and programming our being.

The result is to open our hearts and liberate the love that resides within and awaits its full expression. You might, therefore, consider taking advantage of the opportunities to cultivate love that are offered by your tradition—and other traditions—regardless of whether or not you adhere to conventional religious doctrines. At their best, devotional rituals open a proven channel to the power of love that connects us to the universe. In addition, there is solid research linking positive health outcomes to regular prayer and prayer-like practices.

We usually think of prayer as a way of asking for things we want—what is known as petitionary prayer. However, there are many other forms of prayer, involving heartfelt expressions of gratitude, praise, adoration, and awe that help develop the love muscle.

One possibility in this context is to pray for the capacity to love more and better. Here, the famous prayer attributed to St. Francis of Assisi can serve as a model:

> Lord, make me an instrument of Thy peace;
> Where there is hatred, let me sow love;
> Where there is injury, pardon;
> Where there is doubt, faith;
> Where there is despair, hope;
> Where there is darkness, light;
> And where there is sadness, joy.
> O Divine Master, Grant that I may not so much seek
>   to be consoled, as to console;
> To be understood, as to understand;
> To be loved as to love.
> For it is in giving that we receive;
> It is in pardoning that we are pardoned;
> And it is in dying that we are born to eternal life.

For many interpreters, "dying" is not taken literally but rather as a metaphor for surrendering our usual self-centered orientation to life and opening our consciousness to our higher, truer self, or what spiritual traditions call the divine within. If the full version of this prayer is hard to fit into your busy schedule, try this Twitter-size version: *Lord, grant that I might not so much seek to be loved as to love.*

Come from a Place of Love

"Life isn't happening to you, life is responding to you."

—Rhonda Byrne

One of the most powerful practices I have personally enjoyed came from Patrick Connor, a spiritual teacher who first showed me that how I see things—another person, a situation, a sunset, literally anything—is a direct reflection of my own inner being. Therefore, if my perception is indeed my reality, I should elevate my inner consciousness if I want to improve my outer reality. The more I truly understood how much we shape our own reality, the more I was willing to take responsibility for my moods, perceptions, and intentions . . . and the better I was able to orient myself toward a positive direction.

I already wanted to be more loving and to experience all that it entails. The practice, therefore, wasn't a hard sell: I happily chose love. And I was amazed at how easy the technique was to employ, how applicable it was to virtually every aspect of my life, and how immediate the results were.

Here's how it works: Before interacting with someone—asking a question, offering criticism, sending an email, whatever—I first ask myself if I'm coming from a place of love or if I'm being directed by some more egotistical desire or emotional reaction. If I observe that love and compassion are not part of my intent, I simply adjust internally and add some warm and sincere feelings. Basically, when I practice this, I look before I leap. I take a breath and add some love. Not because I have to, but because I want to.

Asking, *Am I coming from a place of love?* initiates a remarkable sequence of events. It settles me and returns me to a healthier, higher state of consciousness. It also transmits nourishing energy to others. And, almost every time, they respond in kind. It is utterly amazing.

Note that I'm not saying it's wrong to feel frustrated or annoyed or even angry. It's important to realize that coming from love and exercising empathy and compassion does not mean being blind or weak. It does not mean you have to hold hands and sing "Kumbaya" and pretend that conflict doesn't exist. It does not make you sappy or complacent, or compel you to deny your feelings or ignore unpleasant realities. It just means you're choosing to act from a kinder, more relaxed, and more open state of being, and that translates to incredible practical advantages.

When I'm in a difficult situation with someone, asking, *Am I coming from a place of love?* actually helps me deal with it more effectively. I'm better able to tell the other person what's not working for me and why, because I'm doing it from a healthier state of mind and a more open heart. I'm not clenched inside. I'm not feeling hostile. I'm not shut down and unable to listen. I don't feel as compelled to change anyone or score a victory for my ego. The other person invariably feels the energy difference, and he or she reciprocates in kind. As a result, I spare myself the unnecessary annoyance (or agony as the case may be) of making a bad situation worse.

Asking, *Am I coming from a place of love?* is like pausing before you hit Send on a message you might otherwise regret sending. You end up building bridges instead of burning them, because this simple question facilitates trust, cooperation, and love.

I have had an enormous number of encounters improve immediately when I asked myself this one question and then modified my approach accordingly. In addition to not making bad situations worse, I have consistently improved matters. Every time. It *always* makes me feel better.

Coming from a loving place helps us empathize. Our hearts and minds open up. We understand others more deeply. And they feel it. As a result, they open up too. If they were feeling hostile or threatened, they lighten up. They become more understanding, more accepting, and more loving in return, so we get to receive their goodness as well as our own.

Love Yourself

"Self-love is the source of all our other loves."
—Pierre Corneille

It has been said so many times that it sounds like a cliché. But it's true. You really can't love life unless you love yourself. Philosophers and psychologists, from both East and West, agree. Even if they say it in different ways, they recognize that a great deal of dissatisfaction and emotional distress stems from not loving ourselves. The failure to love ourselves creates barriers to both giving and receiving love.

The kind of self-love I'm referring to is not narcissism. It's not an ego trip. It doesn't mean you can't be self-critical. It doesn't mean you have to deny your shortcomings or make excuses for them. Rather, it's a deep feeling of absolute acceptance, warts and all. When we love ourselves, we can see our imperfections for what they are: issues we have the opportunity to work on and essential pieces of what makes us perfect as we are. We feel unconditional love for our children even though they sometimes make mistakes, so why shouldn't the same hold true of ourselves?

But what if you don't love yourself? What if you have trouble getting there? That's when you have to ask yourself a question: "Why not?" What's holding you back? Is an old recording running on Repeat in your head, telling you you're not worthy of love? If not, is it some other program? Whatever it is, seek to identify it, understand it, and figure out where it came from. Then use the programming techniques discussed earlier to neutralize it and replace it with a more productive outlook and program, so that you can better celebrate love and celebrate yourself. *Take back the power.*

But don't stop there. This isn't just a clinical exercise. Nurture yourself as you would any child, or pet, or project. Invest in yourself. The returns will change your world in miraculous ways. Nor do you have to do all this by yourself. Remember that we have access to guides, teachers, therapists, and cheerleaders galore. They want to help. Let them in. Give yourself this precious gift.

The Scary Side of Love

"Love Stinks."
—J. Geils Band

We also need to acknowledge the paradox of love. On the one hand, love brings us joy, expansion, happiness, fulfillment, contentment, and even ecstasy. On the other hand, love makes us vulnerable to loss, grief, loneliness, and pain. But wherever love takes us and whatever it lays at our doorstep, if we open to it completely, it can make us stronger, wiser, and more fulfilled.

Of course, sometimes the pain of love lost, or the fear of more pain and disappointment to come, simply depletes our energy and resolve. In these instances, we should call upon our good experiences to warm our souls and carry us through the dark night. We can focus on our faith in love, as well as our faith in those who have traveled this road before us. And at the very least, we can take some baby steps, ask the right questions, seek out coaches, and appreciate and celebrate the blessings of love that we have.

Love comes in every form imaginable. We can define events as obstacles or opportunities, as problems or puzzles. We can become frustrated or fascinated. We can experiment. But ultimately, we can choose love.

Not in the Mood for Love?

"Feelings come and go like clouds in a windy sky.
Conscious breathing is my anchor."

—Thich Nhat Hanh

There are times when you may not feel like being loving to a particular person or in a particular situation. The feeling is quite normal. I vividly remember being so mad at my wife—and sometimes at others—that I felt no love whatsoever. And I did not want to fake it. Plus, when I felt wronged, I wanted my feelings to be acknowledged and honored rather than be a pretender who caved in and sucked it up. I wanted my due, and I was not in the mood to bestow love or flowers or warm and fuzzy feelings.

I'm sure there are times when you felt the same way. It's quite common. It's also a window into your soul and your psyche, so take advantage of the opportunity and look at what's going on behind the doors of your conscious mind. Get in touch with your thoughts and feelings. Notice if you're reluctant to let go, afraid to open up and tap into the wellspring of love within. If so, ask yourself why. Again, it's normal, and it's nothing to be ashamed of. It's just another opportunity to look and learn.

At the same time, it's important to appreciate that we are not defined by our myriad, and often random, thoughts and feelings. There's no need to punish yourself—or anyone else for that matter—and there is no benefit to be gained from it. If you feel the need to vent, do it in private. Or express your feelings in a letter or email you never send. Talk to a therapist. Whatever it takes to unburden yourself. Then look within. See if you can better identify the old hurts and wounds that were triggered by the current situation and caused those intense feelings to erupt. Old programming can spring from the shadows and catch us by surprise. The important thing is to take it one step at a time, always inquiring, always listening, always feeling. And always loving in whatever way you can.

Experiment with Love

"Accustom yourself continually to make many acts of love, for they enkindle and melt the soul."
—Teresa of Ávila

There's no need to sit idly by, waiting for love to arrive. We can do something about it now. And, because love is both a path and a goal, the journey itself is full of love. As mentioned earlier, love is like a muscle: It needs to be exercised, and when it is used as intended, it grows stronger. The more we let go of the fears that constrain our ability to love, the more love we let in. And the more love we let in, the freer we are to give love away. This free exchange of love—with family, friends, coworkers, puppies, and perfect strangers alike— increases our wellness exponentially. By becoming more radiant with love, we nourish ourselves and those around us, and they in turn light up our lives even more.

Try it. Experiment. Take control. See what happens when you practice the exercises in this chapter, and when you interact with people from a sincere place of love. You don't have to say or do anything inauthentic. You don't have to be weirdly "loving," or suspiciously "spiritual." You don't have to shock anyone with some new you. Just make a slight adjustment within yourself. Ask the silent question, *Am I coming from a place of love?* and turn the invisible dial inside to increase your love volume just a little. Pay attention to those areas where you're tight and resist—usually that's where you can make the greatest gains. Offer a silent namaste. Practice empathy and compassion. Offer assistance. Pray for others. And notice how your mood and attitude change. Notice how, where, and why you feel better, both physically and emotionally.

Then watch how others react to you. Human beings generally follow the Law of Reciprocity. That's why they automatically grasp our hand when we extend it. See if your friends and family members respond with a little more kindness. If you're an executive, a manager, or a team leader, see if the people you lead are more responsive, happier to be working with you, and more willing to go the extra mile. In the end, I think you'll find that the Beatles' equation about the love you take being equal to the love you make is an immutable law of nature.

APPRECIATE and Make Every Moment a Miracle

"There are two ways to live: You can live as if nothing is a miracle, or you can live as if everything is a miracle."

—Albert Einstein

A young friend of mine was a student at Harvard University, a school renowned for providing a world-class education as well as attracting future leaders and cultivating famous alumni. Like most of his Harvard peers, Tommy had been outstanding in high school and in life, graduating with distinction in both academic and extracurricular activities. He was bright, inquisitive, hardworking, and eager to excel. Which is why I was surprised when Tommy told me about his favorite class, a class that was by far the most popular on campus in recent years. Technically titled Psychology 1504, everyone knew it as "The Happiness Course." As it turned out, this wasn't just a Harvard phenomenon. According to Forbes magazine, in 2014 the most popular college course on the Internet was . . . The Science of Happiness, created by UC Berkeley.

Before you scoff and think how irresponsible of an Ivy League institution and a state-funded school to offer something as frivolous as a course on happiness, stop and think for a moment. What is it that we all strive for in life? Isn't it happiness? Perhaps we should be indignant that it's not taught in high school or earlier.

—

I'm for Einstein's second option: Live as if everything is a miracle and appreciate every moment of it. As sages have told us and scientists are discovering today, this is a formula for health, wealth, and happiness, not to mention interpersonal and organizational enrichment. Deep appreciation for whatever the universe lays at our feet, regardless of our expectations, relaxes us, opens our hearts and minds, and leads to a natural flow of practical benefits.

Like love, appreciation is something to be felt, to be given away, and to be received. It's natural, free, always available, and rewarding on every level. It's also a whole lot of fun. It is a practice of perception, thought, and feeling that can be cultivated and integrated into our very being.

The Power of Appreciation

"It is not how much we have, but how much we enjoy, that makes happiness."

—Charles Spurgeon

Pioneering research at institutions like the University of Pennsylvania and Harvard has given us a wealth of information about the transformative power of appreciation. Studies by psychologists and neuroscientists show that there are few quicker or more reliable ways to improve overall well-being and resistance to stress than to cultivate an attitude and habit of appreciation. In one study by Robert A. Emmons, PhD, of the University of California at Davis and Mike McCullough at the University of Miami, subjects were asked to write in a journal once a week for ten weeks. They were randomly divided into three groups and each group was given one of three sets of instructions:

1. List five occurrences from the week that affected you, whether negatively or positively.

2. Name five displeasing hassles from that week.

3. Describe five things from the week that you're grateful for.

At the end of the ten weeks, which group do you think was happiest, complained the least about their health, and felt better about their lives as a whole? The one that focused on gratitude, of course. Appreciation is, quite simply, transformative. It orients us toward the positive and makes us feel good.

Philosophers and spiritual teachers have long been telling us that material success alone does not guarantee happiness. They counsel us to be thankful for what we have; and now a wealth of scientific research has revealed that gratitude is indeed a powerful determinant of positive emotions. (Please note that people often use the terms gratitude, thankfulness, and appreciation interchangeably, and so do I. While there may be some subtle differences, they are close enough to be considered one and the same here.)

Gratitude Drives Success

"Success is not the key to happiness. Happiness is the key to success."
—Albert Schweitzer

It might not be surprising that psychological studies suggest that gratitude leads to happiness. What *is* surprising is that it also contributes to "success." In fact, the data reveals the opposite of what most people expect, i.e., that achieving success will lead to happiness. Instead, it works the other way around. By becoming grateful, we become happier, and then we feel more successful. That's because true success is a state of mind. As Andrew Carnegie said, "There is little success where there is little laughter."

We all know it feels a lot better to win than to lose, but the sense of elation we equate with such success is temporary. Sometimes, it's gone when the celebration ends and we're back in the everyday grind. Sometimes, that familiar empty feeling returns pretty quickly, and we find ourselves striving for another achievement to fill the void. Similarly, when the rewards of success are no longer novel, we begin to take our new status for granted, and once again the need to have more and achieve more takes over. This is why philosophers have always told us not to pin all our hopes for happiness on the fulfillment of worldly desires or the attainment of some honor. Such satisfaction is always transient, and a new desire quickly replaces the one we just fulfilled. Now we have proof of that venerable wisdom from scientific research: We keep setting ever-loftier goals to get another dose of the good feelings we had the last time we succeeded.

Not only does gratitude elicit the same pleasurable feelings we associate with success, but it also promotes many of the factors that lead to success. Psychologists have discovered that positive emotions broaden our minds, allowing us to see more possibilities and pursue options that can be easily overlooked if we're stressed, frustrated, or depressed. In problem-solving experiments, positive emotions generally contribute to better solutions and more successful outcomes over an extended period. And one of the most powerful drivers of those positive emotions is appreciation.

Positive emotions not only feel better, they also attract more people to us and to our causes, be they customers, playmates, partners, or employees. This makes gratitude good not only for our well-being but also for our business. Studies show that appreciative employees have higher levels of satisfaction, optimism, and energy, and they make stronger connections with other people. Clearly, those are great qualities to have in any organization.

Protection Against Desensitization

> "We can complain because rose bushes have thorns, or rejoice because thorns have roses."
> **—Alphonse Karr**

Deep-seated appreciation is also a counterweight to the temporary happiness that comes with attaining an object of desire. You know the feeling: You get that big screen TV you coveted, and a few months later you take it for granted. Substitute a car or golf clubs or furniture or any material object for the TV, and the pattern is pretty much the same. It even happens in relationships. You meet someone special, and you cherish every little thing he or she does and says. But some time later, you barely notice all the things that used to constantly delight you.

Psychologists call this *hedonic adaptation* or desensitization. Over time, we take pleasurable things for granted, and the thrill wanes. On the other hand, cultivating an attitude of gratitude, learning to be more present, and savoring what we have helps to combat desensitization. Gratitude creates a surge of nurturing emotions that replace discontent, desire, and other feelings that diminish our happiness and eat away at our health and well-being.

Appreciating what we have, instead of focusing on what we think is missing, allows us to get renewed joy out of the people, experiences, and things that surround us. Appreciation, rather than negativity, fills our consciousness. And, as an additional bonus, when we bestow appreciation on the people in our lives, they not only return that appreciation, they're also likely to want to do even more for us.

Half Full vs. Half Empty

"I opened two gifts this morning. They were my eyes."

—Anonymous

One summer evening, while kayaking in the ocean, I had an extraordinary experience. The wind and water were calm, the temperature was delightful, and a perfect half moon cast a golden glow over the seascape. For some reason, I gazed at the moon more intently than usual that night, and I realized something that came with the force of revelation: While only half of the moon was lit up, if I looked closely I could see the entire circle. Of course! The whole moon is always there, but we see only the part of it that's reflecting the sun at that particular moment. It's not a half moon. It's a full moon half lit up.

Sometimes metaphors cut right through the intellect and land in our heart and soul. The moon epiphany did that for me. Spiritual leaders have often told us that the universe is perfect. It's complete and whole in itself. It doesn't need to change. Instead, *we* need to change; we need to raise our awareness so that we can better understand and appreciate the true wonder of the world.

Is the glass half empty or half full? We tend to think of those who see the glass half full as optimists and positive thinkers, while the half-empty types are pessimists who dwell on the negative (or perhaps they're "realists," if you're in the half-empty camp).

A predisposition toward optimism or pessimism is a function of perception and orientation, sometimes innate and other times circumstantial. For example, if someone sees his situation as descending to the halfway mark, he might experience the pain of loss as well as the dread of continued misfortune. Conversely, if another person is on the way up, she would experience herself as ascending when she reaches the halfway point. She'd feel pretty good about her accomplishments and believe that her fortunes will continue to rise. They are both in the exact same spot when they get to that halfway point, but they look at where they are in totally different ways.

There are an infinite number of yardsticks in life—an endless list of categories and ways to measure our self-worth—and they're all contrived. The reality is that we get to choose how we view, measure, and interpret every aspect of our lives! Why cede that decision to anyone else?

If, as Einstein urged, we live as if *everything* is a miracle, and if Ralph Waldo Emerson was right that "the invariable mark of wisdom is to see the miraculous in the common," then *the glass is always completely full!* Adjusting our perspective is a central task for anyone who wants to grow and thrive. Opening our mind and heart facilitates a perspective of appreciation, fascination, fun, beauty, and bounty.

But adjusting perspective and focusing on the wonders of life takes practice, since our minds are wired to detect problems and potential disasters. We're problem-solving creatures, and we would be in big trouble if we did not instinctively identify threats. On the other hand, appreciation shines light into the darkness. The real epiphany in the half full/half empty metaphor is this: When we live as if everything is a miracle, the glass *is* always full. Realizing this means accepting that even our perceived problems are part of a perfect wholeness. We can appreciate the challenges of life as well as its joys and pleasures, because that always-full glass contains our curriculum for growth.

When entrepreneurs find a problem in the marketplace, they know they've also discovered an opportunity, because that problem means there is a potential solution that people will clamor for. The bigger the problem, the bigger the opportunity. So why limit our appreciation to life's joys, satisfactions, and gifts? Why not also appreciate our frustrations, losses, sorrows, and mistakes, since that is where the biggest advances may be found?

This approach to life may seem counterintuitive, and it can be difficult to live up to consistently. Nevertheless, it can be done. It's a function of reframing—of discarding perspectives that don't serve us well and crafting new ones that promote a healthier view of life.

We can learn and grow from every experience. Therefore, every experience is an opportunity to see the glass of life as full to the brim. We can choose the most elevating perspective at every moment, as if our happiness depended on it—because it does.

And this applies not just to *our* happiness, but also to that of our loved ones, coworkers, and everyone we come in contact with.

And while we're at it, what if that glass were actually much bigger than we ever imagined or can currently comprehend? Wouldn't *that* be amazing?!

Celebrate Thanksgiving Every Day

"Gratitude can transform common days into thanksgivings, turn routine jobs into joy, and change ordinary opportunities into blessings."
—William Arthur Ward

As I mentioned earlier, Thanksgiving is my favorite holiday. On that one special day, instead of obsessing about what we lack or wish we had, we focus on what we do have. We consciously appreciate and celebrate everyone and everything that adds to our well-being. We give thanks, and in doing so we elevate our energy. When we approach it with true appreciation, the holiday is nothing short of miraculous.

But why limit ourselves to once a year? Why not access that Thanksgiving magic every day? There is always an opportunity to give thanks. That message hit me right in the heart one day many years ago at the kind of occasion that is usually marked by sorrow. It was a funeral service for the father of my friend Peter. The program booklet they handed out called the event "A Celebration and Thanksgiving" of his father's life. The whole ceremony was exactly that!

One additional reason it had a big effect on me is that my wife was ill with ovarian cancer at the time. I had the thought: *If Robbie dies, we will have a celebration* and *a thanksgiving of her life.* When she passed, we did just that, and it was transcendent.

But we don't have to wait until someone dies or for a holiday called Thanksgiving to express our thanks. "Count your blessings" may be an overused cliché, but it turns out to be a proven strategy for making us better, happier, and more productive as individuals, families, teams, and organizations. It's time we balanced the endless exhortations in the marketplace about getting what we want (or what others want us to want) by genuinely appreciating what we have.

How do we do that? How can we shift from habitually focusing on what's wrong, missing, or insufficient to a spontaneous, uplifting appreciation of our present reality? It's not as hard, and definitely not as time-consuming, as you might think. It begins with a conscious decision to recognize and appreciate anything and everything that makes us smile, gives us joy, or adds to our life in any way. There are powerful practices that can foster this kind of transformation, and *thankfully*, I'm fortunate to be able to share some of them with you.

Daily Gratitudes

"Gratitude paints little smiley faces on everything it touches."
—Richelle E. Goodrich

One of the most transformative practices I've ever employed also happens to be one of the most deceptively simple. All it requires is writing down a few things you appreciate or are grateful for every morning. In my case, the exercise called for starting each day by identifying three things I appreciated—big or small, trivial or exceptional—for thirty days. It was fun! It took only a few minutes, and it quickly became a delightful and rewarding habit.

Each morning as I lay in bed, emerging into consciousness, I would think about what I was grateful for and then write it down. (Actually, I posted them to the Notes app on my phone, which was always with me and which allowed me to easily see the growing list.) This was so much better than dwelling on all the perceived problems I had and all the situations I had to deal with. Most mornings, a lot more than three items came to mind. But I stayed with the program and kept it to three, smiling as I thought of more, leaving the rest for another day.

I soon realized that the exercise was working as predicted. By asking myself what I was thankful for, my orientation and attitude underwent a subtle yet powerful shift. My mind was filled with positive thoughts and feelings as I lay in bed. Plus, that time of the morning was extremely fertile ground for autosuggestion. Seeds were planted that yielded a bounty of good thoughts and warm feelings. My consciousness and character were changing right before me.

I found myself thinking about my expanding enjoyment throughout the day. This prompted me to focus on all the good things in my life, just like on Thanksgiving. Then I noticed something astonishing. I became aware that my *subconscious* thoughts and feelings were joining in the fun. Part of my brain was processing appreciation all the time, even when I wasn't fully conscious of it. This exercise was far more powerful than I ever anticipated. I felt more energetic and more content. In my behavior toward others and myself I was happier, kinder, more understanding, and more likely to notice the gifts that others brought to my life—and to let them know I appreciated them.

I hasten to add that none of this was contrived. It was totally natural and authentic. Nor did it turn me into a Pollyanna. I was still quite good at spotting issues that needed to be addressed, only now I expressed my concerns in ways that did not undermine my sense of appreciation or make anyone else feel diminished. Surprisingly, the changes in my behavior actually led to better solutions, as my more relaxed and open demeanor allowed me to listen and focus much better. And others usually responded in kind.

At first I thought I might run out of things to appreciate long before the thirty days were up. To my amazement, that didn't happen. It turned out that I was surrounded by an entire universe of things I could appreciate. It was really quite miraculous and thoroughly enjoyable. So I kept on doing it after the thirty days were up. In fact, I continued for four months in total.

What surprised me most as I continued with the exercise was that I appreciated in similar ways the small and seemingly insignificant incidents, experiences, and attributes (of both myself and other people), as well as the more substantial events. On my mental shelves, each item took up the same amount of space, so supposedly minor things had a comparable impact as major ones. Granted, certain landmark occasions may stand out. For example, the extraordinary joy a parent feels at a child's accomplishment, a special anniversary, a significant athletic victory, or an important business milestone. But when the habit of appreciation takes hold, the little things stand out too—the smile on a toddler, the smell of a bakery, a thoughtful tech support person, the sunshine after a run of cloudy days, an out-of-the-blue phone call from an old friend, not to mention all the mundane gifts we take for granted, like running water and electricity. After a while, the whole tableau of life offers reasons to be grateful. Chronicling them was truly blissful and nothing short of miraculous.

Eventually, the exercise ran its course. I no longer had to deliberately think of things to appreciate every morning because I noticed them spontaneously throughout the day. The shift in my consciousness seemed permanent. It was like climbing a mountain and with each increment of altitude change being rewarded with bigger, grander vistas that elevate your perspective forever.

I have since shared this exercise with many people, and they all had the same response: It's easy, fun, and far more powerful than they expected it to be. On one level, realizing how much there is to appreciate changes how we see the world and transforms our attitude. But actually doing the exercise and experiencing the results makes it much more impactful and benefits us both consciously and unconsciously.

Were the personal changes I experienced really permanent? Well, not entirely. We are all subject to a constant flow of catalysts and programming, from within and without, all of which affects us. So, yes, my gains diminished somewhat over time, but that does not mean they were invalid. It merely demonstrates that, just like every other skill, appreciation has to be cultivated and practiced. Over the ensuing years I have periodically felt the need to take up this exercise again, and it always proves to be just as powerful as it was the first time.

Get Creative

"Creativity requires the courage to let go of certainties."
—Erich Fromm

Our mental language matters a great deal. And the language of appreciation is far more beneficial, far more productive, and far more happiness-inducing than the language of insufficiency, cynicism, and discontent. One of our key tasks, therefore, is to reorient our minds toward a vocabulary of appreciation.

Early in my career, during a course on leadership, the teacher made an important point about the supposed fight-or-flight response to stress: Just because someone came up with the fight-or-flight paradigm, it doesn't mean we have to be limited to that one framework. This got my attention. He went on to say that when leaders are confronted with a difficult situation, they don't necessarily have to stay and fight or run away. They can choose a third option. *They can get creative.*

I was struck by this insight and quickly had an occasion to apply it. My wife and I got into an argument one evening. I got so frustrated at one point that the fight-or-flight impulses kicked in. I was torn between wanting to lash out verbally and withdrawing from the whole mess. Then I heard "Get creative" in my mind. Immediately and intuitively, I dropped to the ground, lay on my back, and started barking like a dog. In retrospect, I have no idea why I did that. Perhaps a dog was part of our argument or a previous conversation; but whatever made me do it, it worked. My wife and I burst out laughing. The flames were extinguished, and we calmly and rationally resolved the issue. In fact, once the stress was dissipated, there wasn't much of an issue to resolve.

"Get creative" became a personal mantra, reminding me that I always have a productive option that can make better use of my brain. Why feel limited to a few choices when there are infinite possibilities? And why limit your options by the language you historically used to define a situation, or the language someone else chose for it?

"Get creative" makes for a much more positive and appreciative mindset. It transforms the challenges of life into sources of fascination, learning, enjoyment, and ultimately opportunity. It gives rise to open-minded, innovative thinking.

Reframing and creativity come together in productive ways in every sphere of life. You name it. Every single experience can be an opportunity to learn and grow and appreciate.

Appreciate Yourself

"Never compare your insides to everyone else's outsides."

—Anne Lamott

Low self-esteem is extremely pervasive in modern society. Perhaps it's a response to living in a competitive world where we have an endless list of constantly evolving things to be measured against. The models of greatness that are relentlessly shoved in front of our faces may not be real, but the barrage of expectation is. Little wonder that few of us feel we can measure up. What to do?

A first step is to recognize the reality of the world we live in and consider the following points:

* Few, if any, people are as wonderful as presented.

- It's absurd to expect ourselves to be as beautiful, smart, wealthy, or entertaining as the top 10% in every category. There will always be someone younger, faster, stronger, richer, or better looking than we are.

- Why should other people get to decide which categories are desirable, especially since their motives are almost always self-serving? This is a no-win game, so why play it?

But all of this is really just a diversion. The real game is not "out there"... it's inside our own heads. Fortunately, it's a game we can craft and play to our own advantage. Once we understand and appreciate that the world we perceive is merely a reflection of our inner realm, everything changes. *If you want to live in a better world, cultivate an appreciation of everything—especially yourself.*

One of the most powerful exercises I've ever witnessed often occurs in kindergarten or first grade. The teacher asks each student to write down their favorite things about every other student on individual pages. At the end, each student is given all of those individual tributes to take home. I've been fortunate to witness what happens when the children share these testimonials with their parents. It's a joyous event with enormous repercussions for all concerned. It elevates the mindset of everyone involved and transforms how they look at others—kids and parents alike. Perhaps that's why this exercise is also used in many team-building retreats for adults.

As parents and teachers, we do whatever we can to nurture positive self-images for our children. For the same reasons, we need to parent ourselves as well. It's an investment that pays enormous dividends.

And here's a bonus: Appreciation is contagious. Once you're infected, you become a carrier in the very best sense.

Spread the Wealth

> "Truly appreciate those around you,
> and you'll soon find many others around you."
>
> **—Ralph Marston**

As we discussed earlier, our nervous systems act like tuning forks, and the energy we emit affects others. For example, it's well known in motivational circles that enthusiasm is contagious. So much so that you can even infect yourself with it when you're not feeling particularly upbeat. Just act enthusiastically and you'll start to feel that way. You can't help it. And when you do that in a group setting, other people get excited, too. They can't help it either.

It's the same with appreciation. As the great psychologist and philosopher William James said, "The deepest principle in human nature is the craving to be appreciated." Why not take advantage of that principle and give out appreciation in copious amounts? Much is said these days about "paying it forward," and sharing appreciation is one of the best, easiest, and least expensive methods.

If you share your sense of gratitude with others, they're also very likely to respond in kind. This keys into karma, a word that has made its way into our vocabulary as shorthand for cosmic cause and effect, a concept found in every culture and expressed in many ways. Positive energy begets positive energy. Each seed of appreciation you plant leads to an abundant, ongoing harvest and celebration. It enhances leverage, leadership, and love.

To get these results, the appreciation has to be sincere. Gratitude has to come from the heart. People can spot phoniness a mile away, and when they do, they will respond with mistrust, not love nor loyalty.

Appreciation is a form of positive reinforcement. However, if we only express appreciation and never offer constructive criticism, people can become desensitized, and the impact of our appreciation will be diminished. Likewise, if we only criticize and never compliment, others will soon tune out our critiques. The trick is to offer suggestions in a respectful and appreciative manner. Remember: While positive and negative consequences both motivate, it's positive reinforcement that inspires people to go above and beyond.

Endless Appreciation

> "Piglet noticed that even though he had a Very Small Heart, it could hold a rather large amount of Gratitude."
>
> **—A. A. Milne**

We're all human. We have our glimpses of enlightenment and our moments of bliss, and then the realizations fade and the cauldron of daily life gets all stirred up with troubles, challenges, and the usual jumble of life. Periodically we have to remind ourselves—or get reminded—to stop and smell the proverbial roses. This is understandable. Our attention instinctively goes to anything that might present an immediate threat. Early humans whose brains were good at identifying threats were more likely to survive and multiply. Today we have basically the same brains, only instead of saber-toothed tigers and marauders, we're barraged with psychological threats that have to be evaluated, prioritized, and dealt with. All this stuff fills our heads, and we can easily forget the vital lessons we've learned.

As a result, you may sometimes find the skill of appreciation hiding underground. It hibernates and maybe even atrophies like an unused muscle. That's when we need a reminder, and this chapter stands ready to serve that purpose for you.

A year or so after I stopped the daily practice of naming three things I appreciated every morning, I found that I was, instead, waking up and immediately focusing on my problems—my aches and pains, pressing situations in business, family issues, and all the items on my plate that I was not looking forward to dealing with. Fortunately, I remembered the daily gratitudes exercise. Picking up the practice again was like getting back on a bicycle after a time away. It came back easily and naturally, and, once again, it worked beautifully. Every morning I thought of three things I appreciated, big and small, serious and silly. Within a few days, my mind started to automatically focus again on thankfulness instead of dread and disdain. Appreciation had once again taken its rightful place at the top of my mind.

And then—to my astonishment and delight—my appreciation list started to include various annoyances and disturbances. One day, for instance, I was amazed to find myself writing down something about a problematic relationship. I realized I was thankful for the person who was rubbing me the wrong way, because the problem he presented forced me to face something I needed to know about myself. Instead of seeing the situation as a nuisance or an impediment, I saw it as a gift. That kind of thing kept happening, and it really surprised me. Why would I be thankful for irritants? Because they made me look at underlying issues and discern what I had to do to change things, myself included.

What I was really appreciating, I realized, was the built-in warning system we all have. Mine was bringing challenges to my attention before they got out of hand, and for that I was truly grateful. I began to see problems as opportunities. I even came to appreciate physical pain for that same reason: My body was signaling that something needed to be looked at. As I became more and more sensitive to subtle physical changes, I had the opportunity to take corrective action before I was really in trouble.

Then something even more incredible happened. One day, instead of writing down three things I appreciated, only one word came to mind. I wrote it down in capital letters: EVERYTHING!

That was the last time I did my daily exercise. I felt I could stop at that point, because I knew that everything in my life had a purpose and a potential benefit. My list felt complete. My perspective had been profoundly reoriented toward appreciation.

If history is any guide, I'll get caught up in daily life again and forget about some of the lessons in this chapter. However, now that I've experienced the vista from the top of Mount Appreciation, it will be even easier to get back up there.

Get into the Habit

"If the only prayer you said was thank you, it would be enough."
—Meister Eckhart

There are many variations of the appreciation exercise. You can make your gratitude list before going to bed, which is also a prime time for programming yourself. You could also list five or ten things instead of three. There are even smartphone apps that remind you to focus on gratitude and keep track of everything you list. Regardless of your approach, the purpose is the same: to instill in your mind the habit and perspective of appreciation.

There are an infinite number of ways to orient yourself toward appreciation. Here are two effective variations. My advice here, and throughout the book is to start with whichever exercises and opportunities appeal to you.

MESSAGE IN A BOTTLE

When you do your daily gratitude exercise, write down each item you're grateful for on a piece of paper, and put them all into a jar. In short order, you'll have a growing collection. Then, anytime you slip into a negative mood and feel like you need a pick-me-up, you can reach into your jar and read a few of the gratitudes.

You'll immediately feel better. And, interestingly, just knowing that bottle of blessings exists can provide an ongoing sense of warmth and nourishment.

There are endless ways to adapt this theme. For example, one friend writes her reminders on little hearts; that way she not only has the pleasure and perception that appreciation affords, but she also gets to experience the sense of love that hearts communicate, both when she first writes down her gratitude and again when she picks some up at random.

SAVOR THE PAST AND THE FUTURE TOO

Take a moment to consider the word *savor*. Its meaning goes beyond "enjoy" or even "appreciate." It alludes to pausing to enjoy or cherish something to its fullest, dwelling on its taste, touch, smell, and total meaning and importance in our lives. Play with this concept. Indeed, savor it.

Much is made nowadays about being in the present and living in the now. That's wonderful advice, but there is no downside to also appreciating the past *and* the future. In fact, if you think about it, there is nothing but the present. It's where our past experiences are remembered and our future experiences are planned and anticipated. Obviously, it's important to keep everything in perspective and to not get stuck in the past or depend too much on the future. But why not include in your gratitude exercises fond memories of the people, places, and events that brought you to this moment? And why not also be grateful for all the goodness to come as you move forward on your path from now to then?

If Not, Why Not?

"All my problems bow before my stubbornness."
—Amit Kalantri

I encourage you to investigate various methods of developing the skill of appreciation. Experiment. Implement the techniques that suit your personality and your daily rhythms. See how they feel when you adopt them and whether or not they bear fruit.

If you think this is good advice, and yet find yourself not doing it, ask yourself why not. It's a window into your soul and psyche, and a great opportunity to learn something new about yourself. Here are some possible reasons you're resisting:

- *You don't quite know how.* If that is the case, you can review the guidelines in this chapter.

- *It seems unnatural and difficult, especially if your life circumstances are especially challenging at the moment.* Try it anyway. Small steps add up. You'll eventually find that appreciation is as natural as smiling when a loved one walks in the door.

- *You're trapped in problem-solving mode.* Like many people, your default setting might be what psychologists call "negative scanning," which is when you automatically survey your environment for trouble. In this plugged-in age, when we're assaulted and tempted 24/7 with things we're supposed to care and worry about, we can get stuck and become hyper-vigilant. That's understandable, but why not add some appreciation exercises to the mix? Perhaps redefine the problems as opportunities. What have you got to lose?

- *You're not centered.* We live in a world of agitation where our minds are constantly stimulated. That makes it hard to be fully in the present, which is the best place we can exercise deep appreciation. Experiment with tuning out for a while, and appreciate the respite as well as the potential lessons to be gleaned. Take a few minutes to breathe, meditate, or stretch, so that your mind is quiet enough to locate your gratitude muscle, and build slowly from there.

- *The appreciation habit is not fully integrated.* Maybe you started doing the exercises and gave up because they didn't seem to work immediately. Be patient and persistent. Be curious. Sometimes it takes a while. And remember, there are many ways to cultivate appreciation; find the approach that works best for you.

- *You could benefit from the experience and expertise of others.* Ask others for their perspectives. What can they see that you can't? What do they know that you don't? And, as with any skill, consider finding a coach to help you advance.

I think you'll find that taking a few minutes a day for a formal gratitude session will have a powerful effect. But why stop there? There are opportunities to appreciate all day long. Keep your eyes, ears, mind, and heart as open as you can, and you'll find that life presents a continuous flow of people, sights, sounds, and circumstances to appreciate. Allowing a silent *thank you* to arise in your mind and fill up your heart—even for a fleeting moment—is one of the greatest gifts you can give yourself—and the world. As Cicero said, "Gratitude is not only the greatest of virtues, but the parent of all others."

10

REFINE and Elevate

"The road to success is always under construction."

—Lily Tomlin

My friend Jim Sharpe is a graduate of Harvard Business School. After receiving his degree, he worked at GE (General Electric), where he managed a manufacturing subsidiary. Eventually, Jim bought his own small manufacturing company that supplied extruded aluminum component parts to other manufacturers. Soon thereafter, his wife Debby joined as CFO. Debby was also an HBS alum as well as an engineer from MIT. They were a powerful team, and they built a successful company with a reputation for high-quality products and excellent service.

At one point, some of their bigger customers insisted that their company become "ISO 9001 certified." ISO is the international standards organization that certifies quality in various industries. Interestingly, it's the process that they certify, not the individual products. It had become so prominent in the manufacturing industry that its seal of approval was a virtual necessity. Jim's customers knew that if any of their key suppliers were not ISO 9001 certified, they would not be certified either. "We won't be able to do business with you anymore," they told him, "because we can't get our product approved unless the component parts are certified."

Jim thought this was ridiculous, and he was not happy about it. He saw no reason to fix what wasn't broken. Plus, instituting the certification process and all the requisite procedures and documentation would be enormously demanding and time-consuming. Why go through the trouble of satisfying some bureaucratic system of standardization when their company already had a stellar reputation and a proven track record? He found it insulting to suggest that their company was somehow not good enough when, by all measures, it was top of the line.

But Jim's hand was forced by the threat of losing his customers to a rival that was ISO 9001 certified. So he hired a consultant to help him through the complicated process. The consultant warned him that the first year would be hell, because they'd have to re-engineer every step of the design and manufacturing process, but in the end he'd be glad he did it. The consultant was right: The first year was grueling for everyone in the company; since every employee was part of the process, everyone had to participate fully. But, to Jim's surprise, what he thought he was doing just to placate his customers actually resulted in better quality, faster processing time, more employee engagement, and bigger profits. Every aspect of the business improved, and a process was now in place to guide continuous refinement going forward. Jim became such an enthusiastic convert that he started giving speeches about ISO 9001.

—

To refine is to improve by making the process or product better. Life can be a glorious journey of constant refinement and continuous growth if you allow it to be. Developing any skill, entity, or enterprise—whether it's motivating an audience, advancing an art, improving a business, or becoming a better lover—is rarely a one-and-done proposition. Mastery takes time and attention. It's a process of ongoing, never-ending improvement, and hopefully, enjoyment. That's why people like Picasso, Steve Jobs, Madonna, Michael Phelps, Jeff Bezos, and Sheryl Sandberg keep pushing the limits—even when they're at the top of their games. It's also why Refine is such an important universal skill.

It's easy to get motivated to improve when the going gets tough and the alarms are sounding—when profits are plummeting, or a relationship runs into trouble, or your team is in last place. But maintaining a consciousness of constant refinement is just as important when things are going well. Success can easily breed complacency, and that can lead to apathy and intransigence in response to efforts to make changes. Even people who are ordinarily bold risk-takers can turn risk-averse when they get too comfortable.

What about the adage "If it ain't broke, don't fix it"? There's a huge difference between trying to fix something that's not broken and improving something that can work even better. In an intimate relationship, it's keeping things fresh, romantic, nourishing, and exciting. In business, it applies to product design, marketing, operations, and everything else. *Waiting for something to break before you fix it almost guarantees that it will break.* And matters become more dangerous as the stakes increase, in the sense that you might be rendered obsolete by a disruptive new technology or technique, or left in the dust by a bold competitor. Just about everything can work better than it does now.

Constant improvement requires constant monitoring. You need to know what's working and why, as well as what's not working and why not. Open your mind, listen to your gut, and scrutinize your domain regularly. Review the chapters in this book from time to time and keep finding new ways to Ask, Listen, Program, Motivate, Structure, Energize, Leverage, Love, and Appreciate.

Humanity's Greatest Achievement?

"Everything must be taken into account. If the fact will not fit the theory—let the theory go."

—Agatha Christie

What's the most important creation of the past few hundred years? While we could make a strong case for numerous technological developments, as well as breakthroughs in medicine, travel, and communication, the greatest overall advance may well have come from a process rather than a product. The process that made possible most of the advancements we think of when we contemplate the achievements of the past few centuries is known as *the scientific method*.

This approach to observing phenomena, and systematically investigating them through rigorous theorizing and experimentation, is how knowledge and technology advance. In science, agreed-upon techniques and procedures lead to experimental data, which lead to new hypotheses and further observations, and ultimately evolve into theories and new predictions, each step adding another brick to the edifice of knowledge. And sometimes, unpredictably, but with surprising regularity, the result is a breakthrough discovery.

The scientific method is so ingrained in our consciousness that we think of it as a given rather than a relatively new development. But it wasn't always so. The basic elements of scientific investigation have been present in every sophisticated culture throughout time. But rigorous analysis, evidence-based theories, and data-driven conclusions have not always been supported by the ruling classes. Nor did societies always direct resources to scientific enterprises.

Why do I bring this up? Because the scientific method is the very embodiment of refinement . . . and it has led to innumerable milestone improvements. We can all benefit from looking at this process as a practical example, and its extraordinary history of accomplishment as an inspiration for our own ongoing efforts to refine, improve, and advance.

Rather than leaving refinement and improvement to chance, you can structure and manage the process, just as you would anything else. Experience is our best teacher. Everything we do generates feedback and an opportunity to do it better next time. And what we learn in one arena is generally applicable elsewhere. We may not be able to leap tall buildings in a single bound (yet), but we can certainly ascend one step at a time, and do so joyfully. Here are some basic practices to consider on your way to the top:

Appreciate Problems

"The Chinese use two brush strokes to write the word 'Crisis.' One brush stroke stands for danger; the other for opportunity. In a crisis, be aware of the danger—but recognize the opportunity."
—John F. Kennedy

Our natural tendency is to avoid problems, but they can be blessings in disguise. If we think of problems as opportunities to improve, or as puzzles to solve, businesses to start or markets to win over, then we realize how potentially satisfying and profitable problems can be.

Scientists, engineers, entrepreneurs, and inventors love identifying problems, because they stimulate creativity and lead to the most exciting breakthroughs, benefits, and new businesses. Marketing and advertising consultants also love problems. In fact, as we saw earlier, sales and marketing professionals are trained to look for the hassles, frustrations, and inconveniences that consumers experience, because they know that when a business offers a solution to a common problem, consumers will beat a path to its door.

Instead of avoiding problems, we should seek them out and see them for what they really are—potential prizes to be claimed, and perhaps disasters to be averted. The bigger the problem, the greater the opportunity.

Invest in Loss

"I've missed more than 9,000 shots in my career. I've lost almost 300 games. Twenty-six times I've been trusted to take the game-winning shot and missed. I've failed over and over and over again in my life. And that is why I succeed."

—Michael Jordan

My Tai Chi teacher often used this expression: "Invest in loss." The saying stuck with me as a succinct reminder that we have much more to learn by attempting something and failing than by staying in our comfort zone and doing what we already know works. This outlook helps enormously when considering something different or risky.

Fear of failure is common, and, of course, we'd all rather win than lose. But when we realize how much we can profit from failure and start responding to it with a learning mentality, we can embrace defeat gratefully and listen well to what it is telling us. As a result, I've come to appreciate missteps and losses as necessary and valuable parts of the learning curve—important personal investments rather than humiliating defeats.

Investing in loss is nothing short of a revolutionary mindset. Mastery is the result of constant refinement, and there can be little learning and little improvement if we are afraid to try something new. *Discomfort may be a doorway; don't run from it.*

Make It a Game

> "You gotta have fun. Regardless of how you look at it,
> we're playing a game. It's a business, it's our job, but I don't
> think you can do well unless you're having fun."
>
> **—Derek Jeter**

Ongoing refinement provides great returns on the energy invested. However, there's an important difference between giving it your all in a game with friends and going all out when the stakes and stress levels are high. We may work just as hard in each case, but one invigorates us while the other drains us. That's why joyful effort contributes more to long-term success, not to mention health and wellness, than constant pressure-cooker exertion. The trick is to make every process as enjoyable as a game you are passionate about. And life is the greatest game of all!

Scientists have studied the relative merits of stress as it relates to performance. They've found that stress can energize and motivate us, but at some point it becomes counterproductive. The Yerkes–Dodson Law is an empirical relationship between arousal and performance, originally developed in 1908 by psychologists Robert M. Yerkes and John Dillingham Dodson. The law states that physiological or mental arousal improves performance, but only up to a point. Research also shows that different tasks require different levels of arousal for optimal performance. For example, difficult or intellectually demanding tasks may require a lower level of arousal (to facilitate concentration), whereas tasks demanding stamina or persistence may be performed better with higher levels of arousal (to increase motivation and physical endurance).

Friendly competition in sports provides a perfect example of how to be energized and at ease at the same time. It's a balancing act that allows us to be 100% in the moment and 100% committed to winning, without becoming so obsessed with winning that it's debilitating. The absence of unnecessary worry and anxiety frees us to give our all to our efforts with abandon and joy, which, ironically, can increase our chances of winning over the longer term.

Stack the Deck in Your Favor

"If the cards are stacked against you, reshuffle the deck."

—John D. MacDonald

Results improve when we make a task easier to accomplish. While much of the information in this book may seem simple to adopt and appear obvious in theory, practice can be another matter. As Yogi Berra put it, "In theory there is no difference between theory and practice. In practice there is."

Let's face it: There are reasons we don't always do what we should do, or even what we want to do. We're human, and we're susceptible to an infinite number of influences, both positive and negative. So stack the deck in your favor. If you want to increase your productivity and enjoyment, try orienting your life in relation to what needs to be done and what ought to be avoided. In addition to implementing practical prizes and penalties, you can also lower the hurdles for desired actions and raise them for any temptations that undermine your goals.

"Activation energy" is the amount of energy required to start something. Essentially, it's the hurdle we have to overcome to do what we need to do. For example, it requires a lot less activation energy to get a cupcake or a beer if it's a few feet away as opposed to a few rooms away or a few floors or blocks away. In the same vein, it's relatively easy to resist an object of temptation that's far away or difficult to obtain; whereas abstaining from one that's close by and easy to get requires a great deal more willpower. The obvious and easy solution to most temptations, therefore, is to keep them out of reach. That's why we never kept soda in our house when our son was growing up (and why I still don't stock things that I'm looking to avoid). Not only was it out of sight and out of mind, but more importantly, my son never developed the soft drink habit.

The 20-Second rule was coined by Harvard psychologist Shawn Achor, author of *The Happiness Advantage*. He noticed that if his guitar was located more than twenty seconds away, he was much less likely to practice than if he kept the instrument within reach and readily available. Combining the two principles, activation energy and the 20-Second rule, we can see that the less time and energy it takes to start doing something, the more likely we are to do it.

Here's a related technique I sometimes use. I have a bit of a sweet tooth. Often, instead of trying to ignore or override the craving, I'll get what I want, take a bite or two, and then quickly throw it away. Note that discarding it only requires an instant of willpower, instead of an ongoing battle. Granted, I may waste some money, but my health and peace of mind are worth a lot more than the price of a candy bar. The same strategy can be applied to a pack of cigarettes or anything else. In fact, in many cases, the more the item costs the better the method works, because at some point the financial pain of throwing away an expensive item makes us decide to not even buy it in the first place. But if we do succumb, we only need that instant of activation energy and conviction to get rid of the unhealthy temptation.

The implications are clear: If you want to cultivate a positive behavior, arrange the necessary components so you can get to them quickly and easily. If you want to break a bad habit, place barriers of time, distance, and energy between you and the object of temptation. While this isn't rocket science, apparently it's something we need to be reminded of. So, if you're trying to lose weight or just be healthier, stack the deck in your favor and stock your fridge with fresh fruits and vegetables and leave the junk food in the supermarket.

Leverage Pride

> "Great champions have an enormous sense of pride. The people who excel are those who are driven to show the world and prove to themselves just how good they are."
>
> **—Nancy Lopez**

Competition is a tremendous motivator, even when there is no tangible reward at stake. If you doubt that, watch high-level athletes battle their teammates in practice sessions. For that matter, watch almost any athletic competition, or any challenge, regardless of the level. These contests harness the enormous energy of ego, self-image, and pride. The better coaches and managers know how to turn that competitive energy into improvements that pay off on game day, or the bottom line, or just getting people to raise their hands and participate.

One of the most famous examples of the power of pride and the impact of self-image is Sir Roger Bannister, the legendary British runner, who was the first to break the four-minute mile barrier (he did it in 1954, with a 3:59.4 time). Up until then, scientists believed it couldn't be done and that a human body had certain inherent limits, one of which was running a mile in less than four minutes. When Bannister proved them wrong, mental barriers came down as well. Within months, other runners were also doing the impossible, and now elite runners consider a four-minute mile slow. Today, the record (3:43.13) is sixteen seconds faster than Bannister's time.

The big caveat is that ego is a double-sided sword and can wreak havoc if it's not managed properly. We all know stories of people who have successfully dug deep to do the seemingly impossible; however there are just as many tales of those who went too far and sacrificed their health, morals, money, and friendships in the name of winning. In addition to being mindful not to risk too much, why not consider choosing positive objectives? To quote my friend Lee Cockerell, who used to run Disney World, "It is never too late to get better, healthier, nicer, more organized, more disciplined, you name it."

Making It to Broadway and Beyond

"The world's a stage and most of us are desperately unrehearsed."
—Sean O'Casey

Reaching Broadway is the ultimate pinnacle of theatrical success, and there's much to be learned from studying the process. Before a play is performed in front of a paying audience, everything about it is refined and improved through collaboration, experimentation, perspiration, and inspiration. "Good enough" is simply not enough to succeed. That's why the script is constantly revised, characters are cast and recast, costumes and sets are reimagined, and the pace is accelerated or slowed based on audience reaction, new ideas, and the needs of the evolving production. Every aspect is in constant flux as everyone searches for the magic combinations that make one approach work better than another. Dialogue is tweaked; scenes are eliminated, added, and rearranged; and the arc of the story is choreographed to make it as intellectually and emotionally compelling as possible.

In this respect, our lives are not unlike a Broadway show. Our businesses, our relationships, and everything else we value are works in progress. We get better and better at them to the extent that we improve our skills through conscious and continuous refinement. And experimentation. We are not born with fully developed ideas, knowledge, or talents. Rather, life presents us with an unlimited number of opportunities to develop and refine. As the old joke goes, "How do you get to Carnegie Hall? Practice, practice, practice."

Everyone Counts

"Feedback is the breakfast of champions."
—Ken Blanchard

Everyone can contribute to the refinement process. To make things better, we need feedback from every person, at every level of the organization—or the family, team, or circle of friends. Each person has a unique set of experiences, a unique perspective, and uniquely valuable ideas. Once again, we're reminded of those all-important skills, Ask and Listen.

People often feel their perceptions are more valid than those of others, and that their ideas and solutions are likewise superior. Someone who is more experienced, or more intelligent, or more anything will tend to use those distinctions as a rationale for discounting the ideas of others. This is especially dangerous when it's done by people in charge. While a company's senior management may have a better view of the bigger picture, the people on the line are up front and personal with customers and have firsthand knowledge of what's going on with them. This is valuable intel, which is one reason why everyone counts. To think otherwise not only hampers improvement, it can also invite a slew of unnecessary complications.

But feedback is not all we need from the people around us. We also need everyone to put their best foot forward and contribute to the refinement effort. We're only as strong as our weakest link. If one person drops the ball, the whole team can suffer. I regularly hear people say that they hate this or that business. Then, upon inquiry, I often discover that it was just one person who left the impression that soured the entire experience and ruined the relationship. Happily, this dynamic also works in the other way—one person or one expression of care and excellence can make a huge difference. Everyone counts.

The 1% Solution

"Change enough of the little pictures,
and you'll find you've changed the big picture."
—Ashleigh Brilliant

What's the best way to eat an elephant? One bite at a time. Likewise, one of the best ways to refine is to make improvements in progressive increments. Starting with easily attainable goals and building on each step of success can be far more effective than brashly choosing difficult goals and risking unnecessary discouragement.

In the best-selling book *Raving Fans*, authors Ken Blanchard and Sheldon Bowles reduce success to three primary points: (1) know what you want, (2) know what your customer wants, and (3) implement "the 1% solution," in which everyone keeps improving things bit by bit. Such incremental improvements are usually easy to identify and apply. And they all add up, even more so over time. Virtually everyone in an organization has something to offer, and the enthusiasm generated by the positive reinforcement that results from each improvement is energizing and contagious.

I learned the wisdom of this approach firsthand when we implemented this process at work. We enlisted the support of every employee and explained that *every* improvement adds up and we *all* have something to contribute. The initial goal was to identify ways to improve every metric by just 1%. Not surprisingly, we achieved that goal relatively easily.

What happened next was remarkable. The self-images of individuals and teams started to change as we kept making incremental gains. They quickly realized that if we could easily find ways to improve by 1%, there was no reason we couldn't do it again and improve by 2% or 3% or more. Before long, the sky was the limit, and the results followed the trajectory of our expectations and beliefs.

One special feature of this approach is that it engages and involves everyone. Almost everyone can improve just about anything they do by 1% (plus they can usually see opportunities for improvement elsewhere). When this happens, a greater sense of belonging, participation, and ownership are created. And, because each person feels vested in the outcome, everyone is energized. As a result, more new ideas are generated and teamwork and morale soar.

The 1% solution applies to all aspects of life, not just business. In fact, the mere decision to improve puts you on the road to better results. Start with small, attainable goals and build up gradually. Want to improve your marriage? Make incremental changes in the right direction. Want to be a better parent? Do one little thing better, then another, and another. Want to lose weight? Take off one pound a week, or a month if need be. Want to swim a mile? Take it one lap at a time.

And make it fun! Who said that working at constant improvement has to be difficult, tedious, or unpleasant? Make it a blast! Why not do what our psyches are always driving us to do: Minimize pain and maximize pleasure. You not only get to choose whether or not to say yes to refinement, you also get to choose how to go about it. If you want the process to be enjoyable, make it so. In fact, make it so enjoyable that you go to bed each night happy and content, and excited about the prospect of playing some more tomorrow.

The Magic of Compound Interest

"Compound interest is the eighth wonder of the world."

—Attributed to Albert Einstein

We all know that incremental improvements add up, but we're usually unaware of just how powerful the compounding effect of those advancements are. I first learned this in the financial planning business. In fact, I still remember the chart I saw decades ago that made my eyes pop:

$10,000 INVESTED OVER TIME					
	Compounded interest rate				
Years	**5%**	**10%**	**15%**	**20%**	**25%**
5	$12,763	$16,105	$20,114	$24,883	$30,518
10	$16,289	$25,937	$40,456	$61,917	$93,132
15	$20,789	$41,772	$81,371	$154,070	$284,217
20	$26,533	$67,275	$163,665	$383,376	$867,362
25	$33,864	$108,347	$329,190	$953,962	$2,646,978
30	$43,219	$174,494	$662,118	$2,373,763	$8,077,936
35	$55,160	$281,024	$1,331,755	$5,906,682	$24,651,903
40	$70,400	$452,593	$2,678,635	$14,697,716	$75,231,638

It's absolutely unbelievable how much a small sum can grow over long periods with higher interest rates. Over forty years, $10,000 can grow to $70,400 at 5% interest, $452,593 at 10%, and over $75 million at 25%!

And you don't need to start with thousands of dollars. Or even one dollar. When teaching children the magic of compound interest, this question is often asked: "If you start with a penny and double it every day, how much will you have at the end of one month?" Kids are astonished to learn that the answer isn't 30 cents, or even 30 dollars, or 300 dollars. Instead, it's $10.7 million dollars (and twice that amount if the month has 31 days)!

Here's a practical example of how this plays out in retirement planning. Financial consultants often pose a quiz question like this to clients:

- Person "A" saves $2,000 per year starting at age twenty-five. *She saves for only **ten years*** and stops at age thirty-five, never adding another penny until she retires at age sixty-five.

- Person "B" doesn't start saving until age thirty-five, but then saves $2,000 per year every single year for the next ***thirty years*** until he too reaches age sixty-five and retires.

- Both accounts grow at the same annual interest rate of 7%.

- How much will both "A" and "B" have at age sixty-five?

- The surprising answer is detailed on the following page: The person who saved for only ten years has more than the one who saved for thirty! $238,732 vs. $215,231.

It's fun to play with numbers. But note that some calculations are not always intuitive, and the power of compound interest is one of them. And this is not just about investments; it's really about life and the benefits of constant refinement . . . and time. Continuous refinement benefits from the same principle as compound interest. It all adds up, and probably more than you suspect. It's a smart investment that anyone can take advantage of.

$2,000/YEAR COMPOUNDED ANNUALLY AT 7%		
AGE	**PERSON A**	**PERSON B**
25	$2,000	–
26	$2,000	–
27	$2,000	–
28	$2,000	–
29	$2,000	–
30	$2,000	–
31	$2,000	–
32	$2,000	–
33	$2,000	–
34	$2,000	–
35	–	$2,000
36	–	$2,000
37	–	$2,000
38	–	$2,000
39	–	$2,000
40	–	$2,000
41	–	$2,000
42	–	$2,000
43	–	$2,000
44	–	$2,000
45	–	$2,000
46	–	$2,000
47	–	$2,000
48	–	$2,000
49	–	$2,000
50	–	$2,000
51	–	$2,000
52	–	$2,000
53	–	$2,000
54	–	$2,000
55	–	$2,000
56	–	$2,000
57	–	$2,000
58	–	$2,000
59	–	$2,000
60	–	$2,000
61	–	$2,000
62	–	$2,000
63	–	$2,000
64	–	$2,000
Total at 65	**$238,732.00**	**$215,231.00**

From Refine to Elevate

In addition to improving whatever product or process we are trying to refine, there are powerful bonuses to this particular skill when practiced on a regular basis. When we set our minds on a course of constant improvement, we are climbing the Stairway of Success. In doing so, we actually change and upgrade the wiring of our brains. Even learning the simplest new skill involves building new neural connections, a process called *neuroplasticity*. Like regularly upgrading our computers with the latest hardware and software, effective methods of practicing and improving an activity optimize the neural circuits that carry out that particular activity. We experience this as the feeling of moving from awkward to comfortable, difficult to easy, unnatural to natural, conscious and deliberate to automatic and unconscious.

But that's not all. Each step of improvement in any skill serves as proof of our fundamental competence. Then the process continues as our rational mind and our newly enhanced self-image combine to fuel more growth. Soon, the road ahead opens up, and we find ourselves in the fast lane. From there it's a short hop, fueled by evidence, to believing we can do anything.

Imagine how this type of confirmation, along with the improved self-image and attendant increase in confidence, can elevate an individual life or the life of a family, team, business, nation, or even a planet.

The Spirit of Experimentation

"If the path before you is clear, you're probably on someone else's."
—Joseph Campbell

If you approach the path of continuous refinement with fascination and openness, it will lead you to places you never anticipated going and probably didn't know existed. That's what makes the process so exhilarating; it's like being taken on a wondrous adventure by a master storyteller. Perhaps even a divine one.

As mentioned early in this book, a therapist once helped me overcome my resistance to a change in behavior by framing it as an experiment: "Instead of changing completely, why don't you just try it for a week and see what happens?" Seeing it that way turned a daunting task into a brief adventure, with very little risk.

I suggest you approach refinement in that same spirit: as an adventurous experiment with very little downside and a potentially enormous upside. This applies to all of the insights and opportunities in this book. Think of yourself as a scientist, contemplating hypotheses, rearranging procedures, designing tests, and following the data wherever it leads you.

This is *your* journey and *your* adventure. Ultimately, it's not about a scorecard, or a ladder, or someone else's notion of what you should aspire to. While scorecards and ladders can be helpful tools, they're just artificial constructs. They're here to assist, not dictate nor demean. Your journey is about your potential and your awakening.

Life can be glorious, with every instant and encounter magical. In fact, it *is* glorious. Opportunity abounds and surrounds us. To truly live and love and evolve, we need only open our eyes and our minds and our hearts.

Wishing you all the best on your adventure!

With love,
Joe

Epilogue

"No problem can be solved from the same level of
consciousness that created it."

—Albert Einstein

"I'm all for progress; it's change that I object to."

—Mark Twain

We wake up, bit by bit. It doesn't happen all at once. There is no on/off switch. Sometimes life makes sense, and then the next day we're confused again. Sometimes, with the help of chemicals, or a good night's sleep, or feeling love, or a great workout, meditation, or any number of actions that shift consciousness, the universe feels just perfect. And then, suddenly, the next day or the next hour—or the next minute, for that matter—we're confused and in turmoil again. What's going on? Or not going on?

Our overall progress seems to be a journey of two steps forward toward understanding and awakening, and then one step (or more) in reverse as we backslide into our ingrained behavior patterns. But, ultimately, we are always moving toward more awareness and greater wisdom, even if that doesn't seem to be the case at any given moment.

A major differentiator is our intent.

Our intent, and the actions that follow, keep us moving toward the light. They help us identify and dissolve the weights that hold us down . . . and rise. Our intent and our actions inform and enable each other. And while it might be nice to think that a guru will be stopping by our village to lead the way, it's actually we who must initiate and perpetuate the awakening.

We must be our own guru.

Spiritual teachers have told us for millennia that wisdom and holiness reside within us as well as around us. Granted, there are teachers and books and circumstances that can help us to see the light, but we must find those teachers, listen to those lessons, ask the right questions, extend our love, experiment, and open up to learning. And when we do, everyone and everything becomes our teacher.

An old maxim states that some people have fifty years of experience while others have one year of experience fifty times. The difference depends on us. It's our choice whether to be open-minded or rigid, whether to explore, to experiment, to be vulnerable, to grant and give love . . . or not. The reality we experience is a reflection of our internal mindset and how we choose to give meaning to things.

A positive and powerful appreciation of all and everything keeps us going, keeps us open-minded, and keeps us loving. The path to true happiness and success is always about waking up, letting go, and letting in . . . especially love. About finding fascination rather than yielding to frustration. Why choose gloomy or pessimistic when glorious accomplishes so much more?

Ultimately, life is what we make of it.

Top Down and Bottom Up

Everything in this book can be applied both individually and institutionally, from the bottom up as well as from the top down. We can all start working on ourselves, our families, and our businesses immediately. But why stop there? Imagine the gains we can make as a society if we also apply the principles and practices in this book to collective concerns such as education and the attitudes of our fellow citizens! What will the world look like when we all understand that we really *can* do virtually anything we set our minds to? What would happen if we properly educated and trained people at every stage of life? What if we showed them how to increase their awareness, how to better achieve their goals, how to serve others more effectively, how to give and receive, and how to appreciate every minute of it? Just imagine! It would be a revolution of the most wonderful sort.

We live at a time of unprecedented scientific and technological progress. Every day seems to bring some dramatic new advance that promises to enhance productivity, comfort, safety, pleasure, and the unfolding of human potential. At the same time, wars of every conceivable kind continue to be waged by misguided individuals; and the same technological advances that enrich our lives also assist those who seek to maximize their power and inflict harm upon others. Terrorists, criminals, corporations, and even children can now— by means of weapons of mass destruction, pervasive social media, cyber warfare, and cyber bullying—wreak havoc on a scope never before imagined. We are decidedly on a precipice.

The solution is the same as it's always been: Increased awareness, which leads to higher consciousness and more enlightened action. If enough people expand their awareness and act more creatively, responsibly, and lovingly, the benefits will reverberate throughout society. It may be a societal problem, but the solution starts with each and every one of us.

Acknowledgments

"If I have seen further than others, it is by standing upon the shoulders of giants."

—Isaac Newton

I was always surprised when I'd read the acknowledgments section of a book. The author had so many people to thank—and for just one book. How could that be? Now I know!

In the end, this practice of appreciation is a wonderful opportunity for the writer to reflect . . . and to honor those who have made it all possible. I am so enormously grateful for everyone who gave me guidance and support. While there's no way that a few pages can ever convey the magnitude of all I received, here goes:

To all those who came before us:

It's amazing how many people have pursued this path of personal growth ahead of us, and have passed on their remarkable life lessons. In a related vein, I've often felt foolish wrestling with an issue for years (or decades) only to find that multitudes of men and women have trod these roads, scaled these mountains, and provided us impeccable directions. Their wisdom is one of our greatest legacies.

The quotes that are sprinkled throughout this book offer a glimpse of the many luminous beings who inspire us on so many relevant topics! Thank you for leaving us your knowledge and insights, your love, your humor, and your energy. They have rippled through time and space more than you could have ever imagined.

And to Mr. McCabe, my eighth-grade history teacher: You probably don't remember me or have any idea how much I learned from you, but your stories and insights and advice have been invaluable.

To my primary collaborators and editors:

Phil Goldberg—generous soul, amazing author, and contributor to numerous books on spirituality, psychology, and wellness. Thank you for being my major co-conspirator. Your lifetime of experience and understanding no doubt saved me from innumerable rookie mistakes.

Lisa Genova—my gift from above. A brilliant writer and neuroscientist who rarely wastes a word. Of all your talents, the greatest are your enormous heart and your instinct for how to tell a story.

Sally Garland—my primary editor at Greenleaf and an absolute delight. Your total appreciation for the subject matter and your measured patience helped me take this to the finish line.

Greenleaf Book Group's *Team Elevate*—you gave me a better title and a gorgeous cover. You gave me assistance and advice. You shepherded this opus through production and printing, marketing and social media, distribution, and much more. Thank you, Sam, Chelsea, Neil, Justin, Tyler, Steve, Sophie, Diana, and everyone else who cared and helped.

To my family:

My parents, who gave me life. You made me what I am. Literally. That was huge. Thank you! You showed me by example what to do . . . and what *not* to do. Robbie Sue, my late wife, companion, coach, and involuntary therapist for twenty-five years. You were love personified. We grew up together (me a lot more, because I needed it way more). And Matthew, my son. You're version 2.0. How lucky I am to have such a talented and caring son. While I still love it when I can figure something out quicker or do something better than you, I like it even more when you surpass me . . . which is more and more often.

To my business partners:
Thank you for indulging me, for supporting me, for disagreeing with me, and for teaching me.

To my mentors, teachers, beta readers, and more:
I could never convey in a few pages the impact you have had on me in so many ways. Nor would it ever make any sense to the reader. Please just know that you have made a big difference.

Alan Shapiro—My tai chi teacher who introduced me to many of the concepts in the book. Interestingly, it was our disagreements that caused me to look deeper.

Allen Ullman—The renegade rabbi and biblical linguistics scholar who loves all and sees so much. You have opened many doors and windows for so many.

Barbara Weinberg—My psychologist buddy who is always available to provide counsel and fact-checking.

Cathy Heenan—Your questions, observations, and suggestions have helped me see beneath the surface and beyond the veils.

Chloe Saad—I used to help you with your homework, and now you're one of my most insightful readers.

Christina Dennis—My loyal assistant who never holds back and is always there when I need her.

Clay Southworth—True lover of the self-help genre, valuable critic, and buoyant spirit.

David Dodson—Role model for human beings, inspiring professor, and wise friend.

David Richman—Teacher, communicator, motivator. Your feedback was just what I needed.

Diaa Nour—Unbridled talent and enthusiasm. May your love of people, sports, and business continue to bear fruit.

Ed Mascioli—My scientist, fact-checker, and dear friend. Uncle Ed to children all over the world.

Emily Southworth—The Pied Piper of fitness instructors, and an artist and musician to boot. You were able to weigh in from multiple angles.

Jeff Speck—My city-planning and TED-Talking cousin who held me to a higher standard.

Jess Mullen—Quietly and competently moving all our projects forward.

Jim Levesque—A teacher of leadership skills with an insatiable appetite to learn and improve.

Jon Picoult—A management and sales guru who understands all the little parts that make the big picture possible.

Joni Youngwirth—The queen of practice management. You could have written this book yourself, but you were too busy in the trenches helping others.

Kate Flood—The driving force at the head of Commonwealth's award-winning communications.

Keith Dennis—A kid in a candy store. Which is a wonderful attribute for a financial analyst and a student of life.

Kol Birke—Business consultant and practitioner of positive psychology. You bring love and light to all and everything.

Laura Becker—"Cousin Ra Ra." Marketing maven, literary aficionado, generator of ideas, and very clever lady.

Lee Cockerel—Former head of Disney World and writer of fabulous books that are crammed with wisdom and show millions how to create the magic.

Lisa Maregni—Copywriter extraordinaire. Thank you for your insights and improvements.

Lynne Mooney Teta—Leader, educator, champion, and cheerleader. You have impacted more people than you will ever know.

Mark Magnacca—Wisdom, courage, caring, and sharing. And a ton of valuable experience that you pass on to the world.

Marty Sandler—Nobody does it better. Renaissance man, raconteur, researcher, writer, and friend.

Pat Porter—Prolific reader, insightful critic, loyal friend.

Patrick Connor—Spiritual explorer with the heart of a warrior. Expanding love and elevating life. So much of what you've shown me is in this book.

Rich Hunter—My COO and Storyteller-in-Chief. One of the most conscientious, practical, and respected people I've ever had the benefit of knowing.

Robert Mazzucchelli—Creativity personified. You bring your art, science, and experience to this project and all others.

Rolando Gadala-Maria—Sincerity personified. You bring wisdom and caring to your clients and friends all over the world.

Sanjiv Mirchandani—My fellow traveler, cheerleader, and dear friend. The world's most interesting man.

Sara Tumen—Reviewing this book was a labor of love for you, and I benefitted greatly.

Steve Kaufman—Esteemed professor, successful CEO, and industry leader. The high and mighty seek your counsel. Thank you for offering it to me.

Tami Holzman—A zest for life, a delightful irreverence, a savvy marketer, a heap of chutzpah, and a lot of love. It all adds up to a great author and friend.

Valentina Castellani—An artist of multiple mediums who pressed me to make the chapter on love more relevant. Thank you.

To those who offered their good names and endorsements:
Many of you did double duty as editors and beta readers. In addition to those listed above, thank you, Adam Grant, Amanda Palmer, Jack Nicklaus, Ken Blanchard, Leanda Cave, Les Otten, Luke Campbell, Shawn Achor, Steve Karol, and Tom Morris. You are all leaders and elevated beings. Thank you for giving so generously of your time to read the early galleys and lend your names to this effort. I am enormously appreciative.

Index

N

O

P

S

About the Author

Joseph Deitch was born and raised in Boston, Massachusetts. After college, he followed his muse and moved to the US Virgin Islands, eventually returning to Boston to pursue a career in financial services, and always trying to merge the ethos of the islands and the entrepreneur.

Joe is the founder and chairman of Commonwealth Financial Network, with assets under management of approximately 150 billion dollars. He is also chairman of Southworth Development, a golf and resort real estate company with properties in the US, the Bahamas, and Scotland.

Joe has dedicated his professional career to the goals of quality and community, constantly trying to craft "the ideal environment." He established the Deitch Leadership Institute at the Boston Latin School, the oldest public school in the United States. He has also been a Broadway producer and won a Tony Award as co-producer of *The Gershwins' Porgy and Bess*.

In 2010, the editors of *Investment Advisor* magazine selected Joe as one of the thirty most influential leaders in and around the financial planning profession over the previous three decades.

Joe is a graduate of the University of Pennsylvania and an alumnus of Harvard Business School.

He divides his time primarily between Miami, Boston, and Cape Cod—depending on the weather.